Arnulfo L. Oliveira Memorial Library

APPROACHING
APOCALYPSE

APPROACHING APOCALYPSE

Unveiling Revelation in Victorian Writing

Kevin Mills

Lewisburg
Bucknell University Press

Associated University Presses
2010 Eastpark Boulevard
Cranbury, NJ 08512

The paper used in this publication meets the requirements of the American National Standard for Permanence of Paper for Printed Library Materials Z39.48-1984.

Library of Congress Cataloging-in-Publication Data

Mills, Kevin.
  Approaching Apocalypse : unveiling Revelation in Victorian writing / Kevin Mills.
    p. cm.
  Includes bibliographical references and index.
  ISBN-13: 978-0-8387-5627-0 (alk. paper)
  ISBN-10: 0-8387-5627-1 (alk. paper)
  1. English literature—19th century—History and criticism. 2. Apocalypse in literature. 3. Bible. N.T. Revelation—Influence. 4. Bible. N.T. Revelation—In literature. 5. Literature and society—Great Britain—History—19th century. 1. Title.
  PR468.A66M55 2007
  820.9'382—dc22   2006026343

In Memory of
Frank and Edith Mills

Wandering between two worlds, one dead,
The other powerless to be born . . .

> —Matthew Arnold, "Stanzas from the Grande Chartreuse," 1855

. . . some transformed apocalyptic voice . . .

> —Elizabeth Barrett Browning, *Aurora Leigh*, 1856

Among stirred clouds and veils withdrawn . . .

> —D. G. Rossetti, "Jenny," 1870

Call it a chapter in Revelations

> —George Eliot, *Daniel Deronda*, 1876

We recreate the horizons we have abolished, the structures that have collapsed;
and we do so in terms of the old patterns, adapting them to our new worlds

> —Frank Kermode, *The Sense of an Ending*, 1967

Contents

Acknowledgments

I AM PLEASED TO THANK JOHN SCHAD, WITHOUT WHOM I SHOULD not have a career at all and without whose constant encouragement this book would certainly not have been completed. Jeff Wallace generously read and helpfully commented on drafts of some chapters. Less definable but equally important have been the help and friendship of Bronwen Price, Graham MacPhee, Simon Morgan-Wortham, Diane Warren, Diana Wallace, Andrew Smith, and in more recent days, my colleagues at the University of Wales, Aberystwyth. My ongoing debt to Christopher Norris is poorly repaid by mentioning him here. Whatever errors or weaknesses may be found in the ensuing pages are entirely due to the influence of these friends. The good bits are all my own.

I should also like to thank Howard Hughes and Andrea Tilley for all manner of diversions, and Robbie for providing doghair for my printer.

Alma and Isla made it all possible, even if they didn't know it.

Parts of this work have appeared in the following publications: John Schad (ed.) *Writing the Bodies of Christ* (Ashgate); *Prose Studies* (Frank Cass, http://www.tandf.co.uk); *Victorian Literature and Culture* (Cambridge University Press); Liam Gearon (ed.) *English Literature, Theology and the Curriculum* (Cassell); *Literature and Theology* (Oxford University Press). I am grateful to the publishers and editors.

APPROACHING
APOCALYPSE

Introduction
Apocalypse Then

AFFINITIES

The great book of God's decrees is fast closed against the curiosity of man. Vain man would be wise; he would break the
seals thereof, and read the mysteries of eternity. But this cannot be; the time has not yet come when the book shall be
opened, and even then the seals shall not be broken by mortal
hand, but it shall be said: "The lion of the tribe of Judah hath
prevailed to open the book and break the seven seals
thereof."

—Charles Haddon Spurgeon, *Revival Year Sermons, 1859*

ON SUNDAY, MARCH 6, 1859, IN THE SURREY GARDENS MUSIC HALL,
the great evangelical preacher Charles Haddon Spurgeon began
his sermon with this appeal to the book of Revelation. His
theme was predestination and the ultimate condition of the
human soul. These opening remarks characterize the opacity,
obscurity, and sealed condition of the Apocalypse as a check
upon the hubris of an age obsessed with progress, ensuring that
whatever the ambitions or pretensions of mankind, the quest for
knowledge would always operate securely within divinely appointed limits and constraints. Through its strange visions, bizarre images, and cryptic locutions ran the impenetrable
boundary of human aspirations that remained in place even for
an age of dramatic and unprecedented expansion and development in science and technology. Spurgeon could not have
known that the publication of Charles Darwin's *The Origin of
Species* in that very year would open the sealed book of nature
and begin the process of reading in its newly illuminated pages
meanings which would have a profound and lasting effect on the
way in which his chosen scripture, and the canon to which it

13

belongs, would be read. The very boundaries that reassured the Christian believer, be they temporal, spiritual, intellectual, or material, were already under threat well before 1859, but Darwin's work would raise the stakes considerably by threatening the ontological framework within which the narrative of divine creation and consummation was produced. This sense of threat, or promise, underlies the deployments of apocalyptic themes, language, and imagery in Victorian writing. For it was not only preachers, nor even evangelicals, who wove St. John's visionary work into their texts. A great deal of Victorian writing adopts, borrows, or quietly assimilates all kinds of material from apocalyptic literature in what might be described as a kind of affinity with the genre. In order to bring to light these investments in an ancient literary mode, it is necessary to say something about the provenance and characteristics of the genre.

Apocalyptic literature, which flourished between 200 BCE and 100 CE and had its roots in Judaism and Zoroastrianism, is familiar in the Christian West principally through the biblical books of Daniel and Revelation. It grew out of the experience of the people of Israel who returned to their homeland after their exile under the Assyrian and Babylonian empires (c. 710–540 BCE). Their experience of restoration did not match the expectations to which the prophetic visions had given rise, and the apocalyptists attempted to address this disappointment. In the words of Klaas Runia: "Apocalyptic . . . takes the prophetic tradition one step further . . ." by opening up a new perspective on the situation.[1] It attempts to situate the experience of the disillusioned remnant of Israel in the context of an overview of human history. The difficulties they face are then seen as part of a larger divine plan according to which the eternal purposes guide all things towards a predetermined end. In the specifically Christian context to which Revelation relates, a disillusionment similar to that of the post-exilic experience surrounded the delayed return of Christ and the deferral of God's earthly kingdom.

In form, apocalypses were prose accounts of a vision or visions, written in the first person, and framed by a description of the writer's circumstances at the time of the visionary experience. Typically they were structured in such a way as to emphasize some revealed message that was intended to communicate a kind of "God's-eye-view" of human affairs. This perspective and the use of a visionary mode had the function of lending credibility to the author's message by claiming a transcendent, supernatural authority. By such means the writers sought to influence the views and to modify the behavior of the reader, or to offer some explanation of the ways of God to men (theodicy).

Dreams and visions were not the only characteristics of the style. Bizarre imagery, a supernatural guide, and the revelation of cosmic mysteries and of the end times were all features of apocalyptic writing.[2] It also usually involved some element of *vaticinia ex eventu* (prophecy after the event). This was a means of disguising an account of recent history as prophecy by writing in the name of some well-known figure from the past (as if I were to write a history of Britain from the seventeenth century to the present day and to publish it in the name of Oliver Cromwell). This was not really intended to deceive, but to provide a historical context for the writer's predictions of the future. History was thus depicted as a unified whole in visions which were extended to encompass the end of the world. Having drawn this rough sketch of the apocalyptic style, it should be noted that the texts which are labelled apocalyptic by scholars are extremely diverse.

At the risk of stating the obvious, Revelation is an apocalyptic text. Its first word in the Greek version (*apokalypsis*—uncovering, or unveiling), actually furnished the label for the genre. But in many ways the book of Revelation, the focus of this study, is unlike other apocalypses: it does not contain accounts of any dreams, it does not indulge in the history-as-prophecy conceit, and it expressly refers to itself as prophecy (a self-attribution lacking in other so-called apocalypses). Structurally it is far more complex than any other known apocalyptic text, whether Jewish or Christian, and it lacks the pessimism characteristic of many apocalypses.[3] Richard Bauckham points out that apocalypses which contain a number of visions do not carry imagery over from one vision to another in the way that John's text does: "As an integrated sequence of visionary material . . . creating one world of images kaleidoscopically presented, the Apocalypse of John is unique."[4]

It is also important to remember that although the "apocalyptic" label is applied to a diverse body of material, the style was never a matter of free invention in the manner of the modern novel. There were traditions concerning the shape and construction of the universe, access to the heavenly realm, the roles of angels and demons, and the relationship between heavenly and earthly events, all of which formed a background against which these texts were written. There was even a repertoire of images upon which writers could draw in describing their visions. But the apocalyptic genre was not just the product of a set of rules which writers could observe in constructing their texts. A background of Hellenic domination following the conquests of Alexander gave rise to a particular need to reassert that, despite appearances, God was in control of human history.[5] One strand of apocalyptic literature offered a supernatural perspective which took in the whole of history and reaffirmed that, however difficult circumstances might be, these things had been decreed; in the long run God would restore the fortunes of his people. Although the political scene was dominated by the Roman military rather than by Hellenic generals by the time that Revelation was written, the same need to understand their historical predicament in the light of God's promises troubled Jewish and Christian minds.

In thinking about the book of Revelation, then, we are dealing with an instance of a genre which grew out of disappointment, and out of a need to re-evaluate the relationship between the extant religious formation and the vicissitudes of human experience. Such a background is likely to have a prima facie appeal to an age in which old religious and social certainties were breaking down, in which wars had been a constant threat, and in which revolutionary hopes had produced little beside fear and bloodshed. The underlying desire to foresee ends, and thus to re-impose order on a threateningly chaotic experience, must have held great appeal for people living in a century of upheaval, change, and the disappearance of familiar, long-standing, and well-established ways of life. The Victorian era was just such a time. With this affinity in mind, this work examines certain structuring oppositions that shape apocalyptic literature and sets out to decode their significance for Victorian writing. They are: human/inhuman, desert/city, veiled/revealed, time/the eternal, and this world/other world.

In attempting to reveal the hidden forces, processes, and events underlying the mismatch between religious expectations and historical experience, apocalyptic thought purports to map out the interconnections between the human world and the heavenly realm which it shadows, or by which it is influenced. The traffic between the human and the inhuman worlds is described in order to reveal the truth about any set of unfavorable (if not unbearable) circumstances obtaining on earth. So a fundamental opposition is set up between the human and the inhuman. This has a peculiar resonance in the Victorian setting, both because the relationship between the human and the divine was rendered ever more unstable and uncertain by scientific, critical and philosophical discourses, and because the rise of evolutionary science inculcated the proximity of human and inhuman into the cultural sphere not as a supernatural threat, but as a natural history. As chapter 1 demonstrates, the question of the relation of human to inhuman in Victorian writing pre-dates the publication of Charles Darwin's *The Origin of Species:* it is present in the works of Carlyle, the Brontës, and Dickens, among others. But Darwin's work rendered the relationship critical by proposing a scientifically feasible model of the evolutionary process and by raising the issue of specifically human evolution. The public debate it spawned focused primarily upon human antecedents rather than upon specialized professional discussion of definitive characteristics and taxonomies. This necessarily had an impact on religious beliefs and profoundly affected the way the Bible was read and understood. New interpretations emerged which effectively recast the narrative of human origins, ends, and meanings.

Another effect of Darwin's work was to blur the distinction between human civilization and the natural world by showing the continuity of human and animal development and by producing a metaphoric which consistently described natural phenomena as analogous to urban structures and processes. In the age of massive industry-serving conurbations, machines, and engines, when the *conquest* of Nature was perceived as a facet of human destiny, the distinction was an important one, definitive of a culture with its roots deep in the Christian belief system. The blurring of the human-animal boundary evokes apocalyptic images of the recrudescence of primordial chaos—the removal of the ontological distinction definitive of civilization. The emergence of the human world out of chaos forms a significant thematic strand to the book of Revelation; there are repeated hints that its visions are as much to do with creation as with destruction. A number of commentators point to similarities between John's language and that of pagan creation mythology in which the world is born as a result of the defeat of primordial

chaos, usually personified as some kind of monster. This defeat
is depicted as both a primeval event and as an ongoing struggle
between chaos and order. Chaos, whether associated with the
darkness of the night, with the boundlessness of the ocean, or
with the wildness of desert regions, is an ever-present force
which constantly threatens to overwhelm the ordered world.
Norman Cohn writes of John's visions:

> In these prophecies the ancient myth of the assault of the forces of
> chaos upon the divinely appointed order, and of the victory of the
> young divine warrior over those forces, is radically reinterpreted. No
> longer concerned with a regularly recurring repetition of primordial
> happenings, it is transformed into a prophecy of the coming king-
> dom—of a world transfigured, for ever immune from the threat of
> chaos, and inhabited by an elect community of transformed human
> beings, for ever immune from ageing, disease and death.[6]

According to the *Enuma Elish* (an ancient Babylonian creation
epic) the world was formed when Marduk overcame Tiamat
(chaos) and cut her body into two, lifting half of it up to form the
sky. This myth was known in Canaan where a different (older)
version personified primordial chaos in the figure of Lotan (a
variant of Leviathan), depicted as a seven-headed monster. At a
number of points the Old Testament contains echoes of such
myths.

The book of Revelation reworks such older mythological formations, drawing on images of fantastical monsters (including a
seven-headed one—Rev. 13:1) and combat myths treating of the
primordial distinction between chaos and order, the desert and
the city. At one level, its description of the New Jerusalem is the
apotheosis of civilization that represents the ultimate and
irreversible defeat of chaos. This triumph is brought about by
cosmic warfare and bloodshed on an unimaginable scale. Urbanization and the rise of new technologies in the Victorian era are
occasionally described in similar terms. Not only do the writers
of the age speak of a war against nature, but they occasionally
also characterize industrialization and urbanization in terms of
a realization of humanity's divine mission to subdue the earth.
Despite this, a perception persists that, far from defeating chaos,
the new cities create conditions for an apocalyptic reversal of
the polarity—locating the desert *at the heart* of the city. Chapter

2 explores this theme, reading Florence Nightingale's *Cassandra* and James Thomson's *The City of Dreadful Night* in this context. Nightingale's use of desert imagery suggests the emptying out of women's time, rendering hollow and chaotic the very core of Victorian civilization—the domestic hearth. On this basis, it argues for a second coming: the advent of a female Christ. Thomson's poem locates the chaos in the human mind rather than in any social space and uses it to fund a reading of Christianity that is simultaneously both apocalyptic and anti-apocalyptic.

Both Nightingale's and Thomson's works are unveilings: Nightingale draws back the curtain of silence surrounding the lot of women in society, laying bare the emptiness at the heart of an entire social system, while Thomson reveals the "real night" of chaos and desperation below the surface of the civilized city. Unveiling is the founding trope of the Apocalypse. These are not isolated examples; the trope of unveiling is endemic to Victorian writing. At the inception of the Victorian era, Thomas Carlyle's *Sartor Resartus* spoke of "the new apocalypse of nature" which would uncover the secrets of the world, rendering it intelligible to human experience.[7] It might be argued that Darwin delivered precisely a new mode of intelligibility by which nature could be read and made to yield a new meaning. Yet, as appears in chapter 3, in Victorian literature reality remains characteristically veiled. This may be a form of denial or a rhetorical acknowledgment that to *unveil* a non-apocalyptic nature is deeply paradoxical. Illustrating this paradox, *Middlemarch* highlights the science that seeks to uncover the "primary tissues" of human life—an uncovering which reveals only another kind of veil—a web. On the other hand, Christina Rossetti's *The Face of the Deep* focuses consciously on apocalyptic themes yet actually unveils or uncovers personal and social forces rather than anything supernatural or inhuman.

As nature revealed ever more of its secrets to the sciences of geology, paleontology, botany, thermodynamics, etc., throughout the period, time remained a mystery which fascinated a number of Victorian writers. Chapter 4 engages with the fact that the human relation to time is of major significance for the Apocalypse, which seems contrived to show that time has a predetermined shape. If Victorian geology and evolution expanded time and abolished the horizons of biblical/apocalyptic time, literary texts renewed those horizons by fantasizing about the manipulation of time, re-imposing upon it a human scale. Thomas Hardy's *Far From the Madding Crowd* demonstrates a preoccupation with the way in which the era of mechanization altered the perception of time. It encodes a bifurcation of temporality between an abstract time, measured by mechanical means, and the older way of understanding time in relation to the rhythms of nature. The new temporality appears as a destructive measure which has a profoundly negative impact on the lives of those entramelled in its constraints. Its inhuman machinery, resisted by the traditional ways of Gabriel Oak, whirrs relentlessly through the novel, as an ever-threatening background noise. While Oak is able to rescue Bathsheba Everdene from its effects, Fanny Robin is ground down and destroyed by its most heartless avatar, Sergeant Troy. The clash of temporalities results in a victory, of sorts, for human time, but abstract time takes its toll and remains an undefeated and menacing presence. H. G. Wells's *The Time Machine* also deals with a new sense of time, but this has less to do with technology than with the scientific discourses that erased the boundaries of creation and consummation during the Victorian period. The novella recuperates narrative closure from the terrifying prospect of endlessness by allowing its protagonist to travel to the end of time—an end based on thermodynamics rather than religion. Both texts, however, demonstrate the late Victorian need to renegotiate the horizons of time, and in doing so both take on some kind of apocalyptic tone.

The Apocalypse takes place between time and the eternal, between the veiled and the unveiled, between the human and the inhuman, between order and chaos. It is neither completely Judaic nor Hellenistic; it belongs to neither Old nor New Testaments; it is both canonical and non-canonical—having a place in the Bible of Western Christianity, but being excluded from the canon favored by the Eastern Orthodox churches. In its curious relationship with both the rest of the Bible and with Christian belief, it opens up kind of third space—a paradoxical central margin. Victorian writing replicates this in various ways, in its evocation of the human within the inhuman, the veiled within the unveiled, the chaotic within the civilized. It often seems to be, in the words of Matthew Arnold, "Wandering between two worlds, one dead, the other powerless to be born."[8] *Jane Eyre* and *Wuthering Heights*, for example, problematize the opposition inside/outside as characters create for themselves a third space on the thresholds of buildings, institutions, and the social order—a space akin to that opened by apocalyptic vision in its occurrence between human and inhuman worlds. Darwinism created its own kind of third space between belief and unbelief, in the agnosticism of Huxley. The poetry of Matthew Arnold and Arthur Hugh Clough plies the margin between faith and doubt. Much of the literature thus looks back to the "dead" world of Christian certainty and forward to a post-Christian era.

Whilst many critics have noticed such images and tendencies, none has identified their specifically apocalyptic resonance, nor attempted to theorize their significance in this context. This study sets out to explore the cultural and literary reasons for the recapitulation of apocalyptic figures in the Victorian period, a time when the processes of industrialization and urbanization were demanding a re-drawing of the lines between civilization and its others—nature, disorder, and chaos.

"Of No Use"

> . . . such sermons would be of no use at Lowick . . . about . . .
> the prophecies in the Apocalypse."[10]
>
> George Eliot, Middlemarch

There are a number of paradoxes involved in finding affinities between Victorian writing and the Apocalypse. Why would a characteristically progressive age in matters of culture and religion look back to a genre of another time and place which traffics in broken-down worldviews and defunct cosmologies? Why would a culture rich in examples of demythologizing discourses turn to a text so irrelevant to the beliefs, ideals, and values of the modern era? Certainly the saintly Dorothea Brooke in George Eliot's great realist novel, *Middlemarch* (1871-72), has little time for the uselessness of apocalyptic thought, at least as it appears in the dry, theoretical sermons of the aptly named Mr. Tyke. She has not picked out the Apocalypse at random, here. There is good reason why its bizarre descriptions of events and processes in a realm far removed from the finely drawn, everyday world of Eliot's works should be held up as the epitome of uselessness: it is everything that realism is not, everything that

it reacts against, rejects, and seeks to relegate to obscure antiquity. What, indeed, could the age of literary realism, utilitarianism, industrialization and urbanization do with such a bizarre,
otherworldly, decidedly non-realist and practically functionless
text? It has none of the direct moral teaching of Jesus' Sermon
on the Mount that would make it a useful target for the demythologising criticism beloved of Eliot and others of her age. It has
none of the barbed wisdom of Jesus's parables, and it is short on
both the practical and doctrinal content of the epistles. It is replete with the fanciful, the improbable, and the downright incomprehensible. It contains no history, no homilies, no facts, no
followable narrative, and not much that could qualify as poetry.
Not even bad poetry. It is peopled with mythical creatures, monstrous beings, and figures of uncertain character and provenance;
it deploys a variety of arcane symbols, cryptic encodings, and numerological puzzles. Of what practical value is it to the Christian in search of spiritual light, let alone to the post-Christian
moral philosopher in search of demythologized, humanist values? It seems—for all these reasons—that the book of Revelation
should be a text with which Victorian thought and culture
should have little to do. Yet, curiously, this is not the case. Far
from it. Dorothea herself has previously made use of it as a
handy source of sublime metaphor:

> "How very beautiful these gems are!" said Dorothea, under a new
> current of feeling, as sudden as the gleam. "It is strange how deeply
> colours seem to penetrate one, like scent. I suppose that is the reason
> why gems are used as spiritual emblems in the Revelation of St John.
> They look like fragments of heaven."[9]

This kind of deployment is a familiar gesture in Victorian writing; the beautiful description of the New Jerusalem in Revelation 21 is alluded to for a variety of purposes by writers as
diverse as Elizabeth Barrett Browning (in many poems, including
her verse novel *Aurora Leigh*, 1856), and Arthur Hugh Clough
(in his *"Amours de Voyage,"* 1858). It turns up in Thomas
Hardy's *Jude the Obscure* (1896) when he needs a suitably grandiose homologue for his hero's boyish vision of Christminster,
and it can be found supplementing Browning's descriptions of
the glories of Rome and Renaissance art in "Christmas Eve"
(1850), and "Andrea del Sarto" (1855) respectively.[10]

Such images of fullness, intensity, richness, or completion are not necessarily deployed in optimism. The promise that gleams in Dorothea's "fragments of heaven" is undercut by her deadly, earth-bound alliance with Casaubon and her involvement in his doomed project to produce the "key to all mythologies"; under Casaubon's hand the biblical text will come to represent a dead weight that, far from opening visionary possibilities of reform, will become a force of repression, holding Dorothea back and eating away at her zeal for social improvement. Clough's protagonist uses the vision ironically to deny the realization of millenial dreams: "I . . . never beheld a New Jerusalem coming down dressed like a bride out of heaven Right on the Place de la Concorde." The Christminster vision of Hardy's Jude ultimately eludes him, and its glorious presence serves only to point up how far and how painfully short of his dreams his experience falls. Browning's use is more nostalgic than it is hopeful, and Barrett Browning alone among these examples alludes to the New Jerusalem as a vision of a brighter future. So, while the Apocalypse is not quite "of no use" in such instances, its appearance is largely wistful or ironic and seems to betoken a sense of loss or frustrating unattainability.

Occasionally its function is even more negative, for Victorian writers turned not only to the image of the New Jerusalem but also to some of the darker visions. In Elizabeth Gaskell's novels characters appeal to images of war and destruction to communicate something of the scale of social upheaval experienced by those caught in the processes of urban-industrial modernization. The battle between unions and masters is likened to "th' great battle o' Armageddon," in North and South (1855), while the political climate operative in Mary Barton (1848) is compared with the chaos unleashed by the horsemen of the Apocalypse: "the distress . . . was riding, like the Conqueror on his Pale Horse, among the people . . . crushing their lives out of them, and stamping woe-marks over the land."[11] Charlotte Brontë, too, invokes the Apocalypse in order to relate political conflict to spiritual causes, so that in Shirley (1849), Castlereagh (British Secretary for War at the time of the Battle of Waterloo) is compared to the antichrist and his pro-war allies to the Satanic legions unleashed before the battle of Armageddon.[12]

Divine judgement often seems close at hand, especially in the period of disillusionment which followed the wars and revolutions of the mid century. Sebastian Evans's poem "The Fifteen Days of Judgement" (1865) is a verse rendering of "Earth's Last Judgement and destruction, / and its fiery reconstruction," based upon the book of Revelation and certain unspecified "Hebrew annals." It ends with a warning that the consummation of the world might be closer than you think: "Sinner! Doest thou dread that trial? / Mark yon shadow on the dial!"[13] Some four years later Matthew Arnold would publish *Culture and Anarchy* (1869) with its apocalyptic fear that the forces of chaos may be unleashed by the "Philistines and Barbarians" and their indifference to "sweetness and light." In such an age, he says: "the warning voice is again heard: *Now is the judgement of this world.*"[14] A similar apprehension appears in Samuel Butler's *The Way of All Flesh*, when the young protagonist worries "that the Day of Judgement might indeed be nearer than we had thought."[17] When, during the same period, Anthony Trollope satirized the mendacity and corruption of London society in *The Way We Live Now* (1875), he occasionally turned to apocalyptic comparisons, likening Melmotte to the dragon who attempts to usurp God's power, and Squercum to the angel Michael who overcomes it (Revelation 12).[16] George Eliot, aware of the currency of such fears and their use in literary works, gently mocks them in *Daniel Deronda* (1876):

> To glory in a prophetic vision of knowledge covering the earth, is an easier exercise of believing imagination than to see its beginning in newspaper placards, staring at you from a bridge beyond the corn-fields; and it might well happen to most of us dainty people that we were in the thick of the battle of Armageddon without being aware of anything more than the annoyance of a little explosive smoke and struggling on the ground immediately about us.[17]

The tone is similar to that of Dorothea Brooke's disparagement of sermons on apocalyptic theology inasmuch as the apocalypse represents, once again, the antithesis of realism. So much so that even were the unlikely events of St. John's visions to materialize in the nineteenth-century world, they would be unrecognizably distant, irrelevant, unimposing. The comic comparison between the biblical image of knowledge covering the earth (alluding to Habakkuk's apocalyptic vision—Hab. 2:14), and the boom in the newspaper trade after the abolition of "newspaper tax" in 1855, serves to force home the point that the modern world, for Eliot, had a profoundly changed relationship with the biblical text.[18] If the Apocalypse was to be of any use at all, it had to be as an index of the times—not in the traditional sense of offering prophetic insight into the spiritual significance of world events, their place in the calendar of progress toward a divinely appointed end, but in the sense that the modern world could be defined by its distance from, and its rejection of, the irreality of the apocalyptic imagination. This distance is discernible in many Victorian literary uses of Apocalypse, especially in realist fiction. Gaskell, Trollope, Hardy, and Butler all come close to such a view in placing their apocalyptic metaphors in the mouths of uneducated, unsophisticated, naive, or just plain bad people.

In *The Nether World* (1889), George Gissing reverses the polarity. He places his apocalyptic vision in the dream of a character called "Mad Jack," yet the vision does not banish the Apocalypse to outer darkness; rather, it draws it close to the real world of urban squalor and despair. In his dream, Mad Jack is visited by an angel:

> There was a light such as none of you ever saw, and the angel stood in the midst of it. And he said to me: "Listen, whilst I reveal to you the truth, that you may know where you are and what you are; and this is done for a great purpose." And I fell down on my knees, but never a word could I have spoken. Then the angel said: "You are passing through a state of punishment. You, and all the poor among whom you live; all those who are in suffering of body and darkness of mind, were once rich people, with every blessing the world can bestow . . . because you made an ill use of your wealth, because you were selfish and hard-hearted and oppressive and sinful . . . after death you received the reward of wickedness. This life you are now leading is that of the damned; this place to which you are confined is Hell!"[19]

The device of the angel bringing revelation is one that Gissing might have learned from St. John, and its effect is much the same as that created by James Thomson in *The City of Dreadful Night*. In both visions Hell is revealed to be an earthly condition rather than an other-worldly place, inverting the apocalyptic process by which the heavenly realm is revealed. This approximation of apocalyptic vision in the establishing of (broadly) humanist values is a central paradox in the literary uses of apocalyptic rhetoric in Victorian writing, and it will appear in a number of guises in the chapters that follow. It might be thought to mark the often-noted uncertainty of the period about the truth-telling status of the Bible and the viability of a Bible-based Christian faith. This is no less marked in the work of George Eliot than any other author of the time, despite the fact that she was at the cutting edge of these developments in introducing modern biblical criticism to the English-speaking world. For her perception of realism, as has been shown, takes the Apocalypse as a limit text—a contrasting background against which realism can be recognized and valorized.

Charlotte Brontë's use of the biblical text forms an interesting parallel in that it encodes an ambiguity about the imposition of narrative endings. The closing lines of both *Jane Eyre* and *Villette* have strong apocalyptic resonances. *Jane Eyre* (1847), of course, ends with a direct quotation of the closing words of Revelation: "Amen; even so, come, Lord Jesus!"[20] Furthermore, they are the words of a man who bears the name St. John. The closing passage also alludes to Bunyan's allegory of Christian experience in *The Pilgrim's Progress,* comparing St. John's missionary endeavor to Greatheart's valiant battle against the demonic Apollyon. This is a venture that Jane has been unwilling to embark upon, having refused to marry St. John in order to return to Rochester. It is possible to see in Brontë's denouement, then, two possible outcomes, one of which offers earthly fulfilment, the other a vision of spiritual destiny. Tellingly, Jane refers to Rochester at this point as "what I love best *on earth*" (emphasis added), as though to differentiate between different modes of construing narrative closure.[23] The fact that Jane has rejected a share in St. John's destiny, and yet concludes her narrative with *his* end rather than her own, could be taken as precisely the kind of paradox already outlined: it acknowledges a need for an end which promises spiritual fulfilment while recognizing that the positing of such an end compromises the demands of fiction that remains true to lived experience.

The later novel, *Villette* (1853), ends with an even more troubled sense of uncertainty. The narrative leaves Lucy Snowe waiting and longing for the return of Paul Emanuel, and she repeats the words "he is coming" in an effort to keep her hope alive.[22] If we miss in this incantation the echo of early Christian

longing for the return of Christ at the world's end, the name
Emanuel—an epithet associated with Christ, and meaning God
with(in) us—is there to remind us of the parallel and to evoke
the apocalyptic closing of *Jane Eyre*. But now the uncertainty
seems to have deepened, and the bereft narrator concludes her
narrative with an unsettling appeal to the reader's own imagination as arbiter of the end: "Let them picture union and a happy
succeeding life."[23] The closure offered in the appeal to the Apocalypse is partially withdrawn but remains as one possible reading of the end: an openness predicated upon closure.

"Transformed, Apocalyptic Voice"

> Life calls to us
> In some transformed, apocalyptic voice,
> Above us, or below us, or around:
> Perhaps we name it Nature's voice, or Love's . . .
> —Elizabeth Barrett Browning, *Aurora Leigh*

Both *Jane Eyre* and *Villette*, in their allusions to biblical language, encode the possibility of ends that transcend the specific
and personal closure enjoyed or desired by the heroines. The personal and the universal inhere in each other so that Jane's sense
of fulfilment partakes of the fullness of the destiny envisaged by
St. John as he works towards the establishing of God's kingdom
and the return of Christ, while the unsatisfactory and unresolved situation of Lucy Snowe at the close of *Villette* reflects
the remoteness of Parousia. Apocalypse thus features as a medium in which the concerns and problems of the individual can
be seen to participate in, reflect, and even embody, a larger process. Conversely, an order which subtends the vicissitudes of individual experience can be seen to inhere in the small-scale
narrative of an enclosed social space. The transformation of the
apocalyptic voice into its characteristic Victorian mode seems
often to be a matter of just such an interweaving of restricted
and general economies on the basis that it offers an overarching,
cosmic narrative closure yet is told in the first person and addressed to specific social and religious situations.

Romantic versions of apocalypse underlie such usage. When,
for example, Elizabeth Barrett Browning refers to "some transformed apocalyptic voice" in *Aurora Leigh*, she seems to be

speaking of what Harold Bloom calls (in relation to Shelley) a "fusion of will and grace,"[24] the coalescence of human and inhuman in the encounter with the sublime. This "fusion" refers to the Romantic sense that the awe-inspiring aspects of Nature communicate to the suppliant a reciprocity which implies that the world cannot be seen merely as an object, or as an "it." The sublime draws the awe-stricken subject into an engagement with Nature, into participating in its struggle and acknowledging their own embeddedness in the natural world. In this interaction human destiny appears in its richest, most fulfilling form. But while the revolutionary fervor that fired the imaginations of the young Wordsworth, Coleridge, and Shelley gave rise to visions of Nature as a material force in the shaping of human destiny, its voice is characteristically transmuted into a sigh of mortality, an echo of the human spirit, or a metaphor for Providence in much post-Romantic writing.

In Barrett Browning's verse novel the voice is apocalyptic, but not in the same way as is Wordsworth's Nature, with its display of "types and symbols of Eternity,"[25] or the voice of Shelley's *Demogorgon* in *Prometheus Unbound*. Barrett Browning's apocalypse consists in the calling of the poetic sensibility towards a renewed vision of personal empowerment: a new, subjective understanding of life and nature. Apocalypse is personal here rather than cosmic, and this is a keynote of its Victorian expression. In the uses already cited this is obvious. Spurgeon's sermon, quoted at the head of this introduction, while it appeals to a generalized human nature, uses the impenetrability of St. John's text, with its closed register of those called to eternal life, as a means of encouraging the individual to "examine [them]-selves then whether [they] have been called" to salvation.[26] Even where the focus is political, as in Gaskell's novels, the apocalyptic moment is voiced by particular characters with idiosyncratic turns of mind and of phrase. Despite its apparent claim to universality, Sebastian Evans's paean to divine judgement comes down to an urge to the individual "sinner" to repent. In such texts we do not hear the sounding of a universal warning, herald, or pronouncement so much as the imposition of narrative shape upon individual experience. Barrett Browning's Apocalypse is apprehended not as the voice of God, nor of an angel, nor even certainly of Nature; it is of uncertain origin. It may arise as a Shelleyan coalescence of the human mind with a personified

"Nature," or "Love," or "Life," or it may be nothing other than an inner voice, be it conscience, intelligence, or imagination.

The ending of Tennyson's *In Memoriam* (1850), provides an interesting counter-example:

> No longer half-akin to brute,
> For all we thought and loved and did,
> And hoped, and suffer'd, is but seed
> Of what in them is flower and fruit;
>
> Whereof the man, that with me trod
> This planet, was a noble type
> Appearing ere the times were ripe,
> That friend of mine who lives in God,
>
> That God, which ever lives and loves,
> One God, one law, one element,
> And one far-off divine event
> To which the whole creation moves.[27]

Tennyson's eulogized friend, Hallam, figures here as the herald, or advance guard, of a new age in human development and knowledge which recalls Carlyle's prophecy of the "new apocalypse of nature." To such people, Tennyson thinks, nature will be "an open book." The advancement of human knowledge and understanding embodied in Hallam itself adumbrates the divine consummation—the realization of God's kingdom on earth. Thus, whereas the direction of much apocalyptic rhetoric and allusion in the writing of the era takes a universal theme and internalizes or personalizes it, Tennyson's poem moves in the opposite direction, taking a personal, subjective grief and teasing from it cosmic implications. But the direction of travel seems to me to be of less significance than the points connected by the journey: Tennyson's Apocalypse may appear to have universal significance, but it does not emerge from currents of public interest or concern. It is not underpinned by war, famine, pestilence, or the manipulation of political power; rather, it flows from the death of an intimate friend and arises out of a process by which the inner agony of grief is documented, analyzed, and, if not overcome, at least assimilated into one's psychological normality.

In the examples already given of uses to which the book of

Revelation is put in Victorian writing, it is possible to observe a range of modulations in the apocalyptic voice; fear of change, nostalgia, hope, irony, socio-political polemic, etc., each impose their own particular subjectivizing spin on the biblical text. But these are more-or-less conscious uses of citation and allusion, deployed to create quantifiable effects, to deepen meaning or enrich possibilites. I would argue that the relationship between Victorian writing and the Apocalypse suggested by these examples is actually somewhat misleading because it distracts the reader from the deeper affinities, the discovery of which serves to reveal otherwise hidden ideological substrates. Obvious references, acknowledged affinities, appear to be elective, deliberate, controlled, whereas the interest of this work lies in the deep-laid cultural assumptions, the buried effects of an inherited biblicism which shape literary choices, endeavors, procedures. It is almost as if the obvious uses of the Apocalypse are there as a palliative against the unmasking of certain shadowy, atavistic proclivities: the desire to regain lost control, the need for a new order to replace defunct systems, the longing for a narrative closure that could give shape, meaning, and purpose to a world rendered unintelligible by constant flux.

The shifts from an agrarian to an industrial economy, from a rural to an urban lifestyle, from a temporal framework dictated by the time of sun, moon, and seasons, to one imposed by train timetables and clocks, all contributed to social and political upheaval and to the loss of familiar cultural landmarks. To this catalogue of destabilizing forces should be added the loss of religious certainty and the decline of the church as a socially cohesive influence. Perhaps these eventualities help to explain why the Victorian era became the great age of the English realist novel. It may be that its culture came to be dominated by a genre which imposed beginnings, middles, and ends on the vicissitudes of human social interaction and attempted to render perspicuous the muddled, entangled, and opaque processes of Victorian life, precisely because the complexity and uncertainty of the times necessitated a transitional narrative between religious order and whatever might emerge from its ruins. If so, then echoes of the Apocalypse are perfectly understandable, since it too belonged to a provisional genre that arose in the limbo between the loss of one world and the emergence of another. The shadows and echoes of the Apocalypse in its images, rhetoric,

and themes serve to locate much Victorian writing in the dystopic space described by Arnold: a space between a dead, or
dying world, and another, as yet "powerless to be born."

APOLOGIA

Having greater cause to say so than he himself had, I would
echo—by way of explaining my choice of texts for discussion—
the words of David Shaw: "though my approach is inclusive, it
is not inclusive enough."[28] In selecting the works for scrutiny in
the following chapters I have sought to focus on those that—to
my mind—best illustrate the particular literary and cultural proclivities under consideration. These are judgements which
might be questioned in terms of their acuity, or their explana-
tory and illustrative value, but they are nonetheless those that
I have formed during the years over which this study has been
conducted. Sometimes these judgements have led me to produce
detailed readings of texts whose relative unfamiliarity may appear to render their selection either arbitrary or even downright
contrary. Chapter 2's focus on Florence Nightingale's *Cassandra*
and James Thomson's *The City of Dreadful Night* is perhaps the
most vulnerable to such a criticism. In defense of the selection
of these two works as foci, I would point out that the framing
discussion takes in a wide range of texts, some of which are considerably better known, but none of which offers quite the same
kind of diagnostic potential or set of possibilities for opening up
the theme. This does not mean that the theme itself is of little
moment; it is my hope that the very range and scope of the con-
textualization suggests that the image of the desert in the city is
of sufficient cultural significance to warrant its inclusion. In this
context, while Nightingale's text may not be the most widely
read discussion of women's time from the Victorian period, it
does illustrate more clearly than any other text of its age with
which I am familiar the sense of desertion or barrenness at the
heart of the domestic ideal. It also offers important insights into
the way in which the civilization/desert duality resonates in the
experience of Victorian women. Again, Thomson's great poem
may not be as well known as some others, but its treatment of
the urban environment is both unique in its scale and intensity
and—at the same time—illustrative of some of the negative re-

sponses to the city in the period. It was also highly influential in the emergence of modernism's urban aesthetics via its influence on T. S. Eliot.

My methodology throughout the book is the same as that described in relation to chapter 2, and where similar concerns might be raised about my discussion of Christina Rossetti's little known commentary on the Apocalypse—*The Face of the Deep*—in chapter 3, my rationale for its inclusion is the same. I would add in relation to Rossetti that I think it would need some justification *not* to examine this text in detail in these pages since it is a direct literary discussion of the Apocalypse by one of the foremost poets of the age and could therefore hardly have been left out. Another contributing factor to my selection of texts has particular relevance to *The Face of the Deep:* the latter is a fascinating, moving, and poetically rich book which deserves to be far more widely read. I hope that by concerning myself with the details of some of these lesser known works, I might foster greater interest in them as worthy of a broader modern readership and intensified critical attention.

1

Human and Inhuman

BEASTS

> I cannot persuade myself that a beneficent and omnipotent
> God would have designedly created the Ichneumonidae with
> the express intention of their feeding within the living bodies
> of caterpillars . . .
>
> —Charles Darwin, letter to Asa Gray, 1860[1]

CHARLES DARWIN'S OBSERVATION OF THE EGG-LAYING HABITS OF A certain species of parasitic wasp is a rather uncomfortable reminder that animals often have a role in theological reflection. At its simplest, their part in Bible-inspired religious rhetoric is as examples of virtue or vice: the ant is the model of commendable industry in the book of Proverbs (6:6); the mule is the epitome of reprehensible stubbornness in Psalm 32:9; in the Sermon on the Mount, moths represent corruption, and birds carefree innocence (Matt. 6:19, 26); sheep are often associated with innocent suffering (e.g. Psalm 44:22, Rom. 8:36), while the generic category "beasts" is used to denote the antithesis of moral responsibility (2 Peter 2:12, Jude v. 10). But it seems unlikely that Darwin's pang of nature-inspired scepticism would ever be replicated in a theologian because the meaning of "nature" in natural science is very different from its meaning within theology—even that branch of enquiry known as "natural" theology. Nevertheless, Darwin's punctilious concern with the detail of natural phenomena did run out in theological debate because it changed the perception of the relationship between humans and animals within western cultures, not simply in raising to popular consciousness the possibility of an ontological continuity between human and subhuman, but also because that perception opened onto far-reaching questions about human nature and its place in the created order. Famously, this debate emerged in the public confrontation between T. H. Huxley and Bishop Wilberforce in 1860, over humanity's closest affinities and the question of whether they were with apes or with angels. That this became an important dividing line between faith and unbelief is a matter of a cultural history that has been traced in detail by James R. Moore in his account of what he calls "the post-Darwinian controversies." He notes that by 1878 at least one churchman saw the situation as a crisis of apocalyptic significance:

> Is there not a great conflict between light and darkness, increasing in intensity every day,—likely to be more fierce? On the one hand the Church of Christ, reviving and strengthening, and full of the buoyancy of life; on the other, her sceptical opponents, ready to destroy her, not with physical weapons . . . but with the weapons of universal doubt. . . . Many events indicate that we are now at the beginning at least of the great struggle which is not to end until the ushering in of the millennial period.[2]

But the apocalyptic dimensions of the question are not confined to the perturbed minds of Victorian divines. The Apocalypse deals with the limits of human experience and with what is imagined to lie beyond them. Most obviously, perhaps, it has come to be associated with the limits of temporality within which human experience is confined. Prior to the rise of the nineteenth-century discourses of geological and evolutionary science, time was limited by creation and consummation—bounded by Genesis and Revelation. The unimaginably extended time implied by rock formation and the slow accretion of infinitesimal changes to living organisms demanded a new negotiation with time. I return to this theme in chapter 4, but for now the focus is on the ways in which the Apocalypse deals with the limits of human nature—its subjection to inhuman forces which exceed, threaten, transcend, or condition its existence and are characterized in terms of personality.

As indicated in the introduction, what the book of Revelation purports to uncover is the heavenly realm—a region of beings, activities, events, and processes beyond normal human perceptions—and to do so in a way that reveals their impact on human affairs. It presumes, as a product of a mythopoeic cultural formation, that human experience is subject to both hostile and beneficent forces beyond its direct observation or control: the human is bounded on every side by the inhuman. Its depiction of the inhuman has two poles, the divine and the demonic, and its narrative focus is on the conflict between these two forces, played out in a cosmic drama. The action is divided between the heavenly and earthly realms so that the events which unfold in human history are shown to be related to, and even caused by, those which happen in the otherworldly region. For current purposes, what is fascinating about the inhuman world of John's visions in the book of Revelation is the way in which its characterizations of the inhuman blend the human and the animal, even in the depiction of the divine. Take, for example, its description of the throne room where God occupies the seat of cosmic power:

> in the midst of the throne, and round about the throne, were four beasts full of eyes before and behind. And the first was like a lion, and the second like a calf, and the third beast had a face as a man, and the fourth beast was like a flying eagle. And the four beasts had each of them six wings about him; and they were full of eyes within: and they rest not day and night, saying, Holy holy, holy, Lord God Almighty, which was, and is, and is to come. (Rev. 4:6–8)

Again, the cosmic Christ, the transfigured and glorified Jesus, is described throughout the text as both lion and lamb: "And one of the elders saith unto me, Weep not: behold the Lion of the tribe of Judah. . . . And I beheld, and, lo, in the midst of the throne and of the four beasts, and in the midst of the elders, stood a Lamb as it had been slain" (Rev. 5:5–6).

Similarly, the depiction of the powers of darkness draws on animal imagery:

> And I stood upon the sand of the sea, and saw a beast rise up out of the sea, having seven heads and ten horns, and upon his horns ten crowns, and upon his heads the name of blasphemy. And the beast I saw was like unto a leopard, and his feet were as the feet of a bear, and his mouth as the mouth of a lion: and the dragon gave him his power, and his seat, and great authority. (Rev. 13:1–2)

Of course, these images are drawn from a repertoire of apocalyptic symbols and cyphers, evident in earlier texts such as Ezekiel and Daniel and other, non-canonical texts. But they also reflect a more ancient, mythopoeic proclivity to draw out the boundary lines of the human, to define human existence in relation to the animals which are both their predators and their prey. In the most ancient literary source, *The Epic of Gilgamesh* (some four thousand years old), we find the character Enkidu who, created half man and half beast, progresses towards full humanity by phatically shedding his animal behavior. His foil is Gilgamesh, created part man and part god, yet who is also described in relation to animals: "two thirds of him god and one third human . . . like a wild bull."[3] The ancient Egyptians liberally mixed human and animal forms in their depiction of the divine: "A god might be depicted as a man, or as a falcon, or as a falcon-headed man. In one context the king is described as the sun, a star, a bull, a crocodile, a lion, a falcon, a jackal."[4] Perhaps more familiar are those classical images of gods and humans who assume, or who are transmogrified into, animal shapes: bulls, swans, eagles, spiders, etc. Celtic mythology, too, often associates the more-than-human with an interconnection between species: the Irish hero, Cu Chulainn, and the Welsh hero, Pryderi, are both born contemporaneously with horses and each is given the animal as a gift.[5]

Victorian literature reiterated the ancient perception of the proximity of humans and animals, even before the publication of *The Origin of Species* lodged it in the popular imagination in 1859. Douglas Jerrold's play *Black-Ey'd Susan* (1829) includes villainous characters called Doggrass and Gnatbrain, and creatures such as sharks, bulls, starlings, gadflies, and albatrosses feature in its metaphors. Emily Brontë created the beastly Heathcliff, consistently associating him with animal features and characteristics (1847). When he first appears his humanity is questioned by Nelly Dean's description of him as an "it"—a creature that does not even seem to be capable of human language: "when it was set on its feet, it only stared round, and repeated over and over again some gibberish that nobody could understand."[6] Even Cathy describes him as "a fierce, pitiless, wolfish man."[7] In the 1840s and 50s, Dickens frequently created names which included animals or evoked their behavior: Guppy, Vholes, Baynham-Badger, Cuttle, Nipper, MacStinger. In the very year of the appearance of *The Origin of Species*, Christina Rossetti wrote "Goblin Market": a poem that blends human and animal in the depiction of the goblin men who sell forbidden fruit: "One had a cat's face, / One whisked a tail, / One tramped at a rat's pace, / One crawled like a snail."[8]

Examples could be multiplied. What the pre–1859 Victorian texts have in common, and where they differ from their ancient forebears, is a sense of the debasement of humans in their association with animals. But it would not be true to assert that this changed in any straightforwardly appreciable way with the rise of Darwinism. In order to understand that the comparison of human behavior with that of animals still represents degradation well beyond the point at which Darwin created the first scientifically plausible theory of their real affinity, one has only to turn to the *fin-de-siècle* period, to the animal-like Mr. Hyde in Robert Louis Stevenson's tale, to the incarnations as dog and bat of Bram Stoker's Count Dracula, or to H. G. Wells's depiction of the subhuman Eloi and Morlocks in *The Time Machine.* Nevertheless, one can still detect in the continued literary proximity of humans and animals an ongoing need to explore the limits of the human—a rolling project to reinforce the boundaries by exposing liminal proclivities.

The limits of the human, its borders with that which exceeds, transcends, limits or threatens it, whether sub-human or super-human, are necessarily drawn out in contradistinction to the animal world, since the only available models for inhuman sentience are to be found among animals. Little wonder then that when mythopoeic human culture projected something stronger, higher, more powerful than itself, it did so by supplementing human characteristics with animal characteristics. In the Victorian context the rise of evolutionary sciences meant that these lines of demarcation, used by now for rather different purposes, had to be redrawn, not only because they called into question the role of the divine in creating and marking out the ontological limits of species, but also because they replaced the static, regional model of specific differences with a temporal process of slow emergence and differentiation. Inherent in the idea of a process is the necessity of the permeability of boundaries, the unavoidable occurrence of blending. In a certain way this echoes the very system that it replaces, drawing the hybrid forms of myth—centaurs, harpies, gorgons, sphinxes, leopard-bear-lions—into the material processes of development. So, in redefining speciation as a temporal, rather than a fixed, categorical phenomenon, Darwin's work on the origin of species set up a series of resonances with the mythologies underlying his culture, principally biblical mythology, and especially, as I hope to show, the book of Revelation. This is not an accident of Darwin's text, but a cultural necessity: in re-imagining the processes of definition in a way that could not but change human self-perception, Darwin was necessarily engaging with the limits of human existence as they had previously been envisaged.

The effects of Darwin's renegotiation of the limits of the human can be felt most strongly, perhaps, in the work of Friedrich Nietzsche. The opening of his early essay "On Truth and Falsity in Their Ultramoral Sense" (1873) has a strongly Darwinian (and almost apocalyptic) tone:

> In some remote corner of the universe, effused into innumerable solar-systems, there was once a star upon which clever animals invented cognition. That was the haughtiest, most mendacious moment in the history of the world, but yet only a moment. After Nature had taken breath awhile, the star congealed and the clever animals had to die.[9]

Nietzsche's sense of both the evolutionary emergence which casts humans as "clever animals," and the brevity of human existence—no more than a bit of a breather for Nature on the new timescale—he clearly owed to Darwin. His later, more memorable image of humanity as a rope drawn between beast and *ubermensch,* is even more clearly Darwinian in origin if not in implication.[10] But while he was, arguably, the nineteenth century's most radical rethinker of cultural values in a Darwinian universe, Nietzsche was not alone in his perception that such values required transvaluation for an evolved, rather than a created, species. In Victorian Britain a number of poets, mostly women, set about the task of redefining some of the culturally most significant terms of their time. Agnes Mary Robinson's poem "Darwinism" (1888), is a useful example:

> Not love, nor the wild fruits he sought;
> Nor the fierce battles of his clan
> Could still the unborn and aching thought
> Until the brute became the man.

> Long since . . . And now the same unrest
> Goads to the same invisible goal,
> Till some new gift, undreamed, unguessed
> End the new travail of the soul.[11]

In this poem, Robinson traces human longing and dissatisfaction to pre-human instincts and ponders whether another stage of evolution might resolve them. There is a quiet revolution taking place in her words which is easy to miss: a question that was once metaphysical, or even theological, has become physical, biological. The "invisible goal" of human development, the fulfilment of human desires, remains "undreamed, unguessed," in a gesture that denies the ends projected by apocalyptic religion. Yet the old language remains, if not intact, at least recognizable: the "travail of the soul" is resonant of St. Paul's image of a creation groaning with longing for its promised consummation (Rom. 8:22–23). The tone remains teleological: evolution is directed towards a "goal" and—most significantly—the human still depends for its definitive form upon that which is *given* to it—the "gift" of some force, power, or being that transcends its condition.

Similar observations may be made about Mathilde Blind's attempt to transvalue human values in her long poem *The Ascent of Man* (1889).[12] It sets out to explore the balance of love and violence in a Darwinian universe, engaging with human suffering as continuous with the struggle for survival in nature. The poem represents a sustained consideration of the processes of civilization in search of some means of transcending our animal origins. "Spirit" or "divinity" are posited as goals of human development—unreached realities foreshadowed in human love—especially the bond between mother and child. Isobel Armstrong has claimed that the poem's search "for a new language . . . to suggest plastic transformation and possibility in matter" is not entirely successful.[13] It is difficult to disagree with this judgement although Armstrong offers no argument or evidence for it. I would argue that its failure to find a "new language" is (perhaps paradoxically) a product of its very investment in Darwin: it is mired in what I hope to show to be Darwin's own inability to escape apocalyptic rhetoric and its related discourses of Christian value and perception.

In the long "Chaunts of Life" section, which takes the reader from the origin of life through to the emergence of "Spirit," the primordial chaos is strangely familiar to readers of the Bible: "over the face of the waters far heaving in limitless twilight / Auroral pulsations thrilled faintly"; "Lo, moving o'er the chaotic waters, / Love dawned upon the seething waste."[14] Humanity emerges from the chaos steeped in violence and bloodshed, but evolving higher faculties of reason and love which give rise to the goal of self-transcendence. In the light of this narrative it is a matter of some interest to ponder the significance of the insistent apocalyptic tone in which war is depicted as a "harvest" (28), the slain as bound in "sheaves" (31; c.f. Rev. 14:14–20); in which the fall of Rome heralds a global drift towards "annihilation" (35), and "Woe" is pronounced over mankind (47); in which the stars fall from heaven amid "rumours of wars" (72), and the return of chaos is an ever-present threat. The apocalyptic resonance is taken into the final section—"The Leading of Sorrow"—with its rhetoric of "unveiling," and the presence of "trampling hooves" that seem to herald the very threats associated with the four horsemen of the Apocalypse: war, famine, pestilence, and death. Again, its introduction of a mysterious guide is a device familiar from Dante, but which originates in apocalyptic tradition (see, for example Rev. 17:1).

Blind's engagement in the process of Darwinian transvaluation leads her to the same kind of gestures as those noted in Robinson's poem, but on a grander scale. In attempting to redefine the human in dynamic, processual terms, she is thrown back on the familiar mythology of creation and consummation. Just as Robinson's poem ends with the "gift" to humanity from beyond, Blind reiterates at the close of her poem the apocalyptic images of inhuman agency: an inhuman guide, unveiling, transfiguration, resurrection, and the eternal:

> And beside me in the golden morning
> I beheld my shrouded phantom-guide;
> But no longer sorrow-veiled and mourning—
> It became transfigured by my side.
>
> And I knew—as one escaped from prison
> Sees things again with fresh surprise—
> It was Love himself, Love re-arisen
> With the Eternal shining through his eyes. (110)

The cultural power of the apocalyptic myth to reabsorb the discourses which threaten to overthrow or supplant it is abundantly evident in the poems by Robinson and Blind. This power is not only attributable to the fact that one cannot avoid speaking of, or speaking to, the discourse one is seeking to overthrow, thereby repeating it, but also to the insistent presence of apocalypse in the desire to bring something to an end, to close it, to replace it. When the target is the human as such, or the cluster of values which we have long taken to be definitive of our species (love, reason, desire, hope, care, etc.), then apocalypticism has already covered the field. In the remainder of this chapter I set out to show that in its very founding text, *The Origin of Species*, the project of transvaluation is everywhere entrammelled in apocalyptic rhetoric. This is not a matter of mere resonances or linguistic echoes; rather it is an instructive instance of the cultural embeddedness of all discourses: another reminder that even when we are dealing with nature—as Darwin was—the discourse is effectively "constrained," as Jacques Derrida puts it, by "a law of the concept of nature," by preformed associations, categories, and even myths.[15]

The Origin of Species may seem to some to be the last place one should look for apocalypse. It might be—and indeed has been—construed as a profoundly anti-apocalyptic work, which conducts scientific enquiries far removed from the kind of theological and teleological values that inhere in the apocalyptic mode. It might also be understood to represent a discourse unrelated to the imaginative and speculative encryptions of history associated with the biblical book of Revelation. But it did give rise in its time to a great deal of theological argument: to debate among theologians as well as confrontation between theologians and scientists, forming a kind of historical watershed in relations between religion and science. So, in a sense that I hope will become apparent during this chapter, it might be said to be the *last* place in which we *should* look for the apocalyptic. That is to say, it might represent the end of an epoch—a paradoxical end to apocalyptic thought. By the same logic, it is also the beginning of a different way of thinking about apocalyptic literature—an evolutionary mode of constructing boundaries, limits, demarcations as such.

The Origin of Species is, perhaps counterintuitively, about last things, because it is about first things. That is to say, it might be understood to have begun the still-current process of rewriting human origins, which is also, as this chapter argues, to rewrite ends. This is a matter of acknowledging that the vision of the end encoded in the book of Revelation depends upon the construction of the origins of the world and of human life narrated in Genesis. Darwin's recasting of the creative (or generative) process, by removing from it all trace of divine intervention (or "special creation") necessarily alters the way in which Revelation is read. Furthermore, *The Origin* has certain surprising rhetorical affinities with the book of Revelation that can fund an intertextual reading of the two works.

One of these affinities—a fundamental one—emerges from an effect observed by Marx and Engels. They argued that Darwin's view of biological phenomena was deeply colored by the historical and cultural conditions under which his work was produced. Following their lead, the remainder of this chapter explores the way in which Nature takes on the characteristics of a mid-Victorian city in Darwin's text. Given this comparison, I argue that his image of the Tree of Life (used to describe the branching movement of species through time) is more closely related to that found in an apocalyptic city in Revelation than to that which appears in the Garden of Eden in Genesis. The Tree of Life turns out to be not a single plant, but a whole species, and this discovery is also the trace of a bio-rhetorical interweaving of origins and ends. A "web of affinities" between the two texts spreads from this perception.

THE POLITY OF NATURE

In *The Origin* Darwin described nature as a "polity" with "districts" and an "economy," in which the structural features of beehives, for example, are compared to the work of architects, masons, and painters.[16] But what place, if any, did the church occupy in this City of Nature? The text of *The Origin*, for the most part, seems to occlude the body of Christ. This might betoken a belief, on Darwin's part, that the church was not relevant to the natural processes that he described, nor those processes relevant to the church. But, for T. H. Huxley, Darwin's publicist and defender, the advent of such theories as that of evolution by natural selection was of deep significance for the beliefs of religious people. He envisaged the "drowning" of religious souls beneath what he characterized as "the advancing tide of matter."[17] Materialistic descriptions of natural phenomena in Huxley's metaphor seem to overwhelm spiritual possibilities. On this account the church must be seen as that Pauline paradox, a "spiritual body" which has no place in the now seemingly universal order of nature.

But materialistic arguments led in other directions simultaneously. For some Christians, Darwinian theory served as a confirmation of their belief that God never intervenes in a natural order, the laws of which he fixed in advance. A. L. Moore, for example, argued that "there are not, and cannot be, any Divine interpositions in nature, for God cannot interfere with Himself. . . . *For the Christian theologian the facts of nature are the acts of God.*"[18] But the nature of nature is still very much in doubt here. In 1860 Darwin himself pointed out certain natural phenomena which would present "the Christian theologian" interested in studying such "acts of God" with some uncomfortable data: the above quotation about the Ichneumonidae is a case in point. It seems unlikely that Moore's version of nature included such a finely observed, detailed knowledge of any specific creature. This highlights the fact that the meaning given to "nature" depends upon the value-system within which it is studied or described. The value attached to the body, whether of Christ or of a simple organism will, to some extent, be determined by the level of observation and the concomitant mode of description applied to natural phenomena. If Darwin's highly differentiated natural world was, for all its closely observed detail, constructed on an urban model, then it should come as no surprise to find that the church, while it is not altogether absent, is well hidden in the recesses of *The Origin*. The rapid growth of Victorian conurbations quickly outstripped the English church's ability to erect new buildings and to adapt its parochial system of government to meet newly expanded urban requirements. The Anglican church did begin a building program in 1818, but it was many years before there was a sufficient number of places of worship in urban areas, so that large areas of Britain's mid-nineteenth-century cities, the urban model for Darwin's natural architecture, were (temporarily) without churches.

Both Marx and Engels saw industrial, capitalist civilization beneath Darwin's characterization of the natural world, like the skull beneath the skin.[19] According to Engels, "the struggle for existence is simply the transference from society to animate nature of Hobbes's theory of the war of every man against every man and the bourgeois economic theory of competition, along with the Malthusian theory of population."[20] The metaphoric profile of *The Origin* tends to support Engels's view. Darwin does sound Hobbesian at times: he refers to "battle within battle" (61), "the great battle of life" (64), "the war of nature" (66); he speaks of "the war" between males competing for females and refers to some carnivorous animals as "well armed" (73–74); he employs the phrases "the great battle for life" (106), "the struggle for life" (167), and "the struggle for existence" (191); he frequently uses the language of invasion and extermination, of victory and defeat, and of supplanting. He is, however, careful to point out that he uses this terminology "in a large and metaphorical sense" (53). Even so, its sheer pervasiveness tends to undermine his avowed control over its deployment. Moments such as the following suggest just this kind of excess: "We ought *to admire*," he writes, "the savage instinctive hatred of the queen-bee which urges her instantly to destroy the young queens her daughters" (165, my emphasis).

Darwin cannot be blamed for the contemporaneous currency of violent and militaristic metaphors. Walter Houghton traces what he calls "the worship of force" in Victorian culture through the work of Thomas Carlyle and Charles Kingsley, to the "self-righteous intolerance" of Puritanism and the religious insecurities of the most aggressive writers of the age.[21] Such aggression found its way into the poetry of both Tennyson and Browning: "it lighten'd my despair," says the narrative voice in Tennyson's *Maud* (1855), "When I thought that a war would arise in defence of the right." While the initial public enthusiasm for the Crimean Campaign (1854–56) is reflected in Tennyson's poem, it was not only military ambition that fuelled this cultural belligerence. In *North and South* (1855), Elizabeth Gaskell hints at an undercurrent of violent domination in the process of industrialization: "we have many among us," boasts the industrialist John Thornton, "who . . . could spring into the breach and carry on the war which compels, and shall compel, all material power to yield to science."[22]

Again, when Mathilde Blind attempted to render in poetic form the cultural implications of Darwinism in *The Ascent of*

Man, she persistently returned to the metaphor of warfare in the natural world, referring to "A dreadful war where might is right," the "drawn battle, / Which ends but to begin again," and "warring Nature's strife."[23] Blind's vision of human evolution as a teleological process of self-transcendence has its roots deep in this rhetoric of violence, and this colors her perception that the goal of evolution is the amelioration of its causes and effects.

That Darwin's use of metaphor in *The Origin* tapped into and helped to maintain this vein of combative language goes some way towards explaining the ease with which social Darwinists were able to make of the theory of natural selection a creed of enforced evolutionary elitism. While Darwin cannot be held responsible for either the widespread cultural emphasis on force or the rise of eugenicist doctrines, his text illustrates the point that metaphors, whatever the intention underlying their production, are never confined by the voluntary limits that govern their deployment.

As Engels suggests, Darwin's language, at times, also betrays its socioeconomic and political provenance: he speaks often of "colonisation," of specialization and the division of labor, and of "kingdoms" and "economies." The stressing of the central theme of genealogy is also politically significant in a text produced by a member of a highly class-conscious society, especially when such a theme employs the pre-Mendelian phrase "allied in blood" to indicate real affinities in nature (see, for example, 340–43). As for the charge of Malthusianism, Darwin invited it. He says on two separate occasions in *The Origin* that his theory is "the doctrine of Malthus, applied to the whole animal and vegetable kingdoms" (6, 54). *The Descent of Man* occasionally adopts a strongly Malthusian tone: "Man tends to increase at a greater rate than his means of subsistence; consequently he is occasionally subjected to a severe struggle for existence."[24]

Gavin de Beer has sought to diminish the role which the reading of Malthus played in the formulation of the theory of natural selection: "All that Darwin derived from Malthus was what has been called an 'analogical leap' from Malthus's fallacious argument on man to a valid argument on plants and animals."[25] Valentino Gerratana also argues that Darwin's perception of his debt to Malthus was somewhat misplaced. Whereas for Malthus the problem of population growth did not arise for plants and animals (superfluity simply being eliminated), for Darwin it was the very motor of evolutionary adaptation in all forms of life.[26] Both de Beer and Gerratana are clearly right as far as the relationship between the social theory and the biological one is concerned, but at the level of imaginative response, the level of metaphor, Darwin's dependence upon Malthus is not so easily dismissed. I would further claim that the relationship between metaphor and science in Darwin's text is far more complex and unstable than Gerratana's argument allows. I hope to show that the image of the Tree of Life in *The Origin* indicates this unclarity as it oscillates between myth, metaphor, and empirical description.

Part of the fascination of reading *The Origin of Species* lies in an imaginative response to its metaphors. Nor is this a perverse "literary" reading of a scientific text. *The Origin* itself is very concerned with the status of its own language, recognizing a metaphoricity that it hopes to overcome. Such a desire has persisted in the delineation of Darwinian thought. As one historian of Darwin's age and ideas puts it: "To arrive at a just interpretation of the controversy over Darwinism, the inquiring historian must *cut through the cake of metaphor* which encrusts the subject" (emphasis added).[27] That one cannot very easily dispense with metaphor, even when dealing with scientific matters, is apparent, in comic fashion, in this quotation: language is too blunt an instrument, it seems, to penetrate to the underlying reality. The very language that asserts the importance of removing the encasing layers of metaphor from the core of scientific truth merely adds another layer of encrustation.

Consideration of the role of metaphor in Darwin's work leads Gillian Beer to conclude that "[m]etaphor depends upon species and upon categorisation," but we might be equally convinced by Paul Ricoeur's insistence in *The Rule of Metaphor* that, as the trope of resemblances or analogies, metaphor also *gives rise* to such classification.[28] In order to classify or categorize flora and fauna into groups, families, and species, comparisons must be made and similarities sought. Thus a dialectic of metaphor and classification is implied which leads to the conclusion that "cutting through the cake of metaphor," as well as being a kind of oxymoron, is a peculiarly self-defeating notion when it is applied to a text whose theme is analogy and speciation.

THE CHURCH INVISIBLE

The body of Christ, according to Paul, is the special creation of the Holy Spirit: "For by one Spirit are we all baptized into one body" (1 Corinthians 12:13). Such specific acts of individuation with regard to bodies are very much the target of Darwin's work. Again and again he makes his point in favor of natural selection by contrasting it with the explanation of the same facts by appeal to special creation: "This grand fact of the grouping of all organic beings seems to me utterly inexplicable on the theory of creation" (380, *passim*).

That Darwin is not concerned with human evolution in *The Origin* does little to stave off the sense (confirmed by his *Descent of Man* in 1871) that mankind's antecedents were, from this point on, to be thought of as having greater affinities with apes than with angels. Bodies, whether of arthropod or anthropoid, whether of crustacea or of Christ, are mere localized hardenings in the primordial soup. The church might still have appeared as the product of divine intervention at some point in the evolutionary process, but Darwin shows no glimmer of interest in such a possibility. However, he is keen to obviate any miraculous incursions into the realm of nature. He writes, rather dismissively, that the observer who rejects the theory of natural selection can only explain geographical distribution by calling in "the agency of a miracle" (285).

The church does appear, momentarily, in the final chapter of *The Origin*, in the guise of "a celebrated author and divine" (Charles Kingsley) who had written to Darwin to express his approval of the latter's "noble conception of the Deity." Given the absence of the church from the preceding account of natural processes, this ecclesiophany seems almost miraculous. It is an uneasy moment, an awkward coalescence, largely by virtue of what is left unsaid. "I see no good reason," writes Darwin defensively, "why the views given in this volume should shock the religious feelings of any one" (388). Now the only reason for mentioning the shocking of religious feelings here is the assumption that some religious feelings will be shocked, comprehensively. The "should" in Darwin's pre-emptive strike at his potential religious detractors is crucial: it is a judgement about the validity of certain conceptions of creation and of nature, especially the creation of mankind in God's image. Darwin is sure that some religious feelings will be shocked, but they *should not be*, they have no right to be.

In the event, the church was (and remains, to some extent) divided over Darwin. James R. Moore has done a very thorough job of tracing the lines along which Christian opinion split in the years following the publication of *The Origin*. Darwin's words, hinting at a fear of religious objections yet able to cite religious approval, betoken a divided church, a broken body. The invisibility of the church in the polity of nature, then, is not the same as its complete absence. When, at last, it appears in the final, prophetic chapter of *The Origin*, as a scene of potential conflict between the "celebrated author and divine" and people with shocked religious feelings, it is perceived as both a threat and an ally. Its place is unclear. This ambivalence is due not only to Darwin's own worries about the religious significance and the likely impact of his theory, but also to the strange ambiguity of the notion of the church as a body. St. Paul theorized about various kinds of bodies: "all flesh is not the same flesh . . . celestial bodies, and bodies terrestrial. . . . There is a natural body, and there is a spiritual body" (1 Corinthians 15:39–44). What kind of body is the church? Is it a body of evolved human flesh—a "body terrestrial?" Or, is it the special creation of the Holy Spirit—a "celestial body?"

THE TREE OF LIFE

At the center of Darwin's churchless conurbation, the "polity of nature," stands the Tree of Life:

> The affinities of all the beings of the same class have sometimes been represented by a great tree. I believe this simile largely speaks the truth. . . . As buds give rise by growth to fresh buds, and these, if vigorous, branch out and overtop on all sides many a feebler branch, so by generation I believe it has been with the great Tree of Life, which fills with its dead and broken branches the crust of the earth, and covers the surface with its ever branching and beautiful ramifications. (106–7)

The Tree of Life as it appears in *The Origin* refers both to the material, developmental processes of natural selection, and to the diagram by means of which Darwin sets out to represent these processes. According to Gillian Beer, Darwin demetaphorized this image by showing that biological descent does, in reality, branch out through time, forming widely ramose system networks: "He did not simply adopt the image of the tree as a similitude or as a polemical counter to other organisations. He *came upon it* as he cast his argument in the form of a diagram. . . . It was substantial, a condensation of real events, rather than a metaphor."[29] But if there is such a process of demetaphorization at work in Darwin's text, which metaphor is thus substantiated?

Perhaps the most obvious candidate in the context of a discourse on origins is the tree as it appears in Genesis. If this is the intended target, then the process is more a matter of demythologization—a profoundly ecclesiastical gesture in the mid-nineteenth-century context—than of demetaphorization. One effect of the publication of *The Origin* was to prompt a rethinking of Christian cosmogony and soteriology—even if the Creator remained after the rejection of a literal six-day creation, it became very difficult to hold on to the idea of a primeval fall into sin. It seems, then, appropriate enough to see Darwin's tree as a demythologized version of Edenic origins. But there are other candidates: the Tree of Life also appears in Proverbs, Ezekiel, and Revelation. Since Darwin's argument in *The Origin* tends to elide the difference between the trees of life and of knowledge, turning scientific data into a diagram labelled *Arbor Vitae*, then the book of Proverbs is perhaps the most relevant biblical model: "She [Wisdom] is a tree of life to them that lay hold upon her" (3:18).

However, if as I have argued (following Engels and Marx), Darwin's nature is modelled on civilization, then his Tree of Life is perhaps best understood in relation to the tree in Revelation, the tree which stands at the center of a city—the New Jerusalem (Rev. 22:2). This might prompt a reinterpretation of the Apocalypse: the New Jerusalem would no longer symbolize the citadel of millennial expectation; rather it would become a figure for the natural world in the process of becoming. The war, famine, and disease of apocalyptic vision could be reimagined as aspects of the struggle for existence, and the last judgement might serve as a metaphor for natural selection. Improbable as it may seem, one strand of theological evolutionism tends towards such an explanation. Ernst Benz, assessing the thought of Teilhard de Chardin, writes: "The idea that all lines of evolution converge in point Omega, leads, without fail, to the idea of *Universal Redemption*. Humanity thus absorbs the Church and final judgement becomes identical with the selection process of evolution in which much is sacrificed and eliminated."[30] The church vanishes. It is absorbed into a soteriologically undifferentiated humanity. Much the same might be said of Henry Drummond's interpretation of the Apocalypse—an interpretation that will occupy our thoughts before the end of this chapter.

Ironically, the very text in which the demetaphorization of the Tree of Life is propagated became a spur to the church to *remetaphorize* its own discourse on origins and ends. This can be seen clearly in the work of Henry Drummond, Charles Kingsley, F. D. Maurice, and Teilhard de Chardin, among many others. Furthermore, the very process of demetaphorization by which natural history is supposed to supplant natural theology, the scientific interpretation supposed to supplant the ecclesiastical, is unstable. This is not just because natural observation, as practiced in Darwin's *Origin*, is shot-through with the mores of western, industrial civilization, but also because the Tree of Life is not a single metaphor; it is a whole species. Among its many functions it represents the church to itself. The absorption of the church referred to by Benz is closely related to the processes of demetaphorization and remetaphorization by which the Tree of Life becomes a diagram of natural selection and vice versa: both are apocalyptic foreshadowings of the church's disappearance.

Demetaphorization is vital to the argument of *The Origin* and forms the core of the final, prophetic chapter: "The terms used by naturalists . . . will cease to be metaphorical, and will have a plain signification" (392). The classification of genera and species, according to Darwin, will be based (henceforth) on descent rather than on analogy. But, of course, analogy could not but remain a vital clue to descent: "I should infer from analogy that probably all the organic beings which have ever lived on this earth have descended from some one primordial form" (391). Since the very process of classification is a matter of analogous thinking, the making of metaphors (metaphor being the perception of the similarity in dissimilars, according to Aristotle), Darwin's demetaphorization can never completely succeed. His metaphor-ridden text bears witness to the difficulty. If this is so, then the Tree of Life not only remains figural but also stands as a figure of the non-reducibility of metaphor to genealogy: a metaphor of metaphors.

This metaphoricity is rendered even more intractable by the fact that the tree metaphor has its own natural-historical genealogy. Dov Ospovat has traced the image from the point at which evolutionary thought broke with Cuvier's teleological method. In 1828 Karl Ernst von Baer used "the branching conception" as the basis for his interpretation of the facts of embryology; Martin Barry wrote of the "tree of animal development," and Henri Milne Edwards developed the case for embryologically determined classification by employing the same metaphor.[31] Darwin effectively reinterpreted the "branching conception," according to Ospovat, by thinking of it in terms of divergence: the diversification of groups inhabiting single regions. The "struggle for existence" enforced this diversification so that different varieties could make use of diverse food-sources. Darwin described this in terms of the division of labor in modern industrial conditions: "The advantage in each group becoming as different as possible, may be compared to the fact that by division of . . . labour most people can be supported in each country."[32] But he also returned the branching conception to metaphorical status by naming it "the Tree of Life." So, while the process of plotting biological genealogies might seem to be a kind of demetaphorization of the Tree of Life, the genealogy of the tree metaphor suggests that the allusion to the Tree of Life is actually a process of remetaphorization.

This is still not the whole story. For not only did Darwin adapt and rename the tree metaphor from earlier writers, but in doing so he furthered the fraught comparison between natural history and philology.[33] In "Darwin and the Growth of Language Theory," Gillian Beer traces the reciprocal relationship which grew up between the theories of evolution and of language development in the second half of the nineteenth century.[34] In *The Origin* Darwin uses the example of linguistic filiation to illustrate the genealogical arrangement of the natural system: "The various degrees of difference in the languages from the same stock, would have to be expressed by groups subordinate to groups; but the proper or even only possible arrangement would still be genealogical" (342). As Beer observes, the terms describing language and descent are interchangeable in Darwin's illustration.

By the time that the *Descent of Man* was written, the exchange between the disciplines was becoming incestuous to the point where, Beer says, "their imagistic interconnections were beginning to flaw argumentative procedures, producing only a self-verifying interchange."[35] Beer goes on to argue that whereas this sharing of terms was, in the period of Darwin's enquiries, "only a metaphorical link between evolutionary theory and language theory," it has since become substantive. Experimental study of the linguistic capabilities and communication systems of non-human primates has established the connectedness of genetic and linguistic versions of filiation.[36]

Hans Aarsleff notes that at this time "language study was beginning to form an alliance with geology."[37] Lawrence Frank insists that, given Lyell's comparison between the fossil record and a "demotic . . . curious document," "it is no wonder that Darwin's Tree of Life in *The Origin of Species* looks, curiously, like a Tree of Language."[38] Beer makes an even more specific connection: "the branching diagram of Darwinian theory shares its pattern with that of the comparative grammarians of the earlier nineteenth century."[39] That "shared pattern" implicates this secondary substantiation of metaphor in the movement of re-metaphorization.

The tangled web of affinities in which language itself appears as a yet-to-be-substantiated metaphor has no locatable center. Which is to say that the Tree of Life belongs to no genre. It always appears as a branching-off from itself of a discipline in search of supplementation. As metaphorical representation of the very surplus of meaning which characterizes metaphor, the Tree of Life exceeds the confines of the demetaphorizing discourse. Since it is at the same time metaphorical, meta-metaphorical, metalinguistic and substantiated non-metaphorical process, and is always at work beneath every genealogical enterprise, it may be described as a figure of textual *différance:* an always displaced, non-originary origin. Described in this way, as the reification within a discourse of the hidden movement which is its very possibility, the "Tree of Life" is named only by means of a catachresis. But this prophetic trope (which calls the yet-to-be-revealed by the name of the apparent) is our only resource in interpreting the processes of speciation, classification, and metaphor.[40]

Observations

The double movement of demetaphorization and of remetaphorization which can be traced in *The Origin*, as the genealogy of species interweaves with the genealogy of the very metaphor employed to depict genealogy, is possibly delusory from top to bottom. Darwin's use of the tree diagram is, after all, susceptible to the criticism which Hillis Miller has levelled at *Middlemarch:* the "web of affinities" which it traces, like Eliot's social fabric, may be an effect of the eye which perceives it.[41] While this is a criticism that could be levelled at almost any text, it is peculiarly appropriate to the case of *The Origin* since, for Darwin, the eye is not altogether trustworthy. In defending the possibility of the evolution of such a "perfect organ" Darwin expressed a strong doubt about the adequacy of the eye to correct "the aberration of light" (164). Despite this caveat (designed to bring the eye within the ambit of evolutionary development), Darwin's dependence upon his own eyes could hardly have been more clearly stated. Throughout *The Origin* he encourages the reader to "look at" certain phenomena, uses phrases such as "when we see" both literally and metaphorically; he refers to "careful observers" (161), "good observers" (230), "observations I have made" (219), and organisms which have "passed under my own eyes" (246). The list could be extended almost indefinitely.

James Krasner's study of the Darwinian eye and its impact upon visual perception in narrative argues that Darwin's work evinces a strong awareness of the problems posed for scientific observation by the eye as an evolved organ. "Darwin," he writes, "abandons the omniscient narrative eye common to nineteenth-century scientific and literary discourse and adopts one characterized by misprision, illusion, and limitation."[42] He goes on to argue that what he calls the "narrative eye" of post-Darwinian writers limits the description of nature with reference to the limitations imposed by the human eye. Krasner shows how writers such as Hardy and Lawrence describe nature not in finely worked detail that takes in the structure of plants, or the topographical niceties of landscape, but in terms of shape, color field, and effects of light. Thus they acknowledged that the human eye has its defects, aberrations, and blindspots, just as Darwin— among others—had pointed out. "Darwin's eye . . . fluxes with

the variability of empirically perceived form. . . . Because evolutionary nature lacks regular biological forms, or stable species,
Darwin portrays the natural world as lacking distinct visual
forms."[43] While Krasner makes a very good case for these claims,
he does not really tackle what remains a profound epistemological problem raised by Darwin's eye: *it is the eye itself* that tells
Darwin that nature lacks stable species and distinct visual
forms. Given the limitations of that organ, how can we know
that the unstable forms are really in nature rather than in the
eye of the beholder? To put it another way, the argument is cir-
cular: if the eye is the limited product of evolution, then evolution is also the product of the limited eye.

So, Darwin's focus on the eye as the diviner of genealogical
connections has important epistemological ramifications. They
surface in Michel Foucault's attempt to state the case for a
Nietzschean filiation of concepts. In order to trace the "number-
less beginnings" of a concept like the "coherent identity" of the
self, Foucault insists, we must possess "a historical eye."[44] But
the eye itself has a genealogy: it "was not always intended for
contemplation . . . it initially responded to the requirements of
hunting and warfare."[45] The uncovering of this conflictual descent, aimed by Foucault (as by Darwin) at the destruction of
evolutionary teleologies, is also the disruption of our ability to
adequately conceptualize what we observe. That is to say: the
eye must be capable of observing the very similarities and analogies, of creating the web or tree of affinities, that prove its own
weakness. Does not the (natural) history of the eye thus blind
the (natural) historical eye? Foucault's blindspot helps us to
identify a similar aberration in Darwin's work. It is an "aberration of light" that allows him to claim the ability to "see in the
dark," as it were: "In the dim obscurity of the past we can see
that the early progenitor of all the Vertebrata must have been an
aquatic animal."[46] Despite this dimness, obscurity and pastness,
the eye, for all its avowed inadequacies, has the power to penetrate the vagaries of formal analogy and to uncover the unimaginably extended progress of human evolution.

The weakness of the ubiquitous eye is also attested by the
presence of its mechanical extensions—the telescope (154), the
camera lucida (196), and the microscope (200). The telescope is
brought in as a seemingly inevitable comparison with the eye:
"It is scarcely possible," says Darwin, "to avoid comparing the

eye to a telescope." This is a curiously incestuous image which involves a "power always intently *watching* each slight accidental alteration . . . and carefully selecting each alteration which . . . may in any way, or in any degree tend to produce a distincter image" (154, my emphasis). A personified Natural Selection, here, must itself be a "good observer," must in fact be gifted with a more reliable eye than it can hope to produce in the organisms which it molds. The prosopopoeia and the metaphor combine to make the empirical project a simultaneously self-generating and self-undermining enterprise. Darwin, like Foucault, cannot look himself in the eye.

With this in mind, the continual references to looking, seeing, and observing render epistemologically questionable the appearances of resemblance between organisms, the formal analogies upon which Darwin's whole project is based. In his *Autobiography*, Darwin explicitly voiced a similar worry about religion: "can the mind of man, which has, as I fully believe, been developed from a mind as low as that possessed by the lowest animal, be trusted?"[47] Despite the fact that Darwin uses this as an argument against his earlier theism, Gerratana points out that this works as much against the denial of God as it does against the assertion of his existence.

The mind and the eye, as is attested by many optical metaphors for thought, are not always wholly distinguishable. Darwin's distrust of the former is of a piece with his bio-scepticism about the latter. Perhaps, then, the disappearance (or at least the relegation) of God in the evolution of Darwin's own thought,[48] and the invisibility of the church in his "polity of nature" are understandable as blindspots. Even if Darwin could have excised all references to the Creator from a possible version of *The Origin*, could he have managed without the telescope, the absence of which he characterized as "scarcely possible"? The telescope, as has been observed, implies a watcher with an infallible eye—an organ, which is, by Darwin's own reckoning, not to be found among the developmental achievements of natural selection.

APOCALYPSE OBSERVED

An apocalypse is an uncovering, a revelation to the eyes of an observer of what has been veiled up to this point. As an account of what has been revealed, St. John's Apocalypse continually draws attention to the experience of seeing: the phrase "and I saw" (*kai eidon*), or a near equivalent occurs with striking frequency throughout the text. From the opening chapter with its promise of universal observation ("every eye shall see him"— 1:7), and its description of the incendiary eyes of the glorified Christ (1:14), to the blessed vision of the righteous whose eyes shall see God's face, in the final chapter, Revelation is a book full of eyes, of looking, watching, and beholding.

Among the churches to whom John was told to write, the Laodicean Christians stand out as people with serious eye-problems: "thou . . . knowest not that thou art . . . blind . . . I counsel thee to . . . anoint thine eyes with eyesalve, that thou mayest see" (3:17–18). They suffer an "aberration of light," a double blindness which means that they cannot see that they cannot see—much like Darwin, when he claims to be able to penetrate the darkness of the immemorial past. The peculiar blessing promised to them if they "overcome" is appropriate: "To him that overcometh will I grant to sit with me in my throne"; that throne is surrounded, according to 4:6, with beasts "full of eyes before and behind." Given this contrast between defective human eyes and the oversufficiency of divine vision (neatly summarized by the diminutive English title, "Revelation"), human finitude is visible as an horizon—it is determined by the eye.

The centrality of the eye to Darwin's famous work is one aspect of a certain apocalyptic tone in *The Origin*. The power of observation is crucial in uncovering the secret knowledge of "the origin of species—that mystery of mysteries" (3). From among its manifold descriptions of organisms and organs, the eye emerges as representative of both the power of natural selection and its weakness, and natural selection thus appears as both the triumph and the tragedy of the human eye. Where Darwin calls in telescope, camera lucida, and microscope, John appeals to angelic guides, and where Darwin relies on the invisible "watcher" who oversees the evolutionary development of the human eye, John surrounds himself with the many eyes of God.

Emanating from the focal point of the human eye, "a web of affinities" (to borrow Darwin's own phrase) is spun between *The Origin* and the biblical Apocalypse. The persistent warfare observed in Revelation is matched by the ubiquitous rhetoric of struggle, battle, and extermination in *The Origin*. Furthermore, just as Darwin saw his deployment of contemporaneous military language as metaphorical, so John reinterpreted an apocalyptic tradition of eschatological "holy war" by redeploying its bellicose imperatives in a metaphorical sense. According to Richard Bauckham: "In the eschatological destruction of evil in Revelation there is no place for real armed violence, but there is ample space of [sic] the imagery of armed violence."[49]

Again, while natural selection determines survival in *The Origin*, the "supernatural selection" of divine judgement determines survival in the Apocalypse. In each case survival is registered in the body. In *The Origin*, the surviving body is marked by its beneficial adaptations, while in the Apocalypse both God's people and those who belong to the beast are marked in their flesh (Rev. 7:3, 13:16). Both texts deal with the question of human destiny, and both do so by (dis)placing humanity away from the center of their descriptions. Both end with more-or-less prophetic utopian visions. Time takes on the character of a nonlinear plot in both texts. "Darwin's account of the origin of species," according to Gillian Beer, "ranges to and fro through time in a way that disturbs any simple sequence or chain."[50] The same could be said, *mutatis mutandis*, of the book of Revelation.

One connotation of apocalypse (*the* connotation for many people) is the end of the world as we know it. On this account Darwin's work might be perceived as the end of the world as God's special creation, and as the end of man as its crowning achievement made in God's own likeness. At the most profound level of comparison both texts seek some means of predicting ends or outcomes, especially the outcome of "the great battle of life." In each case this involves "replotting observed relations of cause and effect or of possibility . . . perceiving underlying patterns by means of analogy" and acknowledging "a world beyond the compass of our present knowledge."[51] If we follow Henry Drummond's interpretation of the Apocalypse, then yet another point of contact between Revelation and *The Origin* is the absence of the church.

Drummond (1851–97), one of the early thinkers of Christian evolutionism, interpreted the New Jerusalem as "a City without a Church."[52] He read into the Apocalypse a kind of civic evolution which would transform "London, Berlin, New York, Paris,

Melbourne, Calcutta" into the "cities of God" (99). This process would eventually eliminate the church which has "literally stolen Christ from the people" (113). In the "struggle for existence," the church is a loser: "the Church with all its splendid equipment, the cloister with all its holy opportunity, are not the final instruments for *fitting* men for Heaven. The City, in many of its functions, is a greater Church than the Church" (122, my emphasis). The city has become the matrix of salvation, supplanting the church. Just as Darwinian theory implies that each positive adaptation in an organism helps not only to ensure its success but also to hasten its own obsolescence in the march of evolutionary progress, Drummond's vision is that the church is the driving force behind its own ultimate extinction: "the great use of the Church is to help men to do without it" (118). The church, then, is viewed as a kind of temporary shelter, constructed to cater for Christian inadequacies rather than to display the glory of God.

Clearly, the rise of the great, unchurched Victorian cities is a cultural factor in this interpretation. A strong sense of the ecclesiastical body's failure to adapt to these changed conditions of existence, and of the concomitant mass desertion of the mid-century church by the common people, can be felt in Drummond's urban prognosis: "The masses will never return to the Church till its true relation to the City is more defined. And they can never have that most real life of theirs made religious so long as they rule themselves out of court on the ground that they have broken with ecclesiastical forms" (119).

Drummond centers his new New Jerusalems on the Tree of Life: "In the midst of the streets there should be a tree of Life." The strange juxtaposition of literal cities and metaphorical trees destabilizes the images of both city and church (in fact, Drummond's text slides between three or four different meanings of the word "church"—building, set of rituals, people, even the paradoxical "City without a Church"). Is this because, like the evolutionary process itself (in which Drummond implicates the church), the church has no single, non-analogical meaning? It is a Tree of Life—a material developmental process that has branched out through time, from a single antecedent form into a multiplicity of communions, denominations, factions, recombinations, sects, cults, and even new religious movements.

Like the New Jerusalem in which the Tree of Life grows, the

church is also caught between heaven and earth, between existing as a celestial and as a terrestrial body. This is part of Drummond's difficulty: "The Church is a Divine institution because it is so very human an institution" (118), he says, indicating its double nature. He also depicts the church as an outmoded institution with which we do not associate Christ: "We never think of Him in connection with a Church. We cannot picture Him in the garb of a priest or belonging to any of the classes who specialise religion. . . . What have . . . the vestures and the postures to do with Jesus of Nazareth?" (110–11). Again, this ambivalence is evident in his sense of mission: while, on the one hand, he calls for the urbanization of the church, on the other hand he issues a challenge to "Christianise capital; dignify labour," and to "church" the city (104).

In Drummond's text, then, city and church are woven together in another web of affinities, and this web is not altogether distinguishable from the Tree of Life. Drummond's version of evolution, it has to be admitted, owed more to Herbert Spencer than to Darwin, but his interpretation of the Apocalypse, with its sense of urban/ecclesial evolution and its depiction of the future of human life based upon cities at the heart of which the Tree of Life grows, does suggest certain affinities with *The Origin of Species.*

The Tree of Life might serve further as a metaphor for the "web of (metaphorical) affinities" which entangles these texts. In Revelation it first appears as a promise to the church (Rev. 2:7). Each expression of the apocalyptic church is identified with a city ("To the Church of Ephesus [etc.] write . . ."). Drummond insists that "Christianity is the religion of Cities," and that John's vision makes this clear in a way "which no eye can mistake" (94–95). The process by which human cities evolve into the cities of God leads us back to that unreliable organ—the eye. The human eye must be sharp enough to catch the analogy (or the "real affinity") between the New Jerusalem and London, Berlin, New York, etc., in order to "discern a new London shaping itself through all the sin and chaos of the City" just as it "was given to John to see a new Jerusalem rise from the ruins of the old" (99). But the weakness of the eye, noted by Darwin, returns to unsettle further the troubled relationship between city and church in Drummond's text: "The distinction between secular and sacred is a confusion and not a contrast; and it is only because the secular is so intensely sacred that so many eyes are blind before it" (102). One is blind to the sacred because it is so secular, and yet one is able to see the New Jerusalem in London. Again, as in *The Origin*, the eye is deemed capable of seeing the right analogies while, simultaneously, its inadequacy is highlighted.

When Darwin introduced *The Origin of Species* as a revelation of "that mystery of mysteries" (3), he may have only subconsciously echoed the prophetic language of some biblical passages. The same may be true of the final chapter in which he makes various predictions about the future of biological study, foretells the "coming day" when a certain present blindness will be overcome (390), dimly foresees a "considerable revolution in natural history" (391), and predicts the opening of "a grand and almost untrodden field of inquiry" (392). This may not be consciously prophetic or apocalyptic, but the church, though largely invisible, is present in the background and perhaps Darwin's deployment of a (de)metaphorized Tree of Life is a shadow thrown across his pages by the church and its ultimate text—Revelation.

If Revelation is the church's vision of the end, *The Origin* has come to represent the end of the church's vision. But origins and ends are always interwoven. Revelation has many affinities with Genesis, and Darwin's consideration of origins ends with a chapter in which the future tense predominates. While it does not predict the end, this chapter does contain a strong teleological suggestion: "as natural selection works solely by and for the good of each being, all corporeal and mental endowments will tend to progress towards perfection" (395). Since natural selection is a genealogical theory, the uncovering of this future perfection depends on the uncovering of the past, and on the covering over of an analogy between past and future. This might be what Darwin would have called a "real affinity," but since the whole project of moving from analogy to real affinity is bound up in the dialectic of speciation and metaphor (which genealogy fails to resolve), we can never be sure that the elision of the (possible) gap between analogy and real affinity is ever more than a metaphorical resistance to metaphor.

If Darwin thought of the "Tree of Life" as having been demetaphorized by the discovery of the process of natural selection, his text can be read as equally involved in the remetaphorization of the same process. Further, it is caught in a web of metaphoricity centered on the human eye—an eye that looks out at nature from within the city, and projects its aberrant light onto the impenetrable opacity of the scene. The city, the church and the natural world all inhere in the meta-metaphorical image of the Tree of Life, weaving the end which the church has given to itself into the fabric of Darwin's materialist discourse. It is an image that connects *The Origin of Species* with the Apocalypse, the terrestrial with the celestial, the city with the church, the physical with the spiritual, and natural origins with spiritual ends.

It appears, then, that Darwin's renegotiation of the processes of speciation, that would alter forever our peception of the relation between human and inhuman, was influenced, albeit covertly, by the ways in which the Apocalypse had woven itself into the cultural fabric. The uncovering and expounding of the theory of natural selection, in its implications for the primordial relations once thought to hold between ontologically fixed categories, necessarily bumps up against the older model of human origins, development, potential, and ends. One can sense this conflict in the work of thinkers such as St. George Mivart, who tried to minimize the damage by recasting evolution as a law put in place by a divine creator: "Creation is not a miraculous interference with the laws of nature, but the very institution of those laws. Law and regularity, not arbitrary intervention, was the patristic ideal of creation."[53] On this basis Mivart argued that "the consequences which have been drawn from Evolution, whether exclusively Darwinian or not, to the prejudice of religion, by no means follow from it, and are in fact illegitimate."[54] Adrian Desmond and James Moore detail some of the ways in which the conflict thus generated played out in debates about the relationship between Christianity and evolutionary theory. Huxley aggressively confronted—and demolished—Mivart's theological rearguard action, stating the case for understanding the new scientific discourse as an indefeasible heresy that should be accepted as offering a "complete and irreconcilable antagonism to that vigorous and consistent enemy of the highest intellectual, moral, and social life of mankind—the Catholic Church."[55] Huxley insisted that Mivart could not be both a scientist and an apologist for Christianity. Darwin himself took up the cudgels before long: he added to *The Origin* a new chapter against Mivart, and added "[a] million odd facts . . . to discredit Mivart's allegiance to theology."[56]

Desmond and Moore also show that Darwin's work was used to advance the cause of secularism in the U.S.A. as he corresponded with radical thinkers such as Francis Abbot, editor of the free-thinking journal *The Index*, and Charles Eliot Norton, founder of the Free Religious Association. Norton's manifesto for the Association, which he sent to Darwin, predicted "the extinction of faith in the Christian Confession."[57] Despite these auguries of the end of the Christian world, the Anglican Church and the society which it served proved adept at reappropriation. When Darwin died, he was buried in Westminster Abbey, and the newspapers and the clergy united to claim him for liberal English Christianity by more or less repeating in various ways Mivart's discredited notion. So while the *Daily News* considered Darwin's theory to be consistent with "strong religious faith and hope," Canon George Prothero, the Queen's Chaplain-in-Ordinary, proclaimed that natural selection was "by no means alien to the Christian religion," once it was rightly understood as acting "under the Divine intelligence."[58] Such attempts at reconciliation may be understood as tacit acknowledgments that if fully accepted on its own terms rather than being translated into theological language, natural selection was potentially inimical to the Christian worldview in many respects; otherwise, why try to reconcile the two? But despite this, as Desmond and Moore observe, it served very well certain ideological purposes that had become interwoven with British Christianity, so that "the Abbey interment gave tangible expression to the public feeling that Darwin, in his life and work, symbolized English success in conquering nature and civilizing the globe during Victoria's long reign."[59] So the act of appropriation by which Darwin was reabsorbed into the Christian mainstream was also an act of partial secularization that took in the church and highjacked its power base; an Abbey in which Darwin is buried necessarily represents a church altered by evolutionary theory:

> The Abbey interment celebrated the vast, unfinished social transformation that England was undergoing. There were new colonies, new industries, new men to run them—not least a "new Nature," as Huxley called it, speaking through new priests. . . . Darwin's body was enshrined to the greater glory of the new professionals who had

snatched it. The burial was their apotheosis, the last rite of a rising secularity. It marked the accession to power of the traders in nature's market-place, the scientists and their minions in politics and religion. Such men, on the up-and-up, were paying their dues, for Darwin had naturalized Creation and delivered human nature and human destiny into their hands. Society would never be the same.[60]

The idea that nature had to be conquered is crucial here because it could be understood as the meshing of theological imperatives to subdue the earth with scientific/technological progress. Natural selection can be grafted onto this project at both levels since it can be interpreted to conform with the notion of divinely ordained progress, and can also serve as an example of a scientific advancement that would actually assist the development of mechanisms of control. If Desmond and Moore are right to claim that Darwin "naturalized Creation and delivered human nature and human destiny" into the hands of Victorian scientists, then one might claim that the teleological dimension inhering in the process is evidence of an apocalyptic response to *The Origin of Species*, or even a subconscious acknowledgment that Darwin's work exists as an intertext of the book of Revelation.

In this light the insistent collocation of nature and the city that has been noted at work in *The Origin* can be understood as a rhetorical betrayal of the cultural desire to colonize, map, and control nature in order to subject it to human ends, to harness it in the interests of human destiny. But the relationship between nature and the city is uneasy and problematical. Darwin's natural polity is violent, diffuse, monstrous, protean, and at times ungovernable, possessing a power "immeasurably superior to man's feeble efforts" (52). To urbanize nature in the way that Darwin's text and the material development of Victorian towns and cities did is also to take into the purview of the urban the threatening, potentially chaotic powers of nature. That is why some Victorian texts seem to evoke the presence of nature within the city as the return of the repressed.

It is hardly surprising, for example, to find in the work of Mathilde Blind—a poet so influenced by Darwinian ideas—an apocalyptic poem born of a momentary recrudescence of nature into the urban scene. The following sonnet is one of two entitled "The Red Sunsets, 1883":

> The twilight heavens are flushed with gathering light,
> And o'er wet roofs and huddling streets below
> Hang with a strange Apocalyptic glow
> On the black fringes of the wintry night.
> Such bursts of glory may have rapt the sight
> Of him to whom on Patmos long ago
> The visionary angel came to show
> That heavenly city built of chrysolite.
>
> And lo, three factory hands begrimed with soot,
> Aflame with the red splendour, marvelling stand,
> And gaze with lifted faces awed and mute.
> Starved of earth's beauty by Man's grudging hand,
> O toilers, robbed of labour's golden fruit,
> Ye, too, may feast in Nature's fairyland.[61]

The strange dissonance between the "apocalyptic glow" of the octet, and "Nature's fairyland" in the final line, accentuates the sense of a mismatch between Nature and the urban environment. Such unease disrupts both the ordinariness of the cityscape and the stability of the socio-political system, so that the red of the sunset is both the intervention of nature in civilization, taking over where "Man's grudging hand" has failed to provide justice for the "toilers," and, at the same time, a revolutionary flag unfurled above the "huddling streets." Both of these modes of disruption threaten disorder, the overthrow of the familiar regime, an apocalyptic reversal. In the next chapter, the implications of this interweaving of nature and city are explored, revealing that wherever natural phenomena reassert themselves within the precincts of the city, an apocalyptic resonance is set up. Owen Howell's dark vision (c. 1850) expresses well the sense of fear and tragic loss such images can produce: "The serpent crawled where once were streets and squares; / Owls and dull birds sat on the mouldering walls / Of crumbling buildings."[62]

As the next chapter will show, the serpent, various birds of prey and other kinds of creatures can often be found lurking ominously in the streets of the Victorian city.

2

The Desert in the City

MODERN BABYLON

THE BOOK OF REVELATION REWORKS OLDER MYTHOLOGICAL FORMA-
tions treating of the primordial distinction between chaos and
order, the desert and the city.[1] At one level its description of the
New Jerusalem is the apotheosis of civilization that represents
the ultimate and irreversible defeat of chaos, a triumph brought
about by cosmic warfare and bloodshed on an unimaginable
scale. The account of its triumph is counterpointed by the destruction of the city of Babylon—a cypher for imperial Rome.
Just as ancient Babylon fell and was destroyed, so Rome would
be returned to chaos by the judgement of God: "Babylon the
great is fallen, fallen, and is become the habitation of devils, and
the hold of every foul spirit, and a cage of every unclean and
hateful bird" (Rev. 18: 2). Echoing the prophet Isaiah's description of the ruined city as a place inhabited by "wild beasts of the
desert" (Isa. 13: 21), the apocalyptic fall of civilization back into
a wilderness is evoked by the placing of wild creatures within
the precincts of the city.

An age of city formation and growth, the Victorian era produced a great deal of literature which, in various ways, reflected
the apocalyptic images of the Holy City and its demonic twin.
Urbanization and the rise of new technologies in the Victorian
era were occasionally described in terms which evoked the construction of the New Jerusalem. While it refers not to modern
British cities but to Rome, one can identify in Browning's
"Christmas Eve" (1850) a sense that the human potential evident in the urban ideal has apocalyptic significance:

> Has the angel's measuring-rod
> Which numbered cubits, gem from gem,
> 'Twixt the gates of the New Jerusalem,

65

> Meted it out,—and what he meted,
> Have the sons of men completed?[2]

The cultural resonance of this urban ideal can be heard, too, in poems such as John Mason Neale's "Jerusalem the Golden" with its evocation of the "City of Angels . . . City of the Lord,"[3] and even in the way Hardy's Jude thinks of Christminster: "he was always beholding a gorgeous city—the fancied place he had likened to the new Jerusalem."[4] The closing lines of Elizabeth Barrett Browning's verse novel *Aurora Leigh* (1856) envisage the future as an urban construct whose materials are drawn, unchanged, from the apocalyptic architecture:

> Beyond the circle of the conscious hills,
> Were laid in jasper-stone as clear as glass
> The first foundations of that new, near Day
> Which should be builded out of Heaven to God.
> He stood a moment with erected brows
> In silence, as a creature might who gazed—
> Stood calm, and fed his blind, majestic eyes
> Upon the thought of perfect noon: and when
> I saw his soul—"Jasper first," I said,
> "And second, sapphire; third, chalcedony;
> The rest in order—last, an amethyst."[5]

If, for some writers, the New Jerusalem served as an urban ideal, one which was being brought within the grasp of Victorian technology, this could not be realized without a struggle. As was made evident in the previous chapter, many writers of the age spoke of a technological and scientific war against nature as though its defeat were incumbent upon the species. Furthermore, industrialization and urbanization were often characterized in terms of a realization of humanity's divine mission forcefully to subdue the earth. These are the words of Prince Albert, speaking in 1850:

> So man is approaching a more complete fulfilment of that great and sacred mission which he has to perform in this world. His reason being created after the image of God, he has to use it to discover the laws by which the Almighty governs His creation, and by making these laws his standard of action, to conquer nature to his use; himself a divine intrument. . . . Gentlemen—the Exhibition of 1851 is to give us a true test and a living picture of the point of development at

which the whole of mankind has arrived in this great task, and a new starting-point from which all nations will be able to direct their further exertions.[6]

The prince consort's apocalyptic vision of the fulfilment of mankind's destiny led, of course, to the construction of the Crystal Palace as a dramatically new kind of venue—a building evocative of Revelation's description of the Holy City as having walls made of "pure gold, like unto clear glass" (Rev. 21:18). His vision places industry and human ingenuity at the heart of new age, and its implicit image of the New Jerusalem is urban: the world will come to London for its inspiration, for its impetus, for its direction. As Janet L. Larson has argued in relation to Dickens's use of apocalyptic symbolism in *Little Dorrit*, one can sense at such moments of capitalist confidence an appropriation of biblical eschatology in the interests of the Victorian ideology of progress:

> In their vanity of "Riches," Mammon-worshippers indulge many "new polite reading[s]" of Scripture, but most extensive is their appropriation of the Bible's most powerful dream in order to enhance capitalist ideology with the fiction that riches are the ultimate apocalypse, the transforming energy that ushers in heaven on earth.[7]

Despite this urban optimism, a perception persisted that far from defeating chaos or establishing God's kingdom on earth, the new cities, gathered and constructed by industrial might, created the conditions for an apocalyptic reversal of the polarity—locating the desert *at the heart* of the city, turning the new Jerusalem into the new Babylon. The imagery of deserts within cities is widespread in Victorian literature. At times this is a matter of alienation and disenchantment, as when Lucy Snowe, the narrator of Charlotte Brontë's *Villette* (1853), describes London as "a Babylon and a wilderness."[8] At other times, it is closer to the Dickensian sense of the city as a place of human degradation and despair resulting from economic and political predation. Robert Buchanan's poem "The Cities" (1874) paints a picture of urban squalor and exploitation where hunger and disease are endemic and where the "bad men" prosper by "treading on human necks." He sums up his view of urban life as "The gorgeous desolation of the Cities."[9] Images of urban desolation

can be found in texts as diverse as Matthew Arnold's early poem
"Alaric at Rome" (1840), where the protagonist's view of the
eternal city is "as one voiceless blank; a place of graves,"[10] and
William Morris's late Victorian view of London as a "brick and
mortar desert" in *News from Nowhere* (1888).[11] At times the
image of the civic wilderness is a matter of sensory deprivation:
George Eliot, occasionally apocalyptic despite her disavowal of
the usefulness of the book of Revelation,[12] wrote of London in
just such terms:

> . . . far as the eye can stretch
> Monotony of surface and of form
> Without a break to hang a guess upon.
> No bird can make a shadow as it flies,
> For all its shadow, as in ways o'erhung
> By thickest canvass, where the golden rays
> Are clothed in hemp. No figure lingering
> Pauses to feed the hunger of the eye
> Or rest a little on the lap of life.[13]

The *mise-en-scène* of Eliot's poem is London as a public space,
seen from a drawing room window (according to its title). But
the desertification caused by various forms of deprivation is a
far-reaching and profound theme which penetrates not only the
public space of streets and buildings, but also hollows out its interior spaces, especially the minds of women, and goes to the
heart of Victorian civilization. I can think of nowhere in Victorian writing where this is made as abundantly clear as in Florence Nightingale's polemical text *Cassandra* (1852)—to which I
will return at the end of the chapter.

London as a public space is also the focus of Dickens's use of
desert imagery in some of his descriptions of the metropolis.
Bleak House's (1853) graphic descriptions of the rotting, fester-
ing, and foetid slums like Tom-all-alones, with its population of
human wretches and various species of vermin and its collapsing
buildings, provides a powerful example. That the rule of chaos is
never far away in the great city is evident from the novel's justly
celebrated opening page:

> As much mud in the streets, as if the waters had but newly retired
> from the face of the earth, and it would not be wonderful to meet a
> Megalosaurus, forty feet long or so, waddling like an elephantine liz-

ard up Holborn Hill. Smoke lowering down from chimney-pots, making a soft black drizzle with flakes of soot in it as big as full-grown snowflakes—gone into mourning, one might imagine, for the death of the sun. Dogs, undistinguishable in mire. Horses scarcely better; splashed to their very blinkers. Foot passengers, jostling one another's umbrellas, in a general infection of ill temper, and losing their foot-hold at street-corners, where tens of thousands of other foot passengers have been slipping and sliding since the day broke (if this day ever broke), adding new deposits to the crust upon crust of mud . . .[14]

London appears to be re-merging with the primeval slime from which life arose, horses, dogs and humans reduced to undistinguishable life forms. People are dehumanized as "foot passengers" as though to suggest that just as they lose their foothold in the mud they are also losing their grip on civilized existence. Then, of course, there is the fog which flows and rolls everywhere, shutting out light, and obscuring form, until the signs of civilization vanish like the dogs in the mud. Little wonder then that the Apocalypse springs to mind before long: "I expect a judgement. Shortly. On the Day of Judgement. I have discovered that the sixth seal mentioned in the Revelations is the Great Seal. It has been open a long time!"[15] At one level this is an ironic comment on the infinitely slow, corrupting processes of the Victorian Court of Chancery: the last trump may well sound and Judgement Day begin before it delivers a verdict. But it is also clear that the law itself—the human achievement which is almost definitive of civilization—is actually the obfuscating medium and the agent of chaos: the lord high chancellor sits "in Lincoln's Inn Hall, at the very heart of the fog . . . Never can there come fog too thick, never can there come mud and mire too deep, to assort with the groping and floundering condition which this High Court of Chancery, most pestilent of hoary sinners, holds, this day, in the sight of heaven and earth."[16]

Lyn Pykett describes the scene in terms that relate Dickens's vision to the historical moment but also evoke the potentially apocalyptic resonances in the imagery:

Here is London in the year after the Great Exhibition, that great expression of London's sense of itself as the centre of a growing empire, represented in highly metaphorical language as if it were just emerging at the dawn of creation, or as if it were declining with the entropic death of the sun . . . the language of the new geology and fiscal metaphors combine in an energetic phantasmagoria to represent London—one of the major capitals of Capital—as the city of modernity, signifying urban chaos and atomization.[17]

It seems that civilization reproduces its opposite—chaos— within itself; at times Dickens's London seems to offer living proof that this is what is happening in the Victorian city. Just such a gesture can be found in "Chambers"—a piece included in *The Uncommercial Traveller* (1861), where once again it is the law that allows the desert to seep into the heart of the city: "I look upon Gray's Inn generally as one of the most depressing institutions in brick and mortar, known to the children of men. Can anything be more dreary than its arid Square, Sahara Desert of the law [?]"[18]

While the idea that the law is an agent of chaos is particularly ironic, it is not the only focus of urban desertification in *The Uncommercial Traveller*. In "The City of the Absent" Dickens visits some of the churchyards that hollow out spaces within the city to gruesome effect:

> One of my best beloved churchyards, I call the churchyard of Saint Ghastly Grim; touching what men in general call it, I have no infomation. It lies at the heart of the City, and the Blackwall Railway shrieks at it daily. It is a small churchyard, with a ferocious, strong, spiked iron gate, like a jail. This gate is ornamented with skulls and cross-bones, larger than the life, wrought in stone; but it likewise came into the mind of Saint Ghastly Grim, that to stick iron spikes a-top of the stone skulls, as though they were impaled, would be a pleasant device. Therefore the skulls grin aloft horribly, thrust through and through with iron spears.[19]

While not precisely an image of the desert, what Dickens conjures up for the reader is a sense of civilization's margins appearing at its very heart, as the impaled skulls suggest cultural practices and affinities far removed from, and opposed to, the sophisticated ideal of modern urbanity. The title of the piece also suggests that the churchyards evoke or instantiate an alternative, paradoxical vision of the definitively populous city as characterized by absence; it is as though the city has a shadow self, a haunting other within its precincts.

This haunting other is most evident at night. In "Night

Walks" Dickens deploys the imagery of the desert to evoke "the night perspective" that defamiliarizes the daytime streets as the sleepless subject of the essay (whom Dickens refers to as Houselessness) wanders between London landmarks—theaters, jails, hospitals. An estranged cityscape emerges that Timothy Clark describes as "detached from the daytime use that defines it."[20] Again, as in "The City of the Absent," the dead trespass upon the territory of the living, seeming to inhabit a parallel London made visible by darkness: "the river had an awful look, the buildings on the banks were muffled in black shrouds, and the reflected lights seemed to originate deep in the water, as if the spectres of suicides were holding them to show where they went down."[21]

When Houselessness enters an old theater the alienating vision of the city specifically takes on the appearance of a desert: "I passed the outer boundary of one of these great deserts, and entered it."[22] The imagery with which he elects to describe the interior is suggestive of apocalyptic desertion and ruin, placing wild creatures within the walls: "The ground at my feet . . . was now in possession of a strong serpent of engine-hose, watchfully lying in wait for the serpent Fire, and ready to fly at it if it showed its forked tongue."[23] After encounters with a subhuman ragged creature on the steps of St. Martin's Church, and with "the most spectral person my houselessness encountered," the essay ends with a return to the sense that what nighttime reveals is that the desert has somehow come into existence along with the city: "in the real desert region of the night, the houseless wanderer is alone there."[24]

The imagery of the desert within the city, the dark tone of the essays and the fact that these perceptions are occasionally seen to be the product of insomnia, make The Uncommercial Traveller appear to foreshadow the themes, imagery, and atmosphere of James (B.V.) Thomson's The City of Dreadful Night (1874). Thomson's dark depiction of the Victorian city's nocturnal character, his inclusion of gory, phantasmagorical, and nightmarish images within the conurbation's streets and buildings have their precursor in Dickens's sense of the chaos lurking just below the surface of London life. Of all the Victorian texts which place such images of desolation and wilderness within the expanding urban sprawls, Thomson's text is the most persistent and the most harrowing. The apocalyptic dimensions of this poem are

well known, but what interests me here are the ways in which
it encodes both apocalyptic and anti-apocalyptic tendencies in
its complex interweaving of apparently disparate themes: insomnia, atheism, and evolution.

"... OF NIGHT, BUT NOT OF SLEEP"

Thomson's insomnia is well documented. Bertram Dobell's
memoir of the poet makes several mentions of it, as do critics of
his work such as Robert Crawford, Edwin Morgan, and William
Sharpe.[25] Although widely acknowledged and noted as a significant biographical detail by critics, Thomson's insomnia has not
been pursued in terms of its relation to the specifically apocalyptic tone in some of his work. It is this curious relationship and
its implications for the reading of his long poem *The City of
Dreadful Night* which form the focus of this discussion.

Thomson often wrote about sleep—the lack of it and the desire for it. "The Sleeper," for example, is an envious and touch-
ing description of a woman drowsing and then falling into
"slumber deep," "Deep sleep, so holy in its calm." The final
stanza is particularly telling:

> Sweet sleep; no hope, no fear, no strife;
> The solemn sanctity of death,
> With all the loveliest bloom of life;
> Eternal peace in mortal breath:
> Pure sleep from which she will awaken
> Refreshed as one who hath partaken
> New strength, new hope, new love, new faith.[26]

Love, hope, and faith, here renewed by sleep, are beyond renewal
in *Dreadful Night*. This becomes clear in section 2, where the
narrator recounts a meeting with a figure who moves around the
city in endless circles repeatedly revisiting the sites where each
of these human proclivities has died in his experience: "Perpetual recurrence in the scope / Of but three terms, dead Faith, dead
love, dead hope" (2.47–48). "The Sleeper" encodes an odd kind
of wonder that sleep so deep and refreshing, so death-like, yet so
invigorating, could be impermanent. The run-on lines "Pure
sleep from which she will awaken / Refreshed as one who hath

partaken," show unbroken syntax, and yet the line break is slightly disturbing in its tendency to make the reader focus on the fact that the sleeper will awake. For those of us fortunate enough not to be troubled by insomnia the observation is banal. In fact, the whole poem is disturbing for just that reason—the fascination with the sleeping figure indicates a degree of alienation in the narrator from normal human experience of sleep. *The City of Dreadful Night* takes this alienation into a far more advanced state in its longing for a sleep that will never be disturbed, from which the sleeper will *not* awake.

Obviously, this sleep is death—viewed as an end to the chaotic experience of insomnia. Such a promise, however, is threatened by the Christian gospel and its apocalyptic coda in their assertion of life after death, of being roused from the grave to face judgement. In Thomson's poem this religious possibility takes on the character of a threat, becoming the focus of an anti-gospel preached in a de-sacralized cathedral: the gospel of eternal death: "This little life is all we must endure, / The grave's most holy peace is ever sure, / We fall asleep and never wake again" (14.49–51). "You are free," the preacher tells his "melancholy Brothers," "to end it when you will, / Without the fear of waking after death" (ll. 83–84). This freedom is predicated upon atheism: "There is no God; no Fiend with names divine" (l. 40). Suicide is a way out only if one can be sure that one will not be called to account for it on the other side of the grave. Or, in Thomson's terms, there is escape from insomnia in death only if one's final sleep is not likely to be disturbed.

Sleep, death, and the desire for resolution coalesce on a number of occasions in *Dreadful Night*. We are told early on that:

> The City is of Night, but not of Sleep;
> There sweet sleep is not for the weary brain;
> The pitiless hours like years and ages creep,
> A night seems termless hell (1.71–74).

In section 5, there is a clearer echo of "The Sleeper," which strongly suggests that the city is, at one level at least, a metaphor for the insomniac condition:

> . . . there comes a morn
> When he awakes from slumbering so sweetly

That all the world is changed for him completely,
And he is verily as if new-born. (5.10–14)

Here, the desire for resolution denied by sleeplessness falls easily into the religious language of a rebirth that completely
changes the world, in stark contrast to the "termless hell" of
section 1 and the longing for eternal death expressed in section
14. Thomson's correspondence suggests that he was well aware
that insomnia divided the truth in two in this way. Writing to
George Eliot, and responding to her complaint of the pessimism
of *Dreadful Night*, Thomson was explicit about both the insomnia out of which the poem was born, and the bifurcation of perception which it engendered: "The poem in question was the
outcome of much sleepless hypochondria. I am aware that the
truth of midnight does not exclude the truth of noonday, though
one's nature may lead him to dwell in the former rather than the
latter."[27] Dwelling in the "truth of midnight" might serve as a
description of much of the poem, but, as we have seen, the possibility of the "truth of noonday" is not entirely absent. These two
truths are two versions of apocalypse—rebirth versus chaos.

Sleep and the lack of it continue to shape the images and rhetoric of the poem throughout; "weary" is the most frequently
used adjective, and death is habitually described as sleep: "that
sweet sleep no power can ever banish, / That one best sleep
which never wakes again" (19.34–35). Sleep offers a kind of ending, a resolution to the images of circling and repetition such as
the "perpetual recurrence" of section 2, the "blindly whirling
mill" of section 8, and the "circling" of section 13.

It might be appropriate to recall at this point that the prophetic utterances of both the Hebrew and Christian Bibles employ sleep as a metaphor for spiritual and moral decline. Awake!
is an oft-repeated alarm call not only in Isaiah and Joel, but also
in Romans, Ephesians, and Revelation. Such disturbing imperatives seem to underlie the sermon in section 14 with its procla-
mation of rest for the weary and "solace" for "wild unrest" (l.
36). It is clear that biblical religion evoked by such lines is too
wakeful for the insomniac poet to bear, saturated as are he and
his poem by sleep deprivation. In turning from the eternal rest
promised by the Christian gospel and by the apocalyptic vision
of the blessed, towards a desire for personal release in the extinction of death, Thomson is moving from a perception of the end

as imminent to one of the end as immanent, recasting apocalypse as an individual release from unchallenged chaos rather
than as its final overthrow.

It is possible, of course, to read Thomson's treatment of sleep
in *Dreadful Night* rather differently, as William Sharpe has
done:

> The controlled anger that engenders the poem consistently opposes
> the sleep, suicide and death which the work at first seems to praise.
> Rather, the poet's harsh honesty acts like cold water dashed over the
> heads of the drugged and weary automatons the City creates. . . . In-
> sisting on the power of poetry to keep the denizens of his city wide
> awake, the poet argues that the only responsible attitude toward life
> lies in the conscious experience of it, in the process of speaking the
> truth.[28]

Since this ignores evidence from poems such as "The Sleeper"
and "Insomnia," from biographical information and from the
kind of internal detail adduced here, it might appear somewhat
tendentious. There seems to me to be little evidence that Thomson is asserting the life-affirming "power of poetry" which
Sharpe wants to see in the poem. Sleep is too positive a force in
Thomson's work for him to have thought of it in biblical terms
as a moral failing. Take the poem "Insomnia" for example, with
its ironic epigraph taken from Psalm 127: "He giveth his beloved
sleep." The poem speaks of "Sleep's fine alchemy" and its
"transmuting" power that can deliver one from "the world of
toil and care and strife," of "Sleep's divine oblivion and repose,"
and of the narrator's "infinite weariness" that leaves him "haggard with endless nights unblessed by sleep." For Sharpe's point
to be valid, Thomson would have had to shuttle between these
two opposed images of sleep in a poem which, according to the
poet's own testimony, was the product of much sleeplessness. It
seems unlikely that a sufferer from chronic insomnia would ever
have pronounced the prophetic "Awake!" over "the City's sleepless sleep" (19.8), or used the longed-for respite as an image of
social and moral decay.

Sharpe goes on to argue that Thomson's City is "a nightmare
from which one cannot wake"—that the city represents the real
condition of the new urban world.[29] But this does not attend
closely enough to either the "truth of noonday" in the poem, nor

to the fact that the problem Thomson faced was the very one of being awake when everyone else was asleep. As he put it in "Insomnia":

> I heard the sounding of the midnight hour;
> The others one by one had left the room,
> In calm assurance that the gracious power
> Of Sleep's fine alchemy would bless the gloom.[30]

Again, as in "The Sleeper," one is struck by the way in which so mundane a sight as people going to bed "calmly assured" of sleeping, is turned into a moment of alienation for the narrator. And this is precisely the kind of alienation endemic in Thomson's nocturnal city—its inhabitants are those who hear the sounding of the midnight hour as though it were an early morning alarm call.

Certainly, *Dreadful Night* contains elements of a critique of urban squalor in its depictions of down-and-outs and street-dwellers, but this vision is engendered by insomnia, and the personal debility is not entirely separable from the material conditions observed by the narrator. Sleepless eyes perceive a world which might exist beyond the weary brain and might not: "For life is but a dream whose shapes return, / Some frequently, some seldom, some by night / And some by day, some night and day" (1.15–17). The problem with taking too clear-eyed a view of the city (too Sharpe a view, one might say), is that night and day are merged: "the truth of midnight" and "the truth of noonday" do not remain discrete, so one can never view the city in either undifferentiated light or darkness. This problem is itself the product of insomnia.

For Thomson, as we have seen, insomnia was a termless wandering that opened up a chaotic desert region beyond the categories of ordinary experience. When others sleep, the narrator of "Insomnia" finds himself "plunging" into "despairs unfathomably deep" as he wanders "Into the desert vastitude of Night, / Arid, wild and black." This condition is precisely the terror engendered by the prospect of time without end:

> Utter despair foresees no termination,
> But feels itself of infinite duration;
> The smallest fragment instant comprehends the whole.

The absolute of torture as of bliss
Is timeless, each transcending time and space.[31]

The dark, seemingly endless hours propel one into a realm of "deep ravines," "torrent brooks," "icy bleakness," "tangled roots," "awful scarps," and "arid sand and gravel;" in short, a wilderness, a "chaos of demoniacal possession." Insomnia returns the subject to that disordered and endless world, to a precognitive condition. The poem "Insomnia," like *Dreadful Night*, is a form of apocalypse—a narrative that attempts to reorder and so control the condition it describes, curtailing the timelessness and infinite duration of its theme by imposing upon them the closure of rhyme, rhythm, and narrative coherence.

In this light, Thomson's imposition of narrative order upon such experiences of inner alterity casts *Dreadful Night* as a myth against chaos that imposes a post hoc diegetic order on the limitlessness of undirected wandering. Narrative uncovers what insomnia covers over—the immanent end. But it also uncovers insomnia itself. It is thus both apocalyptic and anti-apocalyptic, a revelation and a concealment, uncovering both the necessity for, and the impossibility of, the end.

MAN-EVOLVING DOOM

Further evidence for the duality of Thomson's apocalyptic perspective in *Dreadful Night* can be found in its Darwinian intimations. Peter C. Noel-Bentley has argued that Thomson's spiritual journey from "orthodox Calvinist" to "despairing atheist" is evident in the differences between "The Doom of a City" (1857) and *The City of Dreadful Night* (1874).[32] The religious change is a matter, for Noel-Bentley at least, of replacing Calvinist determinism with Darwinian determinism:

> He transferred his dogmatic approach to belief onto science and by doing so transferred the locus of determinism from an essentially benevolent, anthropomorphic, teleological God to an uncaring, non-human, volitionless, and purposeless mechanism. . . . Thomson's religious assumptions never changed: without personal immortality life can have no meaning. . . . Evolutionary science allowed no personal immortality, so life for Thomson came to have no meaning.[33]

Noel-Bentley may be right about Thomson's perception of the meaninglessness of mortal existence, but this is—at best—only half the story. It is clear from the sermon in section 14, and from a number of other places in the poem, that the thought of extinction is precisely what makes life bearable—it promises an end to meaningless existence. By now the apocalyptic duality already discussed should be apparent: evolutionary theory both removes apocalyptic certainty and, at the same time, offers the kind of undisturbed eternal rest that the insomniac craves. Clearly, a Darwinian world is one in which time no longer appears narratable; it is characterized by the very termlessness that makes insomnia so excruciating. Evolutionary time is non-human time that makes of history a relatively new idea, dwarfed and paled by the sheer chaotic vastness of what we now—imposing our will-to-narrative on the formless—call "pre-history." Of more significance for Thomson's poem is that this opening up of pre-human, insomniac time is also the closing down of eternal life as an unwelcome disturbance of death's "sweet sleep." If Darwinian evolution means that the Bible's narrative of beginnings is to be rejected, then we are free to question its narrative of the end, and this, it seems to me, is the one crumb of comfort for those who listen to the sermon in section 14.

The apocalyptic paradox associated with evolutionary science is profoundly connected with the interest in statue-like images which are the focus of Noel-Bentley's discussion. Lapidary figures appear in many of Thomson's poems, figuring objectified human bodies and often associated with sleep, stupor, or death. These images are not distinct; they all cluster around insomnia and its effects. In "The Doom of a City" (another narrative poem that begins with a journey occasioned by a sleepless night), the "doom" of the title is the petrification of the city's inhabitants in a straightforward act of divine judgement. But petrification does not remain a divine prerogative. The fifth stanza of "The Sleeper" describes the slumbering woman as though she were a sculpted form fashioned not from stone, but from porcelain:

> The contour of her cheek and chin
> Is curved in one delicious line,
> Pure as a vase of porcelain thin
> Through which a tender light may shine;
> Her brow and blue-veined temple gleaming

> Beneath the dusk of hair back-streaming
> Are as a virgin's marble shrine.[34]

Porcelain, of course, is a malleable substance that can be fashioned and ossified into static forms. So the woman in the poem is likened to a figure that has undergone a process of hardening and fixing akin to petrification. Despite the fact that this is a human rather than a divine process, the woman's static and lifeless beauty is rendered iconic by a clever play on words that makes a "shrine" of her "temple." That porcelain can be manipulated by human processes into immobile shapes makes it particularly suitable to serve as a mediating substance between the "temple" as flesh (forehead) and as lifeless structure (shrine).

Even the comparatively cheerful and life-affirming "Sunday Up the River" contains a section in which the beauty of the landscape takes on statuary form:

> Yet look how here and there
> Soft curves, fine contours, seem to swim,
> Half emerging, wan and dim,
> Into the quiet air:
> Like statues growing slowly, slowly out
> From the great vault of marble; here a limb,
> And there a feature, but the rest all doubt.
>
> The sculpturing sunbeams smite,
> And the forms start forth to the day.[35]

The ease with which Thomson slips into these metaphors of petrified stasis is evident in a number of ways in the poem with its images of "tideless seas" and time-freezing mental abstraction. The last line of the poem refers to the "Crytal Sea" of Revelation 4:6, suggesting that it is the Christian vision of eternity that suspends time and its effects. But *Dreadful Night,* as we have seen, rejects this possibility for what Noel-Bentley characterizes as evolutionary reasons.

Evolutionary thought offers not only the escape of eternal death, but also the prospect of a non-apocalyptic end: the extinction of human life as one species among many that arise and pass away. One indication of this in *Dreadful Night* can be read in the section describing perhaps the most famous of Thomson's statuary images—the mortal confrontation between the angel and the Sphinx (section 20).[36] Towards the end of the poem, the narrator, weary with his night-time peregrinations, sits to rest before the cathedral: "The great cathedral's western front stood there, / A wave-worn rock in that calm sea of air" (20.5–6). Geological time is evoked and pitted against theological/ecclesial time in this image. Thomson telescopes images of erosion, time, and religion by comparing the cathedral's western elevation to an eroding cliff face, neatly suggesting both the decline of religious certainty and the (scientific) causes of that decline in a single metaphor.

The image of the angel performs a similar contraction, collapsing into the disintegrating figure the evolutionary demise of religion and of humankind. What the narrator sees, at first, is described thus: "Two figures faced each other, large, austere; / A couchant sphinx in shadow to the breast, / An angel standing in the moonlight clear" (20.8–10). As the narrator dozes fitfully the angel is gradually reduced from armed angel (ll. 13–14) to "warrior (l. 27), to "unarmed man" (l. 34), as parts of its form fall to the ground. Eventually it is reduced to "shattered" masonry (l. 40), lying between the paws of the implacable sphinx.

That the wrecked form begins as a statue should not escape our attention, nor should the fact that each stage of its collapse occurs as the narrator dozes. It is the sound of crumbling masonry that recalls him from his shallow slumber. Insomnia is intimately linked with the process of evolutionary decline because what is in view is the nature and scope of human consciousness, its fragility, and the chaos that lies just beneath its surface. The sphinx, after all, is a desert creature whose very presence in the city threatens apocalyptic destruction unless human wit can overcome the danger by solving the riddle whose answer is, precisely, mankind: the very existence of the species depends upon its self-consciousness here, upon self-recognition. It is the desert itself, the region where chaos rules, that poses the riddle—can the human remain human, defining itself against the encroaching chaos represented by the sphinx? If the sphinx wins out, then humanity's very existence is threatened by disorder and evolutionary reversal—angel, warrior, man, non-sentient "rubble."

Such an interpretation is suggested not only by the detail of section 20, but also by what precedes and what follows it. Section 18 describes an encounter between the narrator and a creature which once "had been a man." The sub-human being crawls along on all fours, a stage further down the evolutionary scale than the narrator, who describes himself as having "frame down-bent" (stages suggestive, of course, of the riddle of the sphinx). This crawling creature displays animal hostility and territorial wariness, fearing that the narrator wants his "prize," and threatening to kill him to protect it. His search is for "the long-lost broken golden thread / Which unites [his] present with [his] past" (18.50–51). At the ontogenetic level this cord is umbilical and represents the desire to return to the womb, to the bliss of preconsciousness. This is not the desired bliss of sleep, but is, in fact, uncomfortably close to the insomniac condition. Yet it is also a condition that relieves the subject of the burden of consciousness. So one could argue that in its depiction of the contrasting desires for sleep and for preconscious existence, *Dreadful Night* characterizes the problem of insomnia as the agony of shuttling back and forth between states—of being painfully conscious of one's lapses into preconsciousness, of being caught between humanity and inhumanity, between subjecthood and objecthood.

But the presence of the sphinx and the Darwinian intimations in the poem suggest that the cord should also be understood phylogenetically, as the thread of life itself—the evolutionary chain which connects humanity with its precognitive past and with a possibly postcognitive future. That the creature seeks an alternative to an animalistic future is suggested in the penultimate stanza: "He should to antenatal night retrace / And hide his elements in that large womb / Beyond the reach of man-evolving Doom" (18.70–72). Both ontogenesis and phylogenesis are in view in these lines in the form of the womb and the evolutionary process respectively, confirming the double significance of the "long-lost broken golden thread."

There have been earlier intimations that the future might see the decline of mankind, if not of life on earth in general. In section 8, for example, a mechanistic universe renders apocalyptic prediction impossible, but its demise remains a hidden possibility: "The mill must blindly whirl unresting so: / It may be wearing out, but who can know?" (ll. 40–41). This is later translated into the (then relatively new) language of thermodynamics and the projection of entropic decline:

> These eyes of sightless heaven . . .
> If we could near them with the flight unknown,

> We should but find them worlds as sad as this,
> Or suns all self-consuming like our own. (17.16–24)

A few lines further on such scientific perceptions empty out religious cosmology, mocking the Dantean vision of theocentric fullness and divine order: "The empyrean is a void abyss" (l. 28). Science, like insomnia, effects a decreation which returns the "blindly whirling mill" of cosmic time to a precreation chaos: the "infinite void space." The eroded cathedral and the crumbling angel can be read as restatements of this theme.

What follows the confrontation between the angel and the sphinx is the description of Dürer's Melencolia as the deity presiding over the city. A curious disjuncture here, makes Thomson's description both highly visual and unvisualizable at the same time, in that it is a detailed *verbal* portrait of an *engraving* which the reader is required to imagine as a three-dimensional *statue:* "The bronze colossus of a winged woman, / Upon a graded granite base foursquare" (21.6–7). The poem itself draws attention to the difficulty: "Words cannot picture her; but all men know / That solemn sketch the pure sad artist wrought / Three centuries and threescore years ago" (20.15–17). A two-dimensional image, then, gives rise to two impossible representations: the verbal description and the three-dimensional form. One can sense in this mimetic crisis the disordering of the senses which the city (and the condition of insomnia) produces. Yet Thomson's disordered image is surrounded by suggestions of scientific law and mathematical order, as Noel-Bentley observes:

> Around Melencolia are scientific, specifically geometric instruments. She has measured time and space and has detected evidence in her measurements of a cosmic law (Fate) which cares nothing for men, evidence of an expanse of time which negates humankind's puny little expanse of existence . . .[37]

Noel-Bentley's description actually relates to the description of Dürer's work in another Thomson poem, "The Melencolia of Albrecht Dürer," but the point remains: compasses, scales, hour-glass, bell, and magic square are all present in *Dreadful Night*'s description, and Melencolia sits "Fronting the dreadful mysteries of Time" here, as in the shorter poem. Measurement, investigation, knowledge, give way to the insomniac condition which disorders the world, leaving the instruments of science redundant. Noel-Bentley, it seems, is right to point to Thomson's reading of *The Origin of Species*, in this regard, as that which "confirmed his religious fears."[38] It was the theory of natural selection, above all, that banished both temporal and spiritual horizons in the mid-century and that transplanted into the ordered universe of ecclesial/biblical time the seed of chaos—the prospect of non-narratable time.

In "The Melencolia of Albrecht Dürer," Thomson actually compares the figure of Melencolia with the Sphinx in terms of their common gaze or "eternal trance." It is no coincidence, then, that the description of Melencolia in section 21 should follow on from the reference to the Sphinx's gaze at the end of section 20: "I pondered long that cold majestic face / Whose vision seemed of infinite void space." Melencolia's gaze, here, again reflects the vision/non-vision aporia suggested by her impossible mode of representation: "she gazes / With full set eyes, but wandering in thick mazes / Of sombre thought beholds no outward sight" (21.12—14). The words "beholds no outward sight" evoke the insomniac condition which Thomson repeatedly associates with petrification or statues in so much of his work. Mazing thought, directionless wandering, disorderly and blind, opens the same kind of void space as that which is evoked by the Sphinx's vision—a desert in the heart of the city.

Given these intimations we should not wonder that both Sphinx and Melencolia are caught between species, each representing some sort of missing link: the Sphinx unites human and beast, Melencolia human and divine (her form is colossal, winged, "superhuman"). The facts that Melencolia's wings are folded, that the angel phatically disintegrates, and that the Sphinx is said to be "supreme" (20.46), may suggest a de-evolutionary process before which "infinite void space" stretches in anti-apocalyptic gloom. Yet the wonderful paradox with which the poem ends, with Melencolia's subjects circling before her, would imply that this very anti-apocalyptic notion cannot be sustained: a kind of narrative closure can be seen to reassert itself in the final lines:

> Her subjects often gaze up to her there:
> The strong to drink new strength of iron endurance,

> The weak new terrors; all renewed assurance
> And confirmation of the old despair. (21.81–84)

Renewal is a form of resolution; assurance and confirmation are precisely what constitute narrative ends, even if these modes of assertion are directed towards negative goals. And what is the "old despair" if not the insomniac's terror of sleeplessness, perpetual disturbance, waking after death? Thus, the Sphinx is indeed "supreme," yet the divine/human Melencolia remains the presiding genius. Is this because the Sphinx's vision of "infinite void space" is unendurable and cries out for closure, for assurance, for confirmation, even if that confirmation is nothing but reiteration? Reiteration implies pattern, order, and narrative. Furthermore, if the city represents insomnia then the post-Darwinian decline embedded in its narrative is internally resisted by the desire for sleep in its guise as an isotope of apocalypse. Sleep would represent the end of the city, its vanishing point. The city of dreadful night, then, is also that archetypal doomed city that John calls Babylon, also known as Rome. It is also the New Rome—London, or any modern city that never sleeps.

REAL NIGHT

While Revelation, in common with other apocalyptic literature, thematizes the relationship between the desert and the city, making the threat of encroaching chaos a trait definitive of the genre, it also shows the permeability of the border between them; throughout *Dreadful Night,* there are reminders of this permeability. The city is part bounded by desert, part by ocean—both biblical, apocalyptic images of the disorder against which the ramparts of civilization are shored:

> A trackless wilderness rolls north and west,
> Savannahs, savage woods, enormous mountains,
> Bleak uplands, black ravines with torrent fountains;
> And eastward rolls the shipless sea's unrest. (1.1132–35)

Right away, there are clear signs that the city cannot keep the wilderness at bay. Immediately following on from the lines just quoted we read:

> The City is not ruinous, although
> Great ruins of an unremembered past,
> With others of a few short years ago
> More sad, are found within its precincts vast. (1.36–39)

The proximity of ancient and recent ruins is indicative of a continuing process of desertification "within the precincts" of the city. Not merely contiguous with its other, the city is infected with its ruinous presence to the extent that narrative order itself is under threat from a rupture in the fabric of human history. Material signs of "an unremembered past" both posit and disrupt the succession of generations crucial to narrative order, while their proximity to more recent ruins sets up a potentially destructive reverberation.[39] Recent ruins become monuments to monumentality itself, echoing the loss of memory and petrifying narrative into unreadable signs of an irrecoverable order.

Desert and city remain distinct, each holding onto its name, each definitive of the other, yet both rendered violable by insomnia; the founding distinctions of culture are affected virally by the exchange. In section 3, the frontier between life and death is seen to have been breached by insomnia so that "The lanes are black as subterranean lairs" (1.7), and the eye of the neophyte "Sees spectres also in the gloom intense," (1.14). In this region of compromised defenses, "Death-in-life is the eternal king" (1.25). From this point on spectral, disorderly, and phantasmagorical images abound, from the narrative of desert wanderings recounted in section 4, with its deathly and horrific images of "fleshless fingers," "eyeless sockets," and dripping hearts held in the hand, to the "bodiless voices" of section 6, the "phantoms" of section 7, and the "spectral wanderers of unholy Night" of section 14. The desert has seeped into the city.

Emerging from the dissolution of the distinction between night and day inherent in insomnia, the breakdown of order that collapses the founding binaries of civilization feeds directly into the mixing of species observed in the latter stages of the poem: humanity is subject to the same kind of slippage as are its concepts. This is, more or less, what the sermon of section 14 brings to light: the infinitude that both threatens narrative cogency and, paradoxically, offers closure to the terrors of insomniac temporality: "Infinite aeons ere our kind began; / Infinite aeons after the last man / Has joined the mammoth in the earth's tomb and womb" (14.58–60). Repetition of the phrase "infinite aeons," either side of "our kind," evokes a sense of both (en)closure and infinity at one and the same time, while the internal rhyming of "tomb" and "womb" neatly summarizes the paradox by making beginnings and endings consonant, thus imposing an impossible narrative order on the "infinite aeons" which exceed human temporality.

In John's Apocalypse the imposition of an impossible narrative order is a matter of revelation: Christ uncovers before John's eyes the conflict taking place in regions beyond normal human perceptions in order to explain the disorder of history as perceived at ground level. In Thomson's poem the effect is reversed: the order of normality (of the day) is revealed by the city of night to be no more than a "certain seeming order" (1.20). Denizens of the city see *beneath* this semblance to the underlying chaos, each testifying from what daydreams they have awoken "to this real night" (section 12). Civilization is systematically unpicked in section 12, as representatives of politics, intellectual endeavor, entertainment, religion, law, art, poetry, and the military, one by one come to realize that their world is an illusion grounded in darkness and covering over an abysmal emptiness. It is precisely in this sense that the poem is anti-apocalyptic, reversing the polarities of chaos and order, and inverting narrative hope in order to replace millenarian vision with "confirmation of the old despair" (21.84).

Among those who awaken "from daydreams to this real night" in section 12 is a Christian evangelist:

> From preaching to an audience fired with faith
> The Lamb who died to save our soul from death,
> Whose blood hath washed our scarlet sins wool-white:
> I wake from daydreams to this real night. (12.33–36)

Played out in various forms of christological and ecclesiological parody, which serve the ends of the anti-gospel, the inversion of apocalypse is nowhere made clearer than in these lines. The figure of the slain Lamb and the washing of the saints' garments in his blood come directly from the pages of John's visionary text. Here, John's visions are as daydreams by comparison with the "real night" which the insomniac inhabits, and which nighttime wanderings reveal beneath the surface of the daytime streets.

Thomson's parodies serve the ends of their anti-gospel message by taking on the central metaphor of gospel-apocalyptic tropology, the imagery of desert and city, and by repeating the values inherent in the structuring opposition: the valorization of city/civilization, and the devaluing, or even demonizing of the desert. The opposition belongs to a family of tropes which structure culture and its criticism as a whole, according to Geoffrey Galt Harpham. His book *The Acetic Imperative* argues *inter alia* that the ascetic desert fathers produced the founding tropes of culture by envisaging its alternative—self-abnegation and desert dwelling.[40] Opposed to culture and the city, the desert was the site of demonic torment and trial, but also of purity in being removed from the temptations of the city. Thomson's city is both city and desert—an apocalyptic space in which civilization both *is and is not* its opposite.

Robert Crawford sees in this proximity of desert and city an echo of Dante:

> Dante enters Hell from a *"gran diserto,"* while Thomson's speaker of the famous passage with the refrain "As I came through the desert thus it was" (IV) has entered Thomson's city from a similar locale. The idea of the circles of Dante's Hell where one of the punishments is "roaming incessantly" contributes also to the homeless wanderings of the inhabitants of Thomson's city. . . .[41]

The echo of Dante is clear enough, but Thomson's cosmology, as we have already noted, empties out the Dantean universe making of it a "void abyss"—the city is not a vision of punishment, but an imaginative evocation of infernal terror at the heart of day-to-day (or night-to-night) reality. Dantean intimations serve as indications of the breakdown of the order that structures the Christian universe, subjecting it to apocalyptic decreation. This is why the desert and the city are not in close but discrete proximity to each other, but are actually interwoven and interdependent. The insomniac occupies this space like a latter-day ascetic who involuntarily suffers continual *acedia* and self-abnegation. The city is a non-site, an impossible margin, distinct from the desert beyond its precincts, and yet whose topography and citizenry reveal the illusory character of the "seeming order" that structures the opposition.

It may be that such attempts to rework the gospel-apocalypse nexus can only posit atopia. Their *mise en scene* is a non-site because culture itself, as Harpham shows, is articulated by the very distinction that apocalypse encodes—order versus chaos, desert versus city—and the trial of strength between these modes of existence forms the core of apocalyptic thought. Insomnia, in this light, is an instanciation of the immanent apocalyptic moment—a confrontation or (non)engagement between narrative order and the experiential collapse that is its other. Thomson's text stages just such a moment; it is itself the product of insomnia in conflict with the consciousness into which and out of which the latter irrupts and recedes, producing both apocalypse and anti-apocalypse. What makes *Dreadful Night* so powerful and enduring is that its complex interweaving of apocalypse and its opposite resists both the belligerent optimism inherent in certain cultural events and discourses of the age and the straightforwardly apocalyptic alternative of the doom sayers like Carlyle. It brings to light the tension inherent in both modes of idealism by confronting them with what lies beneath the surface of the city as symbol of both progress and hubris. Paradoxically, it is at its most apocalyptic *and* most anti-apocalyptic in this gesture of unveiling anti-transcendence.

EXILE

While the apocalyptic image of the desert within the confines of civilization can be read—as in *Dreadful Night*—as opening an abyss below the world of everyday experience, it can also be read as opening the way for a new order. Florence Nightingale's *Cassandra* encodes both of these possibilities,[42] revealing both the hidden condition of exile that characterizes the lives of mid-Victorian women and the possibilities for the transformation of society inhering in their largely dormant energies. The text begins with Nightingale complaining of the exile of feminist consciousness.[43] She characterizes Victorian, upper-class women as condemned to a fantasy world by the oppressive social demands and proscriptions which prevent them from being employed gainfully, by the claustrophobic restrictions of family life, and by the way in which their bodies are objectified. The feminist's perception of this common plight isolates her even from her female peers; Nightingale depicts her "wandering alone in the bitterness of life without" (205). In a certain sense Nightingale's text is a feminist reworking of the gospel and apocalypse in which the figure of Cassandra is characterized as a female John the Baptist—wandering in a social desert. In this prophetic role she both criticizes the existing social order and looks forward to the advent of "another order of society" brought in by a female Christ.

The epigraph to *Cassandra* relates the prophetess of classical antiquity to John the Baptist by strategically misquoting the latter's self-description (Matt. 3:3). John's phrase (quoting Isaiah 40:3), "the voice of one crying in the wilderness," becomes for Nightingale: "the voice of one crying in the 'crowd.'" The opening sentence begins with the "one" of the biblical text in order to emphasize the loneliness of the individual consciousness which is exiled from society by its sense of intense suffering: "*One* often comes to be thus wandering alone" (205). The suffering in question is both that of a feminist thinker, alone in her awareness of the injustice under which women suffer, and that of an uncomprehending female audience whose consciousness she feels she must raise: "Such an one sees the evil they do not see, and yet has no power to discover the remedy for it" (205). What the feminist alone sees turns out to be the plight of Victorian women, especially, though not exclusively, upper-class women—their enforced idleness, the denial of their passions, their physical objectification, and their intellectual starvation.

As George Landow has pointed out, the epigraph to *Cassandra* effectively casts Nightingale/Cassandra in the role of prophetic herald of the Christ.[44] By comparing John the Baptist with Cassandra, of course, Nightingale is also preempting the disbelief of the implied reader. "It is my fate not to be believed," she seems to say, "Yet, like Cassandra, I tell you the truth." That the misquotation of the gospels is strategic rather than accidental is evident from the fact that the quotation marks close before the word "crowd," and reopen after it, indicating a deliberate supplanting of the original "wilderness." The effect of this strategy is heightened a few pages on by another quotation associated with John the Baptist. Nightingale asks why people seek a place in *society*, and she does so in the words of Jesus: "what go we out for to seek?" (212). The formulation of this question echoes that put by Jesus to a crowd who had gathered about him. He was asking them why they had gone out into the wilderness to listen to John:

> What went ye out for to see? A man clothed in soft raiment? behold, they that wear soft clothing are in kings' houses. But what went ye out for to see? A prophet? Yea, I say unto you, and more than a prophet. For this is he, of whom it is written, Behold I send my messenger before thy face, which shall prepare thy way before thee. (Matt.11:8–10)

Repeating the gesture of the epigraph, Nightingale's question once more replaces the desert where people gathered to listen to John the Baptist with "society." Cassandra, then, is a feminized John the Baptist—a Joan the Baptist—whose wilderness is society. It is in the social desert among the "crowd" that Nightingale/Cassandra will proclaim her message, preparing the way for a new messiah who, we eventually learn, is likely to be female.

John the Baptist appears in the biblical texts as a marginal figure who occupies the desert region between prophecy and fulfilment. By making Cassandra a feminized version of John the Baptist, Nightingale at once highlights and subverts the social marginalization of women. But the replacement of John's "wilderness" with Cassandra's "crowd" folds the geographical margin (the desert) into the social center (the crowd) so that what appears here is a strange, centerless cartography that locates the desert within the city; such imagery provides Nightingale with one of *Cassandra*'s most outlandish rhetorical flourishes:

> Look at that lizard—"It is not hot", he says, "I like it. The atmosphere which enervates you is life to me." The state of society which some complain of makes others happy. Why should these complain to those? *They* do not suffer. *They* would not understand it, any more than that lizard would comprehend the sufferings of a Shetland sheep. (209)

The distinction is, at least in part, a matter of gender: society is tempered to the male. Why should women air their grievances to those who feel no discomfort? Men simply will not be able to understand. There is biographical evidence, however, to suggest that Nightingale would have classed some women—her mother and her sister, for instance—among the "lizards" for whom the "desert" conditions were comfortable. Intimations of reptilian life—cold-blooded, sub-human—contrast sharply (and bizarrely) with the paschal connotations of the suffering sheep. And yet the geopolitical significance of "Shetland" suggests exile and marginalization as strongly as does the desert associated with the heat-loving lizard. There is no center to this cartographical parable; there are only hot and cold margins. Both of these margins are, paradoxically, within the center, because the wilderness is the crowd, the desert is the city. This is, perhaps, why men appear to be both within and outside of society, belonging in the heat of the desert and on the chilly northern island: "Men are on the side of society; they blow hot and cold." Hot and cold: they belong with the sheep and with the lizards (220). The ambivalence of the male position is seen also in the gendering of Victorian society itself: it is the society "which *He* [God] has made" (206, my emphasis), yet is also referred to as female: "those committed to *her* charge" (212, my emphasis).

Cassandra's exile, characteristic of the prophet, is further entrenched by the rhetorical aporia which marginalizes the center. It is both deepened and undermined. The desert of her lonely wanderings is all the more deserted for being crowded. Here, we approach something like a Derridean *hauntology:* the displacement of a frontier between public and private, between the presence and the absence of others.[45] "Women," Nightingale says, "are accompanied by a phantom" (219). Neither fully present nor entirely absent, the phantom is both a product of fantasy and the condition of prophecy. The "crowd" is always spectrally present, haunting the wilderness where the prophetic task begins. The prophetic commission could only arise in such a scene—where the spectral crowd is addressed in the person of an isolated individual—just as John, in exile on Patmos, received the visions addressed to the seven churches of Asia Minor.

The phantom companion of every woman is the spirit of enforced idleness: "They have nothing to do" (215, *passim*). In place of action, the restless (Victorian, upper-class) female mind raises dreams and phantoms. This is another kind of enforced social exile.

Visions in the Desert

For Nightingale, the preoccupation into which women were often forced by idleness exiled them from the world of action:

"Dreaming always—never accomplishing; thus women live" (218). But dreaming is endemic to the prophetic condition. Nightingale explicitly alludes to the Pentecostal formula by which the apocalyptic prophecy of Joel is claimed to be fulfilled, giving rise to more prophecy: "It is true, our young men see visions, and our maidens dream dreams, but what of?" (230).[46] This worry about the nature of dreams is closely related to the sexual anxiety which pervades the text, and to the prophetic condition.

If the fantasy world of bored women exiles them from the real world by distracting them, it also serves a critical purpose in the prophetic denunciation of the social norms and mores which produce it. The deflection of women's energies into fantasy not only staves off the pangs of extreme ennui but also disrupts an order of society centered on the "sacred hearth": "Mothers, who cradle yourselves in visions about the domestic hearth, how many of your sons and daughters are *there*, do you think . . . ? Were you there yourself during your own (now forgotten) girl-hood?" (206). Inactivity spectralizes sons and daughters rendering their presence uncertain, unstable. The very idleness which Nightingale places at the heart of the domestic order, upon which the stability of that order depends, invites in that which all domesticity opposes—the *unheimlich*.

Dreams also become visions. The distinction thus blurred is a matter of gender: "our young men see visions, and our maidens dream dreams." Disrupting a division of labor, of dream work we might say, memory looks back on youthful dreams as having been of visionary significance: " 'We have forgotten our visions,' they say to themselves. The 'dreams of youth' have become a proverb" (215). These visionary moments have been "noble ambitions, heroic dreams." Another layer of ambivalence in the oneiric rhetoric leaves the dreaming woman suspended between "vain imaginations" and "noble ambitions." Women's dreams take on masculine ambitions: vanity or heroism? The very question is one aspect of the danger of dreaming. A danger to be resisted. A kind of asceticism—a practice of self-desertifica-tion—is evoked in response:

> Many struggle against this as a "snare." No Trappist ascetic watches or fasts more in the body than these do in the soul . . . But the laws of God for moral well-being are not thus to be obeyed. We fast men-

tally, scourge ourselves morally, use the intellectual hair shirt, in order to subdue that perpetual daydreaming which is so dangerous!. (207)

In a rhetorical gesture which will come to have an ironic force, the bodily self-denial of male ascetics is translated into an asceticism of the (female) soul, inverting the social order by virtue of which, Nightingale says, women's bodies "are the only things of any consequence" (220). Unlike male asceticism, the female version disrupts the religious/domestic order: an aberrant practice harnessed to resist an aberrant practice. It is as though, following Cassandra's example, women might find the courage to do what Nightingale says they fear to do: to resist the will of God, "to say, Thy will be *not* done (declaring another order of society from that which He has made)" (206).

What kind of society has He made in Nightingale's estimation? He, God, the generic masculine subject, has made a desert society, a "cold and oppressive conventional" wilderness, in which women's passions, intellect, and moral activity cannot be satisfied: "To say more on this subject would be to enter into the whole history of society, of the present state of civilization" (208). In the very warp and weft of its history, society suppresses all female, non-physical activity, so that one cannot question this endemic oppression without unpicking its fabric.

Yet the male fabric somehow produces a prodigal daughter (God's daughter?) who "fritters away the intellects of those committed to *her* charge" (212, my emphasis). While those oppressed by gender roles are invariably female, the wastefully repressive society can itself be gendered as feminine. Furthermore, while "Men are on the side of society," they also "blow hot and cold:" they are somehow outside of it while constituting it—they belong to both the hot and the cold margins which constitute the center.

Given this ambivalence it is unsurprising (if unsettling) to find that society, for all its essential maleness, is identified with physicality: "We set the treatment of bodies so high above the treatment of souls, that the physician occupies a higher place in society than the schoolmaster. . . . Low as is physical science, that of the mind is still lower" (217–18). On this account, the body, which Nightingale associates with *women*, is of higher consequence for male-engendered society than is the mind. Society's profound but problematical physicality emerges again in the role which Nightingale assigns to Jesus and his co-saviors. She claims that Jesus gave women a different kind of social role, one which transcended mere physicality and servitude: "Jesus Christ raised women above the condition of mere ministers to the passions of the man, raised them by his sympathy, to be ministers of God. He gave them moral activity. But the Age, the World, Humanity must give them the means to exercise this moral activity, must give them intellectual cultivation" (227).

But Jesus, necessarily, occupies a desert place in Nightingale's thought, a central marginality. Not only is he subject to the rhetorical aporia of the cartographical parable, but he also belongs *in the crowd:* he is not alone; he is one savior among many:

> God's plan is that we should make mistakes, that the consequences should be definite and invariable; then comes some Saviour, Christ or another, not one Saviour but many an one, who learns for all the world *by* the consequences of those errors, and "saves" us from them. . . . May we all be Saviours in some way to humanity!. (79)

> What are the saviours to do? Not to do anything *instead* of man. Still it is not intended that every man shall learn all the laws of God for himself. In astronomy, Copernicus, Galileo, Kepler, Newton, Laplace, Herschel, and a long line of saviours, we may call them, if we will, discoverers they are more generally called,—have saved the race from intellectual error, by finding out several of the laws of God. (123)

Society's stress on physicality is evident in this material salvation—the deliverance of the physical universe. But this history of salvation is haunted: one has heard for many in the presence/absence of the crowded desert.

According to this scheme of things humanity is given progressive revelation through the application of reason and science. The more highly developed the society, the closer to religious truth its members will be; the higher the state of a society's theological conceptions, the greater the certainty of belief enjoyed by its members. With this in mind Nightingale looks forward, in *Cassandra,* to the advent of a female Christ, who will save the race from the error of the enforced idleness of its women: "The next Christ will perhaps be a female Christ, But do we see one woman who looks like a female Christ? or even

like 'the messenger before' her 'face,' to go before her and prepare
the hearts and minds for her?" (230). "Looking like" the female
Christ, or like the female John the Baptist, is emphasized in
what follows. Nightingale turns to this imitation because she is
worried by the madness of the question: "half the inmates of
Bedlam begin this way, by fancying they are 'the Christ'" (230–
31). To indulge in this dangerous fantasy is one thing; the imitation of Christ is another:

> People talk about imitating Christ, and imitate Him in the little tri-
> fling formal things, such as washing the feet, saying his prayer, and
> so on; but if one attempts the real imitation of Him, there are no
> bounds to the outcry with which the presumption of that person is
> condemned. (231)

Real imitation. Someone may yet come who is able to mingle in
her flesh the real and its representation. The incarnation of that
which is passionate, intellectual, moral, she will be an embodiment of the non-physical: a phantom.

The wilderness in which Nightingale/Cassandra is exiled by
feminist consciousness is not wholly distinguishable from John
the Baptist's stamping ground nor from the scene of Jesus's
lenten torments. These identifications are based not only upon
Nightingale's self-fictionalization in the figure of a (discredited)
prophet, but also upon her perception that Victorian polite society, for all its avowed piety, casts both Jesus and John in the role
of Cassandra: they are not to be believed. If they were, then "another order of society" would arise—one in which women would
no longer inhabit a desert of inactivity. The order of society
which Nightingale diagnoses places the desert at the heart of the
social order, threatening it from within. This gesture is profoundly apocalyptic not only because the desertification of civilization is a trope which enters western culture through the
bible's apocalyptic texts, but also because it gives rise to the possibility of "another order of society": that is to say that it is precisely the emptying out of civilization, its return to a wilderness
condition, that opens a space for an alternative vision.

Apart from their rewritings of the gospel and their common
investment in a sense of exile—Nightingale's based on gender
discrimination, Thomson's on insomnia—*Cassandra* and *The
City of Dreadful Night* share the agenda of unveiling hidden re-

alities. For both texts the underlying project is the bringing to
light of buried life: a sense that normal, everyday reality obscures certain truths about social existence. In the pursuit of
these subterranean worlds alternative temporalities are uncovered, which, like evolutionary and geological time, expand beyond endurance the duration of tortured experience. For
Thomson this is the "termless hell" of "real night" where "pitiless hours like years and ages creep;" for Nightingale it is "wom-
en's time": the agonizing hours of "enforced ideleness" and the
perception that a woman's time is void, empty, deserted, because it is "of no value" to male-orientated society.[47]

In these shared concerns both texts arrogate to themselves a
certain prophetic function which seeks to lay bare the dangerous
subcurrents that threaten the "seeming order" of civilization.
Thus they raise specters that haunt the streets and drawing
rooms of Victorian cities, and evoke an *unheimlich* presence/ab-
sence at the heart of the domestic ideal, much as Dickens does
in some of his depictions of London. This is not a matter of confronting what Donald Thomas's book *The Victorian Underworld* (1998)[48] reveals in grisly detail—a world of illicit practices
that Victorian domestic respectability would have liked to remain hidden, but of acknowledging the internal rivenness of the
domestic ideal itself, its psychosocial dependence upon a veil of
self-ignorance. Thomson's poem and Nightingale's uncategori-
zable text are not alone among literary texts of the period in
their perception of veiled reality. In the next chapter the focus
will be on the ways in which Victorian writing persistently returns to the image of the veil, speculates about what is beyond
it, and attempts, on occasions, to draw it back and to glimpse
alternative realities.

3

Veiled Unveilings

"A VEIL, A CLOAK, AND OTHER WRAPS"

THOMAS CARLYLE'S CONCERN WITH CLOTHES AND COVERINGS IN *Sartor Resartus* (1834) demonstrates, shortly before the inception of the Victorian era, what would prove to be an abiding interest in the doubleness of perception, its division between empirical knowledge and imaginative insight—reason and fancy, if you like. The book consists of a web of interconnected musings on the various ways in which reality is covered over by enquiry that settles for the limits of empirical investigation. Clothing thus has a metonymic function for Carlyle: clothes hide the body and the body hides the soul; the phenomenal veils the noumenal; time and space conceal the eternal. Nature itself is a kind of cloak: an obscure text written in "celestial hieropglyphics."[1] Hence, early on, we find Carlyle's hero, Diogenes Teufelsdrockh, characterizing Descartes' cogitating subject, consituted by self-awareness, not as the revelation of a founding reality upon which philosophy can build its cognitive structures, but as a mask for such questions as "What is this ME?" From where did I come? How? The answers may lie in Nature, he concludes, "but where is the cunning eye and ear to whom that God-written Apocalypse will yield articulate meaning?"[2] One could say—with hindsight—that the cunning eye and ear would appear before too long in the shape of Charles Darwin, who performed the apocalyptic function of making the "celestial hieroglyphics" of Nature yield articulate meaning in the discovery of natural selection. But, if we cast Darwin in the role of St. John, we should be aware that Carlyle's text encodes precisely what the earlier discussion of *The Origin of Species* revealed: that veiling and unveiling are not discrete, opposable procedures. For, despite the fact that unveiling is the founding trope of the Apocalypse, in Carlyle's formulation, the Apocalypse is not an uncovering, but an obscure text in need of deciphering.

This in itself is a revelation, of course. Such is the burden of

Carlyle's discussion of "natural supernaturalism" in book 3, chapter 8. Here Teufelsdrockh takes on the character of the apocalyptist in the clearest terms when the fictional editor of his work proclaims him a seer who has "courageously pierced through" the various "webs" beneath which reality is hidden: "In a word, he has looked fixedly on Existence, till one after the other, its earthly hulls and garnitures, have all melted away; and now to his rapt vision the interior, celestial Holy of Holies, lies disclosed."[3] What Teufelsdrockh has discovered is that Nature itself is miraculous to the human perspective, since what we know empirically of the universe is extremely limited:

> To the wisest man, wide as is his vision, Nature remains of quite *infinite* depth, of quite infinite expansion; and all Experience thereof limits itself to some few computed centuries, and measured square miles. The course of Nature's phases, on this our little fraction of a Planet, is partially known to us; but who knows what deeper courses these depend on; what infinitely larger Cycle (of causes) our little Epicycle revolves on?[4]

Custom acts as a veil which blinds us to what lies beyond our habitual, everyday observation and assumption. For Teufelsdrockh, we are unaccustomed to questioning the truth-effects of our categories, and, more especially, our nomenclatures. Once we are used to a phenomenon and have named and categorized it, we assume that we have full knowledge of it and it ceases to make us wonder, it ceases to be "Miraculous." So names are "Custom-woven, wonder-hiding garments."[5] The example he lights on and his expression of it are particularly instructive:

> Witchcraft, and all manner of Spectre-work, and Demonology, we have now named Madness, and Diseases of the Nerves. Seldom reflecting that still the question comes upon us: What is Madness, what are Nerves? Ever, as before, does Madness remain a mysterious-terrific, altogether infernal boiling up of the Nether Chaotic Deep, through this fair-painted Vision of Creation, which swims thereon, which we name the Real.[6]

By disrupting the categories which structure consciousness, madness uncovers an ancient cosmogeny in these words—an apocalyptic worldview in which the waters of chaos continually threaten civilized order. As we have seen, this would resurface in James Thomson's insomniacal vision of the chaos which lies just below the surface of the city. Madness, in Carlyle's work, serves a similar function to insomnia in Thomson's poem: it is an index of what lies beneath the veil of everyday perception, and it unleashes the creatures of unreason—demons and specters, here as in both Thomson's and Nightingale's urban desert places. Time and space, the fundamental categories of experience, are for Teufelsdröckh the "deepest of all illusory Appearances, for hiding wonder." They are "spun and woven for us before Birth itself" and they blind us to reality.[7] For Thomson it would be precisely the rending of this experiential veil by insomnia which would produce his apocalyptic vision.

Thomson acknowledged the existence of the veil, even while claiming to know something of what lay behind it: "none can pierce the vast black veil uncertain / Because there is no light beyond the curtain."[8] This wonderfully paradoxical image, that uses the absence of diffusing light to turn the (potentially transparent) veil into an opaque curtain, takes that very opacity as a revelation of the darkness beyond. Something of this play of transparency and opacity is often evident in Victorian writing that employs similar images and has a long history in the era. It may be traceable (most immediately) to the interest of Gothic novelists in veiled forms and figures and the mysteries upon which their plots characteristically turn. Nathaniel Hawthorne's short story "The Minister's Black Veil" (1835), taking its cue from that tradition, weaves a fiction that focuses on the veil as a figure of both revelation and concealment. The protagonist, Parson Hooper, takes to wearing a black veil over his face without explaining to even his closest familiars why he has chosen to do so. In the absence of an explanation the veil can only be taken as a paradoxical signifier of concealment: had he not chosen to wear it, the fact that he was hiding something would have remained absolutely hidden; his choosing to don the veil thus reveals the fact that something is hidden. The members of his congregation are left to speculate upon what it is he is hiding and to interpret the veil in what way they will—as index of either piety or guilt. One of its effects is to make him a more effective clergyman, and this is precisely because the veil, in the obscurity of its true meaning, acts as a mirror to the penitent:

By the aid of this mysterious emblem—for there was no other apparent cause—he became a man of awful power, over souls that were in agony for sin. His converts always regarded him with a dread peculiar to themselves, affirming, though but figuratively, that, before he brought them to celestial light, they had been with him behind the black veil. Its gloom, indeed, enabled him to sympathize with all dark affections.[9]

At the end of his life, refusing to allow removal of the veil even on his deathbed, the parson offers some kind of explanation for his strange habit:

> What, but the mystery which it obscurely typifies, has made this piece of crape so awful? When the friend shows his inmost heart to his friend; the lover to his best-beloved; when man does not vainly shrink from the eye of his Creator, loathsomely treasuring up the secret of his sin; then deem me a monster, for the symbol beneath which I have lived, and die! I look around me, and, lo! on every visage a Black Veil![10]

Again the veil takes on the character of a mirror: the parson interprets his material veil as a physical reminder of the multiple concealments practiced in everyday life—the hiddenness endemic in the human condition: the concealing garment is thus a revelation of spiritual truth. But if Edgar Allan Poe's interpretation of the story is accepted then the interplay between covering and uncovering is even more involved: "The *moral* put into the mouth of the dying minister will be supposed to convey the *true* import of the narrative; and that a crime of dark dye, (having reference to the 'young lady') has been committed, is a point which only minds congenial with that of the author will perceive."[11] In which case the revelation of the meaning of the veil is in fact another form of concealment contrived to mask the minister's true guilt.

The veil in Hawthorne's story serves as the nexus of a number of different—but related—concerns that seem endemic in Victorian literature. These concerns are spiritual, physical, moral, social, and psychological and are all related to the question of the relationship between appearance and reality. When Dickens took up the image of the veil in a story in *Sketches by Boz* (1839), a play of hiddenness and revelation emerged that was directed towards the social dimensions of the question. In "The Black Veil" a young medical practitioner is visited by a veiled woman whose quest is as mysterious as her appearance. She is seeking medical attention for someone else, but does not want the young doctor to attend until the following morning. He in turn is mystified at her insistence upon delaying his attendance as she seems to indicate that the life of the third party is at stake. In one sense the veil she wears simply heightens the sense of mystery surrounding her strange request. But by virtue of Dickens's clever analogy making, the veil also serves as an index of social divisions and urban alienation.

The first indication of social division occurs when the doctor sends his orphaned, parish-dependent messenger boy out of the room in order to speak to the veiled woman in private: "Leave the room, Tom. Draw the curtain, and shut the door."[12] The curtain recalls the veil, and the reader is forced to sympathize with the excluded Tom, since they too are shut out of the mystery. But that Tom's exclusion is far more than a metaphor for the reader's position is made evident by the presence of another curtain. When the doctor makes his way to the address the woman has left for him, he crosses into an area of the city that the narrator describes as "a straggling miserable place . . . a dreary waste," which is cut off from the rest of the city by a curtain of extreme poverty.[13] In this environment the reader is reminded of both the veil and the earlier curtain—the one that excluded Tom—by another that hangs across the window of the house where the veiled woman lives: "An old yellow curtain was closely drawn across the window up stairs, and the parlour shutters were closed." And like the area of the city in which it is located, "the house was detached from any other."[14] The multiple closings off and shuttings out clearly indicate social and economic exclusion—whether of the parish boy, the veiled woman or the deprived township.

When the mystery is solved the woman's veil is finally removed and, at the same time, the curtains are opened. But the revelation does not mitigate the misery; rather it shows it to be inexorable: the woman is the mother to a hanged son; she has asked the doctor around on the merest chance that he might be able to revive the young man whose social deprivation had led him into crime and a sentence of death. Thus Dickens's use of the veil serves a dual purpose: its occluding presence draws attention to the various kinds of exclusion that produce misery and abjection, and at the same time it emphasizes their very hiddenness. So the veil takes on meaning by embodying what it also conceals.

Tennyson's poem "The Two Voices" (1842) stages a dialogue between hope and despair, and appeals to a veiled truth hidden behind the appearance of the world. Here again the impulse to interpret the veil is strong, but is driven by metaphysical rather than by social imperatives. In the fourth stanza the veil is embodied in the cocoon of a dragonfly: "An inner impulse rent the veil / Of his old husk: from head to tail / Came out clear plates of sapphire mail."[15] The image seems emblematic of the emergence of hope, suggesting that despair is temporary, though the means of its overthrow is not yet apparent. But by the end of the poem a more subtle meaning has been created by the appearance of another veil: "To feel altho' no tongue can prove, / That every cloud, that spreads above / And veileth love, itself is love."[16] As with Thomson's curtain and Dickens's veil, Tennyson's veil itself becomes meaningful not because of what it conceals, but because it is itself a revelation. The veil partakes of the character of what it conceals, becoming revelatory by taking on a synechdochic function. When Tennyson later sought reassurance that mortality was not an intimation of meaninglessness, he returned to the image of the veil: "What hope of answer or redress? / Behind the veil, behind the veil."[17] Again, the repetition of the phrase focuses attention on the veil as a symbol of an ignorance that may open onto as yet unknown grounds for hope: its presence is ambiguous. It thus takes on a self-referential character, functioning both to veil and to reveal its own true significance.

A similar trope is employed in Christina Rosssetti's poem "Winter: My Secret" (1857), but here the focus is psychological.[18] The poem teases the reader with the promise of some kind of revelation that may or may not be forthcoming: "I tell my secret? No indeed not I: / Perhaps some day, who knows?" As the poem progresses, Winter clothing becomes a metaphor for the concealment of inner truth:

> To-day's a nipping day, a biting day;
> In which one wants a shawl,
> A veil, a cloak, and other wraps
> . . . .
> I wear my mask for warmth: who ever shows

His nose to Russian snows
To be pecked at by every wind that blows?

Then the coming of spring, with its shedding of the heavier layers of dress, seems to hint at the possibility that there may one day be some kind of unveiling, but the poem ends with the repetition of the teasing "perhaps": "Perhaps my secret I may say, / Or you may guess." The overall effect is to focus attention on the act of concealment, on the veil itself, since we are told that it is possible that the real secret is that there is no secret: "Suppose there is no secret after all." At one level Rossetti's poem seems to replicate, or at least to dally with, the dominant gender ideology according to which womanhood is delightfully mysterious, veiled, and intriguing. The idea is expressed succinctly in Coventry Patmore's *The Angel in the House* (1854): "No mystery of well-woven speech, / No simplest phrase of tenderest fall, / No liken'd excellence can reach / Her, the most excellent of all."[19] But the image in Rossetti's poem is also consonant with those that focus on the play of appearances and reality, revelation and concealment, betokening an uncertainty about what, if anything, might lie behind the veil of the phenomenal world.

For E. S. Dallas, writing in 1866, a perception of the reality which lay beyond appearances was fundamental to the processes of artistic expression:

> It is in the hidden sphere of thought, even more than in the open one, that we live and move and have our being; and it is in this sense that the idea of art is always a secret. We hear much of the existence of such a secret, and people are apt to say—If a secret exist, and if the artist convey it in his art, why does he not plainly tell us what it is? But here at once we fall into contradictions, for as all language refers to the known, the moment we begin to apply it to the unknown, it fails. Until the existence of an unknown hidden life within us be thoroughly well accepted, not only felt, but also to some extent understood, there will always be an esoteric mode of stating the doctrine, which is not for the multitude.[20]

Instantly forgetting his own insistence that "all language refers to the known," Dallas attempts to make his own use of language adequate to the task of urging the "thorough" acceptance and understanding of the "unknown hidden life." Thus art will always have a secret at its heart, but it will be that oxymoronic

thing—a "well accepted" and "to some extent understood" secret. The doubleness of the rhetoric, that wants to assert the existence of an obscured field that is somehow known to artists
and to their appreciators, but which is inaccessible to "the mul-
titude," may lead us to suspect that what is hidden here is not
so much the secret life of the artistic soul as the agenda to which
Dallas is working. The stark elitism of the "esoteric mode" is
half disguised as an aesthetic judgement, raising a question mark
against the ideological value of the veil. But to whatever political ends it may be turned, it is human finitude that leads Dallas
to his theory of art. The "secret" is that of what he calls the
"Hidden Soul"—something like a forerunner of the Freudian unconscious, but having a Romantic/mystical dimension; it consists in the submerged regions of the mind and extends beyond
the limits of conscious life. Quoting Prospero he asserts: "Our
little life is rounded with a sleep; our conscious existence is a
little spot of light, rounded or begirt with a haze of slumber—not
a dead but a living slumber, dimly lighted and like a visible darkness, but full of dreams . . . unknown and indefinable . . . a Hidden Soul."[21] What Dallas is unable to make clear is just how the
"Hidden Soul" has come to his attention; how can he possibly
know what is hidden, or even of its existence? It is as if he is
making much the same inference from ignorance as did Thomson: in a gesture typical of the age, he is reading the veil itself.

A comparable strategy is applied to a range of phenomena by
writers of the time. Death, however conceived, is the margin of
the knowable world and is, therefore, often depicted in Victorian
writing as forming a veil, as when the speaker in James Henry's
short poem "Very Old Man" (1854) sees its darkness adumbrated
in his failing sight. He thus spends his time "Hoping or fearing
something from [me] hid / Behind the thick, dark veil."[22] Edward
Fitzgerald's translation of "The Rubaiyat of Omar Khayyam"
(1859) imagines death as a locked door and as a "Veil past which
I could not see."[23] Olive Schreiner wrote in 1883 of the "veil of
terrible mist over the face of the Hereafter."[24]

A variety of other uses can be noted. In *Jane Eyre* a veil is used
to suggest the mysterious complexity of identity when Jane sees
Bertha Mason looking at herself in Jane's own mirror and wearing Jane's wedding veil.[25] As Gilbert and Gubar note, the episode
suggests that "the specter of Bertha is . . . the most threatening
avatar of Jane . . . Jane's truest and darkest double . . . the fero-

cious secret self Jane has been trying to repress"—an embodiment of her unconscious desires.[26] Similarly, in *Wuthering Heights* the fact that Cathy has never developed a full adult identity, but has insisted that she *is* Heathcliff, leads to a delirious failure to recognize her own image in a mirror: the mirror has to be veiled in order to hide her from herself.[27] Identity is still the main issue in the ways that the sensation fiction of the 1860s uses veils to deceive and to dissimulate: in *Lady Audley's Secret* (1862) Robert Audley vows to himself that he will "tear away the beautiful veil under which she [Lady Audley] hides her wickedness";[28] in *East Lynne* Lady Isabel Vane "was never seen out of doors without a veil."[29] That the uses of the veil are so multifarious is attributable, in part, to its familiarity as an item of female clothing but is also traceable to the fact that its doubleness as a mask for, and as a signifier of, hiddenness makes it an irresistible image for an age of uncertainty about the relationship between appearances and reality.

Even nineteenth-century English realism, for all its commitment to perspicuity in representation, acknowledges a degree of doubt about the project of true and accurate portrayal of the real. In *Middlemarch*, for example, language itself functions as a veil at times. The narrator, echoing the Carlylean perception that metaphors condition understanding, insists that "all of us, grave or light, get our thoughts entangled in metaphors, and act fatally on the strength of them."[30] Again, the text repeatedly draws attention to the ways in which bad grammar, the endurance of writing beyond the cultural context of its production, and the changing significance of words all contribute to the slippage between language and the reality that the novelist wants to convey in words.[31] The problem with representation necessarily deepens and intensifies the doubleness of perception that cannot rest with appearance, that pursues an underlying reality that remains characteristically veiled, even for the writer of realist fiction. *Middlemarch* demonstrates the problem in its creation and deployment of revelatory/concealing tissues.

Doctor Lydgate, Eliot's forward-thinking medic, is said to admire the French anatomist Francois Bichat:

That great Frenchman first carried out the conception that living bodies, fundamentally considered, are not associations of organs which can be understood by studying them first apart, and then as it were federally; but must be regarded as consisting of certain primary webs or tissues, out of which the various organs . . . are compacted. . . . No man, one sees, can understand and estimate the entire structure or its parts . . . without knowing the nature of his materials. And the conception wrought out by Bichat, with his detailed study of different tissues, acted necessarily on medical questions as the turning of gas-light would act on a dim, oil-lit street, showing new connections and hitherto hidden facts of structure.[32]

The obvious comparability between this passage and that which details the famous parable of the pier-glass (see chapter One, note 41, above) is instructive, and together they suggest something of the problem associated with observation in the period, caught as it is between the apparent and the inferred. The scratches on the pier-glass foreground those very issues in that they focus attention on the observing consciousness. The parable relates specifically to Rosamund Vincy, who understands the world as a pattern formed around her, a design which centers upon her needs and desires, ordered by "a Providence of her own."[33] An image of the observing consciousness, the candle held up to the pier-glass forges random scratches into a concentric pattern. Characterized as an egocentric illusion, the pattern is a veil of light which conceals the truth about herself from Rosamund while revealing it to the reader. But it is also a veil which, according to Hillis Miller, hides Eliot's own procedures from herself as realist author. After all, earlier in the novel she has described her own procedure in suggestively similar terms: "I have so much to do in unravelling certain human lots, and seeing how they were woven and interwoven, that all the light I can command must be concentrated on this particular web."[34] In what way does Eliot's "light," "concentrated" as it is on a "particular web," differ from the illusion-making candle held up to the pier-glass?

In the delineation of Bichat's theory, quoted above, the image of pattern-making again reveals a web or tissue which is supposed to be revelatory. But the apparently unproblematical reference to what living bodies are when "fundamentally considered," disguises (briefly) the fact that observation reveals nothing that cannot be attributed to the will to impose a pattern on phenomena. That is to say: the "primary webs or tissues" are an effect of the "fundamental consideration" to which they themselves give rise. Or, at least, this seems to be the implication when the metaphor which Eliot lights upon, once again, is that of light itself—the very condition of appearance, of the phenomenal. Bichat's work is compared to the lighting of streets in a way that reveals what is previously hidden. That this is both a revelation and a concealment is evident not only in the fact that what comes to light is another kind of veil ("primary webs or tissues"), but also in the fact that the rhetoric has first to plunge the reader into darkness in order to create the effect of revelation: the streets illuminated in the metaphor, the "new connections and hitherto hidden facts," appear out of an obscurity deliberately imposed in order to make the web appear revelatory.

What emerges from these uses of the images of veiling and unveiling in Victorian writing is that those who produced them were bumping up against the limits of empirical knowledge—a knowledge that did not satisfy the imagination. Seemingly uncomfortable within their own epistemological constraints, the writers of the age refused to settle for the world they could observe. This was precisely the form of discontent which gave rise to apocalypticism and which drove its practitioners to assert that, at times, they were permitted in visions and dreams to look through divinely engineered ruptures in the fabric of time and space. Victorian writers did not assert the occurrence of such openings, but looked longingly at the veil and attempted to read it for its inferences of what lay concealed beyond it. "From the veil can nothing be inferred," Teufelsdrockh ironically asserts with regard to the fabric with which his babyhood carrying basket was overhung;[35] from the veil much certainly was inferred by Victorian writers in his wake. It is this process of inference that makes Christina Rossetti's study of the book of Revelation so telling an account of the need both to posit the existence of some kind of an epistemological veil and to assert the existence of unfathomable depths lying beneath it. This is a quest not only for depths beneath the surface of the phenomenal world, but also for a depth dimension to texts; as Rossetti's hermeneutical procedure demonstrates, the two are not altogether distinct.

The Anxiety of Ignorance

"If thou canst dive, bring up pearls. If thou canst not dive, collect amber"

—Christina Rossetti, *The Face of the Deep*[36]

In 1892 Christina Rossetti published a devotional commentary on the Apocalypse, entitled *The Face of the Deep*. Little read today, it represents an attempt to make the Apocalypse useful as a guide to Christian living without attempting to plumb its perceived spiritual depths. The hidden depths of John's divine visions, Rossetti repeatedly tells her reader, are beyond her interpretative reach. A complex rhetoric of surfaces and depths is therefore deployed in order to focus attention on moral and spiritual issues rather than on the more abstruse prophetic aspects of the book of Revelation. But this attempt to scour the surface of the text in search of "amber" (as she puts it in her preface, contrasting this process with "diving for pearls") gives rise to an unresolved tension between her perception of the inadequacy of "shallow" or "surface" religion, and her sense that one can find truth on the surface of the text.

The remainder of this chapter conducts a close reading of Rossetti's work in order to discover what gives rise to the perception that the text of Revelation contains unsearchable depths. Arguing that the illusion of depth on a surface is definitive of reflection, I show that what Rossetti sees on the surface of the text is a series of reflections: of her own time, her own place, and herself. This, in fact, helps to explain the enduring allure of the Apocalypse: interpreters have always seen in its visions reflections of their own times and situations. But whereas this has led generations of male readers to assert their hermeneutic mastery in apocalyptic sects, cults, and religious movements, Rossetti's text reveals, by its humility and self-abnegation, the fact that the Apocalypse acts as a mirror of the historical, social, and cultural conditions under which interpretations are produced.

This is not to say that Rossetti set out to historicize the biblical text—far from it. Her concern seems to have been to offer readers ill-equipped to penetrate the mysteries of the text a way of reading which would make an elusive and worrying portion of sacred scripture accessible at a level within their hermeneutical purview. In other words her aim is to dehistoricize the text—to render an ancient work spiritually enlightening to a modern audience. Paradoxically, the depth to which she and her readers are denied access appears as an effect of the very "superficial" reading in which she claims to be engaged: the rhetorical superficies prove, on close reading, to posit the very profundities which they are said to be incapable of reaching.

There are two moments in *The Face of the Deep* which are significant for understanding the main title to this "Devotional Commentary on the Apocalypse." The first occurs in the section devoted to the letter to the Church in Sardis (Rev. 3:1–6). She employs the phrase "the face of the deep" here, in one of the many poems which punctuate the text:

> As froth on the face of the deep,
> As foam on the crest of the sea,
> As dreams at the waking of sleep,
> As gourd of a day and a night,
> As harvest that no man shall reap,
> As vintage that never shall be,
> Is hope if it cling not aright,
> O my God, unto Thee. (88)

If understood in terms of this usage the title would be a negation of the work's value: "the face of the deep" would represent the ground of a false hope, the surface upon which rests a shallow, evanescent, and vapid optimism. As this is the only occurrence of the phrase "the face of the deep" in the entire text, it enjoys a certain interpretative privilege, and given Rossetti's own frequently expressed doubts about the validity of her attempt to come to terms with the book of Revelation, it can be understood to indicate something of the ambivalent nature of the work. In fact, it is the only clue to the significance of the title in the first 364 pages of pious, word-by-word exposition. The second possibility does not occur until page 365.

When it eventually appears the second possibility comes in the form of a methodological apologia:

I take this opportunity of calling attention to my ignorance of, sometimes, a very critical point in the text on which I venture to meditate; and if in consequence I misrepresent the person of the speaker or the word spoken, I ask pardon for my involuntary error. Only should I have readers, let me remind them that what I write professes to be a *surface* study of an unfathomable depth: if it incites any to dive deeper than I attain to, it will so far have accomplished a worthy work. (365, original emphasis)

Such gestures occur throughout the book. Again and again Rossetti draws attention to her own lack of status as an interpreter: repeated phrases include: "If I dare so think," "If I am not mistaken," "If such an inference is allowable," "If I may." That she feels out of her hermeneutical depth in the Apocalypse is evident in a number of places: "Without hazarding conjecture beyond my depth" (363), "If I may venture so far out of my depth" (403), "I can neither explore height nor depth" (440). While this tendency seems at times to be the index of humility before the sacred text ("Far be it from me to think to unfold mysteries or interpret prophecies," 146), at other times it gives rise to an almost despairing anxiety over the task which she has taken on: "The whole subject is beyond me; the prophecies leave me in anxious ignorance" (342).

It is clear at such moments that the notion of interpretative depth is being associated with competence and authority. Conversely, Rossetti's worry about her own hermeneutical shallowness appears to be a product of her sense that truly fruitful study dives deep and brings up pearls and that such study is the fullest expression of true religion:

a religion without depth is not Christ's religion. The necessity of depth is set forth in the Parable of the Sower: the seed enters not at all into the first refuse soil, and barely penetrates into the second; in the third it perishes from a different cause; in the fourth and good ground alone does it take root downward and bear fruit upward. (37)

The vertical movement of religious growth, sending roots downward and shoots upward, is thwarted by textual study which fails to penetrate the surface and which is deflected into a horizontal search for possible intertexts.

In one particularly telling apology for her inadequacy as an interpreter, Rossetti draws attention to her failure to understand the significance of the ten days during which the unfortunate church in Smyrna will be called upon to suffer tribulation (Rev. 2:10): "It may be that even the excellent souls addressed understood not what period that cipher indicated. At any rate I assuredly understand it not. But wisdom transcends understanding; and doubtless this word is capable of instructing us, God helping an honest endeavour" (62). What follows is a catalogue of biblical tens designed to "fortify hope by cheerful meditation." These include the ten commandments, the ten strings of David's harp, the ten talents delivered up by the good and faithful servant to his lord, ten virgins with lamps, the ten degrees by which the shadow retreated on Hezekiah's time-defying sundial, the ten lepers healed by Jesus (nine ingrates plus one thankful Samaritan), and the ten days of vegetarianism endured by Daniel and his three compatriots at the court of Nebuchadnezzar.

These hopeful and fortifying intertexts are offered in place of understanding. Consequently, Rossetti, conscious of a lack of hermeneutical depth, diffuses meaning across a broad textual surface. A similar movement is observable on more than one occasion. Her exposition of 8:10–11, for example, follows a curious path from consideration of a falling star to remarks about the morals of writing. She proceeds according to the dictates of a spontaneous intertextuality, characterized as the effect of the evocative power of these verses: they are "liable," Rossetti says, "to recall to the mind even involuntarily by verbal association the sacred verses: 'For ever, O Lord, Thy word is settled in heaven. . . . Thy word is a lamp unto my feet, and a light unto my path'" (252). On the strength of the association between stars as luminaries of the earth, and the word of God as a light to the reader (combined with the fact that the fallen star is said to poison a third of the earth's waters), she goes on to speculate on the value of secular knowledge. She wonders if human intellect might not sometimes prove as hazardous as the water-polluting star: "For in the text we behold light introducing men to the darkness of death; an emblem of unsanctified knowledge and its tendency. The star is a genuine illuminator: so may the knowledge be genuine knowledge; yet not being mixed with faith in them that hold it, it becomes to them perilous or even deadly" (252).

This is a constant worry that repeatedly feeds into her concern about the legitimacy of her apocalyptic project. In the final chapter the connection becomes quite explicit: "To study the Apocalypse out of idle curiosity would turn it, so far as the student's self were concerned, into a branch of the Tree of the Knowledge of Good and Evil. And what came of Eve's curious investigation of the original Tree we all know. Obey to the limit of knowledge, and in all probability obedience may extend knowledge" (531). Certain aspects of *The Face of the Deep* suggest that the issue is, at least in part, a matter of gender ideology, of what it is proper for a woman to know,[37] but it is also a matter of what knowledge is legitimate within the bounds of faith and obedience. Ignorance, which she describes on one occasion as "often a safeguard and a privilege" (54), turns out to be quite a good thing in a writer (at least in one who writes about the Apocalypse), not only because it leads one to move across the surface of the text in search of fortifying scriptures, but also because it addresses ignorant readers at their own level. Never one to flatter her audience, Rossetti writes:

> There is one advantage in ignorance writing for ignorance; the writer sets before the reader resources common to both. Only we must all beware of becoming as blind who lead the blind.
>
> Yet, after all, neither knowledge nor ignorance is of first importance to Bible students: grace is our paramount need; Divine grace, rather than any human gift. Acquirements and deficiencies sink to one dead level when lacking grace. . . .
>
> Such considerations befit my own ignorance. . . . (114)

Of course, Rossetti's surface reading does not operate on the "dead level" of graceless deficiency; rather it moves to and fro across the face of the deep. The difference is a matter of depth, or, at least, of the perception of depth in the surface—a depth effect denied to the "dead level."

Returning to the intertextual progress of the comments on Revelation 8:10–11, here too the question of the legitimacy of secular knowledge leads Rossetti back to Eve: she whose genuine knowledge proved fatal. From Eve she moves to the antediluvians as exemplars of useless knowledge and "unassimilated truth," who were forewarned of the flood, yet of whom it was said that they "knew not until the flood came, and took them all away." This leads her to quote Paul's advice to Timothy with regard to useless knowledge: he is to avoid "profane and vain babblings, and oppositions of science falsely so called." Rossetti then speculates on how much worse it is to propagate error than to hold it, and this thought, in turn, directs her towards consideration of the morality of writing: "Among all channels of in-struction, speech is the readiest and is universal. A noble gift entailing a vast responsibility." Thence to James's discourse on the importance of bridling the tongue, and, by extension, the importance of bridling the pen: "And what is true of the tongue is in ample proportion true of the pen: this likewise may bless, edify, diffuse sweetness; or may become a fire, a world of iniquity, may propagate defilement, and kindle impious fire, being itself set on fire of hell" (253).

I have described this passage in some detail because it is illustrative of Rossetti's technique throughout her study, and because it makes clear her perception of the way in which those among the readers of scripture who are ill equipped for pearl-diving can "collect amber," as she puts it. But it illustrates, too, that this movement across the surface of the biblical text masks a worry about the legitimacy of this very procedure—a worry that not to dive into the depths of apocalyptic mystery may be to practice a false religion, a religion without depth. At the end of the above quotation, where Rossetti worries that hellfire may blaze at any moment from the nib of her pen, it is manifest that she cannot altogether separate what she has explored in chapter 2 under the rubric of the "depth of Satan" from the surface of the text: as she moves across the face of the deep, she seems ever to be teetering on the brink of a demonic abyss.

Commenting on the phrase "depths of Satan" in Revelation 2:24, Rossetti asks: "Why dive into such depths, when deeper depths are open before us?" (80). She then quotes Romans 11:33 as proof text for the openness of divine depths: "O the depth of the riches both of the wisdom and the knowledge of God! how unsearchable are his judgements, and his ways past finding out." For Paul, as for Rossetti, depths are ultimately beyond our ken; they are "unsearchable" and "past finding out." Those "deeper depths" are not really open to us at all; they are always unreachable, so that one is left to wonder whether they are anything but effects of the text's surface, anything, that is, other than the reader's own reflection on its surface.

By contrast, one seems to be in mortal danger of being immersed in demonic depths unawares; depths which eventually outfathom those so-called "deeper depths" of wisdom and knowledge: "Christ in his mercy preserve us from ever sounding that *surpassing* depth of Satan" (131, my emphasis). That this is a matter of falling into interpretative error becomes clear in chapter 12: "Whilst studying the devil I must take heed that my study become not devilish by reason of sympathy. As to gaze down a precipice seems to fascinate the gazer towards a shattering fall; so it is spiritually perilous to gaze on excessive wickedness, lest its immeasurable scale should fascinate us as if it were colossal without being monstrous" (321). So while one is never fully equipped to explore the ocean of God's immensity, one is only too likely to hit rock bottom in the Satanic abyss. Rossetti freely admits to terror at the prospect of unwittingly taking such a dive: "I exceedingly fear and quake lest I should fall away" (193). Yet Satan's depth, like the divine largesse, is "immeasurable," suggesting that even in falling one can never comprehend its scale. This rhetorical inconsistency alerts the reader to the fact that like its divine paradigm, Satan's chasm is another textual effect. A textual comment on a text, it is explained by means of a quotation from another textual comment on a different text: "A quotation from my sister's *Shadow of Dante* speaks to the point," Rossetti tells us. Her sister's point is that Dante never makes evil appealing; discerning readers "feel *in the depths* of [their] nature" how loathsome are those who become besotted by sin (321, my emphasis). Deep calls to deep on the intertextual surface of Rossetti's Apocalypse.

Veiled Unveilings

The depth that remains unfathomed appears only by contrast with such intertextual gestures. Towards the end of the book, still apologizing for having written it, she writes: "I suppose that no insight or profundity of mortal man ever has been adequate to the full exploration of this Apocalypse. I feel certain that no natural shallowness need render it a dead letter to man, woman, or child" (531). It is always Rossetti's sense of her own inadequacy, of her own hermeneutic shallowness that causes her text to slide across the surface of the Apocalypse like crowns across a sea of glass. Thus, commenting on the promise to the Church in Pergamos (Rev. 2:17), that they will be given to eat the "hidden manna," she writes: "The subtlest and profoundest of men cannot explain mysteries; the simplest person can appropriate and exult in them. *On the very surface* of this great promise it transpires that as Christ is life to the faithful soul now, so He will be life to the indefectible soul then. This for the present suffices" (72, my emphasis). Again, the eschewing of subtlety and profundity in opting for a reading of that which is "on the very surface of the text," creates the illusion of inaccessible and unfathomable depths. The face of the deep, then, is a mask, a dissimulating appearance akin to that which marks the spiritual condition of the Church in Sardis: "thou hast a name that thou livest, and art dead" (Rev. 3:1).

Dolores Rosenblum's examination of the use of masks and veils in Rossetti's poetry is relevant here. Rosenblum notes that the surface/depth dichotomy not only encodes a contrast between appearance and reality, but that it has, too, a specific biographical significance:

> Like most Victorian poets, Rossetti is sensitive to the disjunction between surfaces and depths, between appearances and the buried life. More than others, however, she is concerned with the point of juncture, literally the face that is looked at and the eyes that look out from it. Her poems are full of references to faces, masks, veils, shrouds, and, less frequently, bodies fixed in an attitude—all surfaces to be regarded.[38]

She goes on to argue that, as an artist's model who sat for sketches and portraits from an early age, Rossetti was peculiarly conscious of being looked at, and was acutely aware of the gap between external image and interior self.[39]

Poems such as "L. E. L." (1859) and "In Progress" (1862) are based on this kind of distinction. "L. E. L." depicts a woman whose social persona seems both to imprison and to protect her true self: "Downstairs I laugh, I sport and jest with all; / But in my solitary room above / I turn my face in silence to the wall. . . . They praise my rustling show, and never see / My heart breaking for a little love . . . Perhaps some saints in glory guess the truth, / Perhaps some angels read it as they move"[40] Typically, Rossetti offers her subject an other-worldly hope: while members of the subject's social circle are blind to her suffering, there may be heavenly readers capable of penetrating the veil of polite behavior. But whether or not there are such true observers, an apocalyptic transformation ultimately will remove the need for the private grief which causes the rift between inner and outer selves: "Then love shall fill thy girth, / And love make fat thy dearth, / When new spring builds new heaven and clean new earth." A similar impulse can be detected in "In Progress." In this case the woman at the center of the poem is masked not by artifice, but by a care-worn appearance produced in "long-unbroken silences" and by "drudging daily common things." The poet imagines a future transfiguration that will cause "Her head to shoot forth seven stars from where they lurk / And her eyes lightnings and her shoulders wings."[41] The transformation is apocalyptic in tone in that it both evokes the vision of a woman crowned with stars in Revelation 12:1 and suggests a moment of judgement, of the unveiling of spiritual truth in the manifestation of her hitherto masked inner being.

Consideration of this sense of personal hiddenness opens up yet another depth dimension in *The Face of the Deep:* the depth of the human soul. Pondering the moment in Revelation 6:8 when Death and Hell are given power over a fourth part of the earth, Rossetti, noting that this power does not extend over the whole earth nor beneath the earth, writes: "It is a surface scourge: kiss the rod, and thou shalt abide as the profound sea whose surface is lashed and ploughed by winds, but whose depths repose in unbroken calm. Alas for shallow persons who are all surface!" (207). She goes on to evoke the parable of the sower once more, as a caution against shallowness. That the self is divided here between a tempestuous surface and a calm depth is a subject to which I will return. Here I wish to note the rhetoric of selfhood as depth or the lack of it. Just a few pages further on, Rossetti characterizes religious poverty in similar terms, but with a startling difference:

> Man is a still wider sea, a still deeper ocean, a more insatiable abyss: this life and the resources of this life can never fill him. . . . The vast bed of ocean corresponds with the ocean whereof it is the bed: so man's vast emptiness corresponds with the Immensity of God Who fills him; they correspond, God having fulness where man hath emptiness. (213–4)

"Empty depth" now describes the plight of those who lack deep religion, replacing and contradicting the notion of shallowness associated with the parable of the sower. Man has also been transmogrified from the creature that must dive into the divine depths, into a receptacle for God's fullness: the pearl-diver has become the ocean bed. Once again the rhetoric of depths appears subject to the kind of slippage associated with the horizontal movement of textuality, rather than with the vertical movement which Rossetti associates with true religion.

What does Rossetti see on the surface of the Apocalypse which makes her believe in the existence of unfathomable depths, of Christ or of Satan or of the human soul? She sees what interpreters of the Apocalypse have always seen in its other-worldly visions, alien life-forms, and cataclysmic happenings: she sees her own world, her own time, herself reflected. I want now to examine each of these three reflections in turn, remembering in the process that reflection is the illusion of depth on a surface.

ALREADY IN ENGLAND

For all its apparent concern with universal values and ends, there is a very clear geographical and cultural specificity evident throughout Rossetti's commentary. London, the Anglican Church, England, and Ireland each find mention in its pages. Events on either side of the Irish Sea seem to Rossetti to be adumbrations of eschatological woe: "are not coming events already casting their shadows before? Glance at recent troubles in Ireland: mark boycotting and its results. Look at home; at strikes and unions, so far as any terrorism resorted to is concerned" (349). But most of the reflections of the age are less overtly eschatological. The Anglican Church appears as the branch of the "Holy Catholic Apostolic Church" to which must be applied the words addressed to the churches in Revelation: "To the Church of England now, as to the Church of Ephesus then" (56, 540). Despite this will to align the Anglicans with the noble Ephesians who, it is said, have "laboured and not fainted" (Rev. 2:3), Rossetti opts for a more general inference in commenting on the letter to the Church in Sardis. The believers of Sardis, of course, are a pretty hopeless bunch among whom, John has the Spirit say, there are but a few "which have not defiled their garments" (Rev. 3:4). Rossetti comments: "*A few* in a whole city, *a few* out of an entire population. Shall London cast the first stone at Sardis?" (92, original emphasis). In eliding the difference between the city and the church, comparing Sardis with London rather than with the Anglican church, Rossetti deflects attention away from the failings of the institution which she elsewhere calls "the beloved Anglican Church of my Baptism" (540), making them the failings of the city at large. She was willing, it seems, to accrue to that august body the blessings due to the Ephesians, but unwilling to expose it to the divine ire earned by the defective Christians in Sardis. This is a clear indication both of the specific, deep, personal feeling with which she regarded her church, and also of the selective way in which she applies apocalyptic warnings to her own place and time.

In a similar vein, England as a whole is subjected to certain apocalyptic criticisms that reflect Rossetti's particular biases and predilections. If, on one occasion, she considers England's apocalyptic fate in elegaic mode, bewailing "our beloved England" as subject to the day of God's wrath (217), other passages suggest that the nation might actually deserve a little fire and brimstone. The religious defection of the English in the 1880s, for example, takes on a portentous quality:

> Already in England (not to glance at other countries) the signs of the times are ominous: Sunday is being diverted by some to business, by others to pleasure; Church congregations are often meagre, and so services are chilled. Our solemn feasts languish, and our fasts where are they? Yet each for himself and God for us all, we can if we choose "remember the Sabbath-day, to keep it holy"; jealous of its essentials, not wedded to its accidents. (243)

If this emphasis on the decline of religion seems, in the face of colonial and domestic injustice on a vast scale, to exemplify what Jesus meant by straining at a gnat and swallowing a camel, then Rossetti's remarks on the fall of Babylon go some way to redressing the balance. Picking up on the language of the merchants who mourn the city which made them rich (Rev. 18:16), Rossetti lists a few places and people for whom she would cry "Alas!" Those from the (biblical) past include Sodom, Tyre and Dives, while those who merit an "Alas" in the future are all who are unprepared at the final hour (421). Her "Alas" for the present day is saved for England and its social inequities:

> Alas England full of luxuries and thronged by stinted poor, whose merchants are princes and whose dealings crooked, whose packed storehouses stand amid bare homes, whose gorgeous array has rags for neighbours! From a canker in our gold and silver, from a moth in

our garments, from blasted crops, from dwindling substance, from righteous retribution abasing us among the nations, Good Lord, deliver us. . . .

If any shipmasters and crews, sailors and sea-traders, have yet to lament and quake, well may arrogant England amid her seas quake and lament betimes. (422)

Despite its awareness of conditions for the underprivileged denizens of late Victorian Britain, and its rhetoric of economic injustice, this lamentation serves to raise a suspicion that the real focus of prophetic concern, here, is the need to insulate the current order of things from the kind of cataclysmic upheaval that may diminish the world status of beloved England.

A concern for England's international prestige underlies a similar argument in favor of international and interracial harmony. Here muted echoes of imperialism sound in her cordial welcome:

Language discriminates into groups; whilst speech, man's universal heritage, by grace brings home to our hearts the world-width of brotherhood. By grace the concentrated, I will dwell among mine own people, expands until we say with delighted welcome, Thy people shall be my people. By grace nations become bound and welded together in the unifying presence of God. (185)

One has only to replace the phrase "by grace" with "by main force" in the final sentence of this passage to understand the proximity of imperial ambition and missionary endeavor in the British expansion of the last twenty to thirty years of the nineteenth century. Just a few pages further on Rossetti is quite explicit about the connection: "If all our forefathers had preached adequately by word and by example, wrestled in intercession, invested liberally in alms, spent themselves in missionary enterprise or at least in missionary zeal, doubtless Christ would have gone forth mightily with them to annex nations and races" (199). What such rhetoric obscures, by virtue of its cultural assumptions, is the fact that the Apocalypse is *inter alia* an attack upon imperialist economics, upon the annexing of nations and races.[42] Revelation 18, with its description of the fall of Babylon ,is especially virulent in its anti-imperial rhetoric. In this light Rossetti's refusal to mention the city of Rome in any of her interpretative comments is particularly noteworthy.

Revelation's allusions to the imperial capital are at times very thinly veiled. Following the vision in which John sees a woman dressed in scarlet and purple, "drunken with the blood of the saints," sitting on a seven-headed, scarlet-colored beast, the text explains: "The seven heads are seven mountains, on which the woman sitteth" (17:9). A few verses further on the allusion is made even more plain: "the woman which thou sawest is that great city, which reigneth over the kings of the earth" (17:18). Despite the text's nudging and winking Rossetti refuses to recognize the woman: "who then, what then, is she?" (411). Her explanation evokes the language of hermeneutic shallowness, speaking of what the woman may "on the surface" represent (400), of being out of her depth (403), and of "veiled reality" which "may elude discovery" (404). In her avowed perplexity she relates the seven hills to seven virtues through seven stages of life, and to their potential corruption by the world: "innocence in infancy, reverence in childhood, holiness in youth, aspiration in maturity, patience on the decline, perseverance in age, hope in death" (405). In place of the critique of imperialism, and diverting attention both from Rome and the "New Rome," cities with which she was biographically linked, we find Rossetti celebrating the virtues constitutive of domesticity. Once more the deep is that which eludes discovery, and that which appears on the surface is a reflection of Rossetti's own geographical and cultural location: imperial England's home front.

Sometimes those reflections take the form of forays into social comment. These are not confined to lamentations over the decline of organized religion and remarks about the inequities evident in the contrast between Britain's mercantile wealth and its abject poverty. Rossetti is also aware that there are around and about her newly popular occult practices, the tendencies of which seem to her antichristian: "I will have nothing to do with spiritualism,[43] whether it be imposture or a black art; or with mesmerism, lest I clog my free will; or with hypnotism, lest wilful self-surrender become my road to evil choice, imagination, conduct, voluntary or involuntary" (271). This is part of Rossetti's meditation on Revelation 9:21: "Neither repented they of their murders, nor of their sorceries" and represents an attempt to make the need for repentance appropriate to her own age: "Certain heathens . . . worship devils. This literal gross act is not perhaps likely to tempt nineteenth-century Christians" (271), but modern "sorceries," she implies, are little less corrupting than their first-century antecedents and their contemporary "heathen" cognates.

Sixty or so pages further on, philanthropy and socialism join the list of modern trends which run counter to revealed truth:

> Satan, a master of his weapons, brings out of his counterfeit treasure things new and old: his own blasphemy, along with worldly deceits and carnal obstructions. . . . I must beware of "polished corners" which form no part of the sole Temple; of fair-seeming superstructures which are not founded upon the one only Rock; of spiritualism which is not spirituality; of philanthropy divorced from dogma; of socialism in lieu of Christian brotherhood. (336–37)

Here, the issue is not so much the relevance of repentance as the awareness of Satanic dissimulation. The Apocalypse functions, appropriately enough, as an unmasking or unveiling of the face of evil in late Victorian Britain.

So, if John's text reveals to Rossetti unpleasant truths beneath the surface of late Victorian society, it does so by means of a reflection on its surface—a surface which Rossetti claims to be unable to penetrate. The veil drawn over those depths—a veil which the Apocalypse purports to remove, of course—appears to be that which grounds the reflection of Rossetti's own time: *the biblical text has contemporary relevance only as an impermeable, reflective surface.* A similarly revelatory veil makes the Apocalypse a site of self-reflection for Rossetti.

"I MEAN MYSELF"

P. G. Stanwood has observed that in *The Face of the Deep* "Rossetti is engaged in a self-study." He points out that she quotes the final line of George Herbert's "Miserie"—"My God, I mean myself"—as a means of counterbalancing the self-righteousness implicit in her remarks about the final condition of the unrighteous.[44] This focus on the relationship between self and sacred text is characteristic of the work as a whole, with its many personal poems, prayers, self-critical observations, and even the occasional illustrative anecdotes drawn from the author's own experience.[45] Jan Marsh, too, notes that *The Face of the Deep* "can be read biographically as a partial record of her spiritual experience in these narrowed years."[46] It may be that the book in its entirety is an elaborate disguise, a veil which allows Rossetti to write about herself under cover of apocalyptic secrecy: a simultaneous veiling and unveiling. It should be noted that, at times, she is quite explicit about using the text of the Apocalypse as a looking glass: 'instead of attention being directed to the ends of the earth, our eye must be turned within" (396). "Know thyself," she writes on another occasion, and then quotes James's comparison of the Word to a mirror (548). This might be read as a maneuver designed to legitimate the commentary's continual focus on individual morality and personal righteousness at the expense of politico-economic considerations, but it also serves to underpin the autobiographical detail, giving it a hermeneutical basis in the biblical text.[47]

In a manner which mirrors the very apocalyptic process under scrutiny, the self-study proceeds with a double movement of revelation and concealment which Dolores Rosenblum has called "a structural principle" of Rossetti's poetry.[48] It might be said of Rossetti's poetry what Rossetti herself says of John's Apocalypse: "underlying or parallel with the primary meaning, is often discernible a further signification which may be unfolded to us even while the other continues occult" (195). Just as John's text claims to uncover certain truths about contemporary history while cloaking figures and events in cryptic symbols and numerological riddles, Rossctti veils her self-revelation, in this case, in devotional exposition. A biocritical analysis of *The Face of the Deep* is beyond the ambit of the present work, but the self-reflective elements of Rossetti's text, by which I mean the moments at which the text constructs (and deconstructs) a subjectivity, are of immediate significance.

Rossetti's sense of division between the external image and the interior self, between the false face and the true depth, is played out in her consideration of the self confronted with ultimate judgement and with the person of Christ. In that face-to-face encounter the surface yields to the deep gaze of divine eyes: "His eyes are light, all-seeing. . . . Thou, Lord, Who hast beheld all sinners from the first sinner, and wilt behold us all even unto the last; turn Thy face from our sins, but turn it not from us" (33). This plea is followed by a short poem which refers to "That look which pierced St. Peter's heart" and to being searched through and through with a look. Again, in commenting on Rev. 2:18, Rossetti writes: "'Eyes like unto a flame of fire.'— Omniscience from which nothing is concealed; unto which nothing is veiled, disguised, obscure" (74). This attests to a need for recognition not found in human society—already noted in the poems "L. E. L." and "In Progress"—but also for a reunifying of the self. The divine gaze is characterized as having the ability to meld surface and depth into a complete image, healing the rift between public and private selves. Yet this is repeatedly expressed in terms of face-to-face encounter: "Hidden in God's Presence worshipped face to face" (69); "That I may behold thy Face, / For Thee I desire" (183); "Till we gaze on Thee face unto Face" (308).

Given the pervasive rhetoric which contrasts faces with depths and which makes the former synonymous with shallowness and deception, it seems necessary to ask whether Rossetti's desire for a face-to-face encounter with Christ can be taken at face value. It certainly seems to reflect a genuine longing for psychic wholeness—a wholeness which much of the book's rhetoric of subjectivity problematizes by means of opposing gestures. On the other hand it may be that there is at work a countervailing desire: to keep certain depths well hidden in case they reveal not a profound mystery but an all too familiar face. In order to work towards the unmasking of that face it will be necessary to explore briefly the ways in which the text deals with subjectivity.

Selves are characterized in contradictory terms as stable entities with eternal value, but also as riven and permeable. Permeable in that love opens us to others in a way which blurs the boundaries of selfhood: "Heavenly large-heartedness seems scarcely to know *me* from *thee*" (181, original emphasis). Riven in that they are subject to violence and internal conflict. Thus the sharp two-edged sword that proceeds from the mouth of the glorified Christ in John's opening vision is perceived as a threat to self-identity: "That which probes and sunders me will never of its own proper nature slay me; for life it is not death, that thus cleaves its way into my heart of hearts" (37). Like the fiery eyes, the sword pierces to the heart, but unlike the eyes it sunders rather than renders whole. This is the context in which the religion of Christ is said to be a religion of depth (see above), but that depth is both welcoming and threatening: it both offers wholeness and threatens "a dividing asunder of our very selves."

The divided self appears on other occasions in different guises: the division is that which is marked by self-enmity when Rossetti refers to "that deadliest of all our enemies, self" (103); a little later it is the division which keeps the self in the dark about its true condition: "Lord, grant me grace to strip myself of any subterfuges which hide me from myself but never from Thee; of any whitening which overlays my foulness" (133). A degree of self-loathing is all too evident in these formulations, and the same is true of the passages that suggest a more stable identity:

> I who am myself cannot but be myself. I am what God has constituted me: so that however I may have modified myself, yet do I remain that same I; it is I who live, it is I who must die, it is I who must rise again at the last day. I rising again out of my grave must carry on that very life which was mine before I died, and of which death itself could not altogether snap the thread. Who I was I am, who I am I am, who I am I must be for ever and ever.
>
> I the sinner of to-day am the sinner of all the yesterdays of my life. I may loathe myself or be amazed at myself, but I cannot unself myself for ever and ever.
>
> "O Lord, I am oppressed; undertake for me." (47)

Eternal self-identity seems a heavy burden for Rossetti to bear. Biographical evidence suggests that an element of self-loathing crept into Rossetti's psyche at around the age of fifteen as a result of a breakdown in her health. Jan Marsh explains the change thus:

> incestuous abuse of some kind—possibly in the form of mutual masturbation that gave Christina unwanted knowledge of arousal— offers a convincing explanation of the dark and disturbed aspects of her inner life that would account for her teenage breakdown, personality change, inexplicable rages and recurrent depression. That it probably coincided with puberty made it all the more disabling.
>
> Whatever the actual experience, it was not something that could be talked about, and perhaps like many abuse victims she banished the knowledge from conscious memory.[49]

This may be what lies in the depths which Rossetti's text carefully avoids exploring. It would help to explain why the encounters with Christ are couched in a double rhetoric of confrontation with eyes that see into the heart of hearts, and of the face-to-face meeting which echoes the public-private dichotomy of many of her poems: a split desire to be made whole and yet to preserve the secret.

That the face of the deep unmasked may be the face of Rossetti's father is suggested by her short story "Commonplace" dating from 1870. Some twenty years after her father has been lost at sea, the heroine, Lucy Charlmont, is depicted walking along a beach, "absent eyes fixed on the monotonous waves, which they did not see. Gradually a morbid fancy grew upon her that one day she should behold her father's body washed ashore, and that she should know the face: from a waking fancy, this began to haunt her dreams with images unutterably loathsome."[50] A face from the deep haunts Lucy with "loathsome" images of her father. The fear of seeing again the father's body is all too evocative of inappropriate contact, as is the terror of the deep yielding up its dark secret.

The reflections of her country, her time and herself—some of them deeply personal—that can be read in Rossetti's commentary on the Apocalypse suggest that although St. John's text purports to be an unveiling of divine mysteries, its very obscurity turns it into a revelation of human desires, anxieties, concerns. In this sense Rossetti's text reiterates towards the close of the Victorian era what Carlyle observed at its opening: that the veil was a key image for such an age of epistemological and religious uncertainty. What was inferred from the veil reflects some of the underlying assumptions that played across Victorian literature and culture and reveals its deepest fears and most cherished illusions.

"Raise the Veil"

Rossetti's perennial interest in the disjunction between public appearance and private reality reflects something of the complexity and paradoxical nature of the image of the veil as it persists in the literature of the period. As has been shown, from Carlyle's epoch-making work to writings of the *fin de siècle*, the image finds its way into all kinds of Victorian texts. When William Thackeray employed the metaphor of veiling in *Vanity Fair* (1848) it was as both a cover for, and an index of, moral impropriety, arising from his refusal to describe the scandalous behavior of Becky Sharp, choosing instead to "throw a veil" over some scenes.[51] By the end of the period such veils were being removed in the uncovering of a range of hitherto unacknowledged proclivities and desires. Hugh Stutfield identified the trend in an article in *Blackwood's Magazine* in 1895. Upbraiding writers of what he called "neuropathic fiction," he observed that they openly discussed "matters which would not have been tolerated in the novels of a decade ago. . . . Emancipated woman in particular loves to show her independence by dealing freely with the relations of the sexes. Hence all the prating of passion, animalism, 'the natural workings of sex,' and so forth, with which we are nauseated. Most of the characters in these books seem to be erotomaniacs."[52]

The process (perhaps) began with the emergence of the figure of the detective in the work of Edgar Allan Poe, Charles Dickens, and Wilkie Collins. Poe's Dupin (in "The Murders on the Rue Morgue" and "The Purloined Letter"), Dickens's Mr. Bucket (in *Bleak House*), and Collins's Walter Hartright (in *The Woman in White*) became agents of unmasking, of revelations that brought to light deeds done in secret by outwardly respectable figures. At the time when the uncovering of clandestine activity was providing the sensation fiction of the 1860s with its characteristic plots, John Ruskin voiced a demand for society to unblinker itself in other ways. His collection of essays on political economy, *Unto This Last* (1862), ends with a plea to "Raise the veil boldly; face the light," where the veil represents a refusal to acknowledge social injustice.[53]

More and more of that hidden life, whether sexual, criminal, or economic, was to be uncovered as the nineteenth century entered its last decade. George Moore's controversial novel *Esther Waters* (1894), for example, not only exposed the horrors perpetrated upon unmarried mothers, including the murderous practice of "baby farming," but also took the reader to the very scene of his heroine's seduction, all but naming the act. His naturalistic style, learned from Zola, is profoundly anti-apocalyptic inasmuch as it is anti-transcendent, focusing attention not on what is veiled by the phenomenal world but on details of that world covered over in earlier forms of realist fiction. At the same time George Egerton's collections of short stories *Keynotes* (1893) and *Discords* (1894), and Menie Muriel Dowie's *Gallia* (1895), contained frank accounts of the female sexual desire that had been implicit in earlier texts like *Jane Eyre* and *Cassandra*. In such a cultural climate Rossetti's *The Face of the Deep*, with its deeply felt concern with moral and religious decline, might be characterized as an ambivalent reaction to such uncoverings, betokening both a need to acknowledge that decline and to re-cover the world emerging from beneath the wraps of Victorian propriety by focusing attention on transcendent certainties. It illustrates David Shaw's claim that the veil is a profoundly ambivalent symbol for Victorian minds: "An obsessive curiosity about what lies behind the veil is always matched by a fear of knowing too much."[54] That Rossetti should turn to the Apocalypse in such a climate is not surprising, given its plotting of relations between an uncomfortable reality and a hidden world in which divine order is ultimately victorious.

The signs of the times that Rossetti reads off against the biblical text, then, are designed, in part, to locate her age in the cosmic progress towards consummation, but they also serve to mask the unpalatable specificities of her time in ignoring the kind of revelations that so worried Stutfield. The tone of the work is, therefore, not one of exultant despair like that found in, say, Matthew Arnold's apocalyptic poetic drama "Empedocles on Etna" (1852). Arnold's gloom reflects a "weary" and "ignoble world," that inspires the suicidal protagonist's desire to throw off the "stifling veils" of mind and thought in order to embrace the "All" which lies beyond.[55] Rossetti's sense of apocalyptic drama is less philosophical and more conventionally religious. Yet her work does encode a degree of ambivalence which is shared with Arnold, a doubt which James Longenbach identifies as to whether "the coming apocalypse is one of consciousness or of culture."[56] No doubt, Rossetti would have denied the more limiting implications of the subjective possibility, but the fact that so much of her interpretative procedure issues in self-reflection is emblematic of the personal dimensions and functions assumed by Victorian apocalyptic rhetoric. At the same time, as is obvious by now, there are definite cultural affinities at work in her writing that make Rossetti's text illustrative of a broader tendency rather than merely the idiosyncratic expression of her own beliefs, or a series of metaphors for the vicissitudes of the inner life. But the distinction of Rossetti's approach, that which sets it apart from Arnold's and from the modern sense of the apocalyptic to which it helped give rise (expressed most powerfully in *The Waste Land*), is that she refuses to translate the mythological narrative of temporal closure into one of mere cultural decadence. In the age of the abolition of temporal horizons she maintained an atavistic attachment to an older perception of time as bounded by inviolable divine limits. The next chapter explores the ways in which that process of abolition, unmarked in *The Face of the Deep*, was dealt with in texts that both acknowledged and resisted its implications.

4

Time After Time

"Pierce through the Time-Element, glance into the eternal"
—Thomas Carlyle, *Sartor Resartus*

IN *SARTOR RESARTUS* TIME FEATURES AS ONE OF THE REALITY-concealing veils which Teufelsdrockh's vision peers through to God's "Everlasting Now" or eternal present. He dreams of owning a "time-annihilating hat" that would allow him to travel through the past and future at will, "from the Fire-Creation of the World to its Fire-Consummation."[1] If this seems impossible or unimaginable, he argues, then we should consider memory and hope as evidence that the past is not annihilated, nor the future non-extant; "Yesterday and To-morrow both are." Furthermore, time and space are "but creations of God," and God is eternal; therefore, time past and time future must both continually exist for him. Such a perception owes its characteristic cosmology to the Apocalypse; the author of that text claims to have "pierced through the Time-element and glanced into the eternal," gaining a god's-eye-view of the processes of history.

By the end of the Victorian era the defeat of time as a bar to direct scrutiny of the past and future would be transformed from a product of apocalyptic discourse to one of science fiction: H. G. Wells envisaged travelling through time not by virtue of visionary experience or some supernatural talisman, but in a machine. This is hardly surprising given that various kinds of automated, time-bending machinery had been brought into existence between the publication dates of *Sartor Resartus* and *The Time Machine*. But the contrast between the two also throws into sharp relief the shift in the perception of time from one that

is fundamentally cosmological to one that is essentially technological. The struggle between these two temporalities is dramatically represented in Thomas Hardy's fiction, especially *Far
From the Madding Crowd* (1874), and I will turn to that novel
shortly in order to explore the conflict. Yet, as I hope to show in
considering Wells's novella, the shift to a technological apprehension of time could not be accomplished without negotiating
with the Apocalypse and in certain ways repeating it.

Underlying the Victorian change in relation to time was the
development of powerful and versatile steam engines which
were to revolutionize travel, manufacturing, and—before the
end of the century—food production and distribution, each region of change in its own way impacting upon the perception of
time. In one direction the development of the steam engine led
to the emergence of the new science of thermodynamics, initially through the work of the French scientist Nicolas Sadi Carnot on the efficiency of early nineteenth-century engines,
published in 1824. Carnot's work, the significance of which was
slow to be realized, was eventually built upon in the mid-
century by James Prescott Joule and William Thomson (later
Lord Kelvin). Joule established that all forms of energy (whether
mechanical, electrical, or heat) were fundamentally the same
and were therefore interchangeable, a discovery that formed the
basis of what came to be called the first law of thermodynamics.
In 1850 Thomson formulated the second law of thermodynamics, which says that heat cannot pass from a colder body to a hot-
ter one. The implication of this is that entropy is increasing and
that the universe is, therefore, winding down and may eventually reach a mean temperature which would be too cold to support life. It is the idea of "heat death" that informs Wells's vision
of the end of the world as depicted in *The Time Machine* (1895).
In 1862 Thomson calculated (erroneously as it turned out) the
age of the earth based on its rate of cooling. The effects on time
perception of these discoveries was twofold. In the first place
they imposed a new, non-mythological temporal horizon on life.
Initially this seemed to conflict with the expansion of time necessitated by geology and evolution, but as the different sciences
progressed they ultimately contributed to the supplanting of
biblical time with its modern scientific replacement.

Thermodynamics also impacted on the perception of time in
that it led to the invention of the refrigerator. This was an inno-

vation based upon the discovery by Joule and Thomson of the fall in temperature when gases expand—the so-called Joule-Thomson effect. Quickly turned into a practical technology, by the end of the 1870s refrigeration had been installed in ships that were thereby enabled to import into Britain previously unshippable, perishable foodstuffs, from countries such as Argentina and New Zealand.[2] Thus, when Oscar Wilde's image of the aging portrait of Dorian Gray that preserved the youth and beauty of its subject appeared in 1891, it did so at a time when refrigeration offered a familiar time-defying method for staving off the effects of decay and corruption.

Steam-powered rail travel too altered the perception of time for two reasons: it allowed travel at speeds far faster than had ever been experienced before, cutting journey times to a fraction of their former duration, and brought about the standardized measurement of time across Britain in order to make an accurate timetabling system possible. Noon was no longer when the sun was at its zenith in the midday sky, but when the clock said it was twelve. As will become clear a little later in this chapter, this would prove an irresistible image for Thomas Hardy in the writing of *Far From the Madding Crowd*, with its persistent contrast between cosmological and mechanical modes of temporality. It also produced massive physical change which formed a material sign of the times. In Gaskell's *Cranford* (1853) and *Cousin Phyllis* (1864), it serves as the index of a cultural shift which separates the older generation from the younger, suggesting the growing influence of urban manners and values upon rural life. So significant was the railway to this change that one of *Cranford*'s characters, Captain Brown, is killed by a train as he rescues a child from the line. But its presence impinges upon the physical and cultural landscape perhaps most dramatically in Dickens's *Dombey and Son* (1848).

In that novel Dickens describes an apocalyptic scene in London's Camden Town as though it were the result of a devastating earthquake. Its traces include demolished houses, deep trenches dug in the ground, precarious ruins teetering on the brink of collapse, and a chaos of carts, tools, and debris:

> Everywhere were bridges that led nowhere; thoroughfares that were wholly impassable; Babel towers of chimneys, wanting half their height . . . carcases of rugged tenements and fragments of unfinished

walls and arches ... wildernesses of bricks and giant forms of cranes.
... There were a hundred thousand shapes and substances of incompleteness, wildly mingled out of their places, upside down, burrowing in the earth, aspiring in the air, mouldering in the water, and unintelligible as any dream.[3]

Once again, as in the opening of *Bleak House*, Dickens depicts the return of chaos, creating a dystopic space within the bounds of the city. While the focus here is on the effects of spatial disruption, its temporal effects emerge from the same source before the end of the novel. For the cause of this devastation in *Dombey and Son* is the coming of the railway, specifically, the building of the London end of the line from Birmingham, construction of which began in 1834.[4]

The tearing up of the fabric of the city also serves as a metaphor for what the city—as a set of values, practices and institutions—does to the individuals held in its thrall: as a result of his obsession with his business Dombey's life and the lives of his family and employees are shown to be fragmentary, unfinished, and out of place. At one stage in the narrative the image of life disrupted by chaos is reinforced when Dombey's house itself, under structural alteration, becomes a "wilderness of bricks": "no furniture was to be seen through the gaping and broken windows in any of the rooms; nothing but workmen, and the implements of their several trades, swarming from the kitchens to garrets."[5] Thus the image of disruption caused by the coming of the railway is traced to its source in the commercial and economic enterprise of one of the city's leading capitalists. When Dombey's senior employee and the embodiment of the greed, corruption, and ferocity of the capitalist venture, the villainous Carker, is killed by a train, it appears, not as in Gaskell—a symbol of the death of a way of life—but as a stroke of Dickensian poetic justice. His death occurs after a journey which terrifies, disorientates, and displaces him until he is "unable to reckon up the hours ... or to comprehend the points of time and place in his journey."[6] Ironically the part of the journey which has been by rail has scrambled his sense of time, as his exchange with a waiter makes clear:

"What day is this?" he asked of a waiter, who was making preparations for his dinner.
"Day, Sir?"

"Is it Wednesday?"

"Wednesday, Sir? No, Sir. Thursday, Sir."

"I forgot. How goes the time? My watch is unwound."

"Wants a few minutes of five o'clock, Sir. Been travelling a long time, Sir, perhaps?"

"Yes."

"By rail, Sir?"

"Yes."

"Very confusing, Sir. Not much in the habit of travelling by rail myself, Sir, but the gentlemen frequently say so."[7]

While the expansion of the rail network led to the standardizing of British time, to its centralized measurement and control, it seems that it also served to break down familiar categories and demarcations of space and time.

But, as is evident from *Sartor Resartus*, a profound concern with time in the literature of the age pre-dates the emergence of the scientific and technological discoveries and advances that would create the double effect of producing both disorientation and a new kind of control. It might be seen to stem from Charles Lyell's *Principles of Geology* which appeared in 1830–33 and paved the way for Darwin in arguing the case for an immensely protracted period of rock-formation, disdaining earlier cataclysmic models and their temporal implications. It has often been noted that Tennyson's *In Memoriam* evokes Lyell's work in its references to the fossils that emerge from "scarped cliff and quarried stone," and to the vanished forms of life now "sealed within the iron hills."[8] But even earlier in the Victorian period John Clare seems to have imbibed something of this emergent temporality. His sonnet "I am" (1842–64) is the lament of a soul that has fallen from eternity into space and time and experiences these fundamental categories of human experience as a kind of imprisonment:

> I was a being created in the race
> Of men disdaining bounds of place and time:—
> A spirit that could travel o'er the space
> Of earth and heaven,—like a thought sublime,
> Tracing creation, like my maker, free,—
> A soul unshackled—like eternity,
> Spurning earth's vain and soul debasing thrall
> But now I only know I am,—that's all.[9]

While the verse is strongly Platonic in its commitment to a hier-archical dualism of soul and body, it is also redolent of its own age of incipient rail travel, and of various new forms of mobil-ity—both physical and social—that allowed people to disdain "bounds of place and time" in ways that had never before been possible. At the same time the imposition of measured and stan-dardized time might itself be perceived as a kind of fall from a state of natural grace, from the freedom of not being bound by the strict demands imposed by mechanized time, labor and travel. Clare's late romantic vision of the free spirit falling into a world of shackles and constraints associated with the limita-tions of time adumbrates some of the concerns that Hardy would explore in *Far From the Madding Crowd.*

Two Kinds of Time

"And the stars of heaven fell unto the earth . . ."
                                                   —Revelation 6:13

". . . and there fell a great star from heaven, burning as it were a lamp . . ."
                                                   —Revelation 8:10

Much of Hardy's fiction dwells on a tension between historical continuity (often associated with nature and rural life) and the changes wrought by industrialization and urbanization. This has been perceived by critics, especially in relation to *Far From the Madding Crowd,* as a moral hierarchy:

> At bottom Hardy's story juxtaposes two different worlds or modes of being, the natural against the civilised and it insists on the superi-ority of the former by identifying the natural as strong, enduring, self-contained, slow to change, sympathetic, while associating the civilised with weakness, facility, modernity, self-centredness.[10]

Given the spatial register of its title, *Far From the Madding Crowd* might seem to make of this hierarchical structure a model of regional difference, dividing city from country, the urban from the rural, with nature offering a site of pastoral es-cape from the corrupt values of civilization. Of course, more re-cent criticism has problematized the over-simplicity of such

neat oppositions, demonstrating the ways in which, for example, the novel's title is rendered ironic by the fact that the putative distance from the "madding crowd" does not prevent the
inhabitants of rural bliss from being subject to financial ruin,
sexual betrayal, consuming jealousy, murder, fire, and storm.[11]
So, while Hardy can seem reactionary at times, lamenting the
passing of an old and deeply embedded culture, there are more
complex ideas about the relationship between the natural and
the cultural at work in a novel like *Far From the Madding
Crowd*. Nevertheless, the ironic aspect of the title when perceived solely in terms of space is somewhat diminished (though
not completely undermined) if a temporal meaning is allowed to
play alongside the more obvious spatial sense of the word "far."
For the novel encodes two starkly opposed modes of construing
time, which do indeed correspond to "two different worlds or
modes of being": sidereal, or cosmological time, and abstract, or
mechanical time; the dramatic conflict of the story can be read
as a trial of strength between them. But while the conflict is
sharp to the point of being murderous, there are also traces of an
interdependence between them in that they occasionally seem
to supplement one another.

Mechanical time is that measured by clocks and calendars,
whereas cosmological time is that associated with the rhythm
of the earth in relation to the solar system and is told by observation of the heavens and the changing seasons; both stars and seasons play significant roles in Hardy's novel. Gabriel Oak
emerges, early on, as a man in tune with cosmological time. In
fact, he is almost an embodiment of it: his name alone, in its
collocation of the angelic (Gabriel) and the earthly (Oak), connects him with both the heavens and the seasons. One of the
first things we learn about him is in relation to the telling of
time:

> Mr Oak carried about him, by way of a watch, what may be called a
> small silver clock; in other words, it was a watch as to shape and
> intention, and a small clock as to size. This instrument . . . had the
> peculiarity of going too fast or not at all. The smaller of its hands,
> too, occasionally slipped round on the pivot, and thus, though the
> minutes were told with precision, nobody could be quite certain of
> the hour they belonged to.[12]

This failure of mechanical time associated with Oak is the flip side of his identification with cosmological time:

> The stopping peculiarity of his watch Oak remedied by thumps and shakes, and he escaped any evil consequences from the other two defects by constant comparisons with and observations of the sun and stars, and by pressing his face close to the glass of neighbours' windows, till he could discern the hour marked by the green-faced timekeepers within. (2)

Just as the information supplied by the failing timepiece has to be supplemented by appeal to the stars, so that appeal is itself supplemented by the viewing of other people's clocks. When we later see Oak's cosmological observation in action, a similar process of supplementation is in evidence:

> The dog star and Aldebaran, pointing to the restless Pleiades, were half-way up the Southern sky, and between them hung Orion . . . Castor and Pollux . . . were almost on the meridian: the barren and gloomy square of Pegasus was creeping round to the north-west; far away through the plantation Vega sparkled . . . and Cassiopeia's chair stood daintily poised on the uppermost boughs.
>   "One o'clock," said Gabriel. (13)

While Oak can read off sidereal time with a glance at the night sky, the information he gathers from the process registers in his consciousness as clock time: " 'One o'clock,' said Gabriel." That is to say that despite the fact that cosmological time is everywhere threatened and compromised by the mechanical time that is in the processs of supplanting it, Oak, as the human representative of the former, both resists and requires the new temporality. This reveals a tension at the heart of the novel's treatment of time: cosmological time is already partially obscured, and Oak personifies a nostalgia for its erstwhile rhythms and durations, a nostalgia that is not simply for past *times*, but for time itself. An embodiment of atavism, he is yet also the future: it is he who wins Bathsheba, who represents her future, and their joint story is, in a sense, beginning at the novel's close.

Thus, as he carries around his ineffectual timepiece and peers in at the clocks of his neighbors, Oak's effortless harmony with the natural world is expressed most fundamentally as a matter of temporality. He is characterized as master of the time to which, as a farmer, Bathsheba Everdene is subject. Nowhere is this clearer than in the storm episode (chapters 36–37). On this occasion Oak reads the signs of the impending storm, saving Bathsheba's crop from being spoiled, and beginning the process by which she comes to depend upon him. Without wishing to enter into the long-running and vexed debate of the gender politics surrounding *Far From the Madding Crowd*, it seems to me that Bathsheba becomes, to some degree, the plaything of time— the subject for whom two modes of male-constructed temporality, embodied by Oak and Troy, respectively, compete.[13] This emerges from the fact that cosmological time serves Oak's sexual desire in that his mastery of it furthers his cause of obtaining Bathsheba, while an opposed temporality, associated chiefly with Sergeant Troy, comes close to destroying her.

Troy's temporary control of Bathsheba is based upon his ability to create an illusion of the cosmological time which Oak serves (and by which he is served). Troy famously conquers Bathsheba with his dazzling demonstration of swordplay in which his blade flashes around her body seeming almost to carve her form in the air around her. As the sword rushes around the enthralled woman, the language is evocative of the stars in which Oak reads the time: "In short, she was enclosed in a firmament of light, and of sharp hisses, resembling a sky-full of meteors close at hand." Unlike the stable constellations so familiar to Oak, the illusory "firmament" summoned by Troy's martial dexterity which "encloses" Bathsheba is flashy and evanescent, as fleeting as a meteor shower. A little further on the text refers to the same effect as "the luminous streams of this *aurora militaris*," indicating both its superficial likeness to Oak's world and its short-lived duration (211). As though to confirm that this astral display eclipses Oak in Bathsheba's mind and cuts her off from cosmological time, Troy's sword is said to "well-nigh shut out earth [Oak?] and heaven [Gabriel?]" (211). This is precisely the fatal illusion. Bathsheba misreads Troy's character because she fails to grasp that he creates an illusion which blinds her to Oak's true worth. The doubt about which world she belongs to has been sown early on in the novel when Oak momentarily mistakes the "artifical light" of her dwelling for a "star low down" (14); the ambiguity of the light adumbrates the precariousness of its owner's position with regard to time: her temporary alienation from Oak and from the "natural" temporality he embodies.

Bathsheba's apparent distance from the natural order is clearly signalled when, fearing Boldwood's anger against Troy, she drives to Bath. Before she sets out she is observed looking at the evening sky, unable to read its significance: ". . . the unresting world wheeled her round to a contrasting prospect eastward, in the shape of indecisive and palpitating stars. She gazed upon their silent throes amid the shades of space, but realized none at all. Her troubled spirit was far away with Troy" (237). In this contrast with Gabriel's ability to read the stars she is already isolated from him and is "far away with Troy" in time though not in space.

Yet, at a more profound level, that she is deeply rooted in the world of nature is evident from the seasonal pattern of her emotional life. Peter J. Casagrande has shown that her attachments to male characters are strongly suggestive of the seasonal cycle: her associations with Oak occur in the winters of the first and second years of the novel's duration and their marriage takes place on the Christmas day of year three; her dalliance with Boldwood is in the late winter (around St. Valentine's day); Troy dies in December. After these winter encounters, she is described as "reviving with the Spring."[14] Now, we are told, she begins to spend "more of her time in the open air" and to attend to "farming matters" (447). This revival, and the attendant return to the soil, of course, herald her return to Oak and their ultimate union. It is significant, then, that on going into the porch of a church at this time she hears children singing the words of Cardinal Newman's "Lead kindly light" (published just six years before Hardy's novel), evoking once more the contrast between the guiding star of Oak's astronomic skill and the *ignis fatuus* of Troy's *aurora militaris*. As though to confirm Oak's status as "kindly light" and as herald of a return to cosmological time, he appears beside her as she weeps in a moment of repentance and purgation.

Sidereal time also marks Fanny Robin's decline and fall. As she makes her agonizing way to the workhouse at Casterbridge, having been forsaken by Troy, we read of her dependence upon a dog who acts as a guide and support. If we are reminded of Oak's observation of the dog star (Sirius), then it is not without reason. In some mythological formations Sirius is the canine hunting companion of Orion—he who pursued the seven sisters (Pleiades). It is Troy who, by betraying her trust, has led Fanny to the workhouse, and the dog seems to be his representative. (Interestingly in this connection, the image of Troy as a dog is furthered by the fact that he is shot in chapter 53, echoing the shooting of Oak's dog in chapter 5). But in case we are not reminded of the dog star, Hardy prompts us a little: ". . . the Casterbridge lamps lay before them like fallen Pleiads" (308): Fanny appears as one of the sisters who has fallen to the hunter. By way of marked contrast Bathsheba's star is observed at the beginning of the novel to be "low down," but it never quite falls. The image of fallen stars inevitably evokes the Apocalypse, but Hardy uses it to indicate the defeat of "natural" time and a set of values that inhere in the slowly disappearing rural way of life. Consciously or otherwise this was an apocalyptic occurrence for him.

Just as Oak embodies the time of nature and the cosmos, the new time—measured mechanically—is embodied by Troy, who (as Geoffrey Harvey observes) "lacks the countryman's sense of continuity and time."[15] It is associated with change, rootlessness, and discontinuity. The reader is first made aware of a time other than the cosmological variety through architecture. Bathsheba's house is described in terms of historical styles that have contributed to its current state: "Classic Renaissance" and "Gothic extraction" (80). Already, then, a temporality associated with change, and even conflict, is at work in the fabric of the building. By contrast, when the great barn is described in chapter 22, its ancient construction, uninflected by architectural style, is as relevant to its modern as to its original function; it breaks down the distinction between ancient and modern because its form is perfectly adapted to its function and its environment, despite its antiquity. Its function also associates it with seasonal time, so that it stands outside of the architectural categories deployed to describe Bathsheba's house. Yet, at the same time, its contrast with the house not only pits continuity and stability against change and conflict, but also relates the barn to the very thing it resists—the process of cultural obsolescence: in its difference from the modern it symbolizes the very change it is harnessed to devalue. It thus serves as a symbol of rural stability and as a reminder that that very stability is already obsolescent. Something of this paradox infects the entire narrative, so that at the close Bathsheba is rescued and restored to the traditional concerns of Oak, but mechanical time has triumphed in Fanny's case: she is dead. Troy too is dead, but this is not the end of his time: the time-telling machines with which he is associated continue to tick. Again, just as the barn appears as a symbol of stability only inasmuch as it contrasts with the architecture of changing fashion, so the temporality embodied by Oak depends upon a contrast with the clock dependency of the new time. Its characteristic mode of calculation runs out in the mechanics of the time it eschews, both in the sense that sidereal time is constantly translated into clock time, and in the sense that Hardy himself has to impose upon his material a narrative time which itself belongs to a changing history of literary styles, fashions, and representational modes akin to those that shape the history of architecture.

"Grotesque Clockwork"

Having subtly suggested the influence of an abstract historical time associated with the cultural eras of shifting taste and style—renaissance, gothic, medieval, ancient, modern—Hardy then establishes a connection between historical time and clock time. Both belong to what I have called "abstract time": both have to do with non-cosmological modes of construing temporality, with mechanical or artificial modes of measurement. The connection, appropriately enough, is made by Troy.

In chapter 26, Troy and Bathsheba meet in the Haymead. Troy appears here in hunting mode, using all his skills as a silver-tongued flatterer to ensnare Bathsheba. Her resistance, almost predictably, is based upon time as reckoned by the season and the pressing urgency of the hay harvest. "I won't listen to you any longer. Dear me, I wish I knew what o'clock it is—I am going—I have wasted so much time here already!" (201). Her desire to know the clock-measured time signals her desire for Troy and her distance from Oak: had the latter been present he, presumably, would have been able to tell her the time by the position of the sun. In Gabriel's absence Troy's response, of course, is to give her a watch:

> The sergeant looked at his watch and told her.
> "What, haven't you a watch, miss?" he inquired.

"I have not just at present—I am about to get a new one."
"No. You shall be given one. Yes you shall. A gift, Miss Everdene—a gift."
And before she knew what the young man was intending, a heavy gold watch was in her hand. (201)

Unlike Oak's unreliable timepiece this, Troy insists, "is an unusually good one . . ." Not only so, but it "has a history." Engraved inside the back cover is a crest and motto of the Earls of Severn. The motto, it turns out is: *Cedit amor rebus*: "Love yields to circumstance," and in accepting it Bathsheba yields to an alternative temporal mode where "circumstance" disrupts the patterns and rhythms of a close-to-nature existence: she moves from cosmological to abstract time: out of the continuity and stability of the rural world into clock time and the processes of history. Her near disastrous involvement with Troy comes close to leading her away from the rural world of Oak. The contrast is made at the critical moment which spans the end of chapter 31 (quoted above) and the beginning of the following chapter. Chapter 31 ends with Bathsheba failing to read the night sky, being (in spirit) "far away with Troy," and then chapter 32 begins with the signal sound of clockwork on the air:

The village of Weatherbury was quiet as the graveyard in its midst, and the living were lying well-nigh as still as the dead. The church clock struck eleven. The air was so empty of other sounds that the whirr of the clock-work immediately before the strokes was distinct, and so was also the click of the same at their close. The notes flew forth and with the usual blind obtuseness of inanimate things— flapping and rebounding among walls, undulating against the scattered clouds, spreading through their interstices into unexplored miles of space. (238)

Space, on this occasion, is not the backdrop to a familiar and interpretable pattern of stars; rather it is an unexplored emptiness resounding to the meaningless noise of a blind mechanism. Furthermore, the whirring which fills the air does so in the apparent absence of human life, at a time when the village seems dead.

While this menacing herald of death does not ultimately bespeak the demise of Bathsheba, it echoes the earlier grinding of a similar machinery that does destroy Fanny Robin. For Fanny, too, in her relationship with Troy becomes entangled in abstract time. This emerges in chapter 16 when she goes to the wrong church, missing her wedding in the process. As he waits for her at a different church Troy is closely associated with a mechanical, clock time, controlled by a hidden "grotesque clockwork":

> From the interior face of the west wall of the tower projected a little canopy with a quarter-jack and small bell beneath it, the automaton being driven by the same clock machinery that struck the large bell in the tower. Between the tower and the church was a close screen, the door of which was kept shut during services, hiding the grotesque clockwork from sight. At present, however, the door was open, and the egress of the jack, the blows on the bell, and the mannikin's retreat into the nook again, were visible to many, and audible throughout the church. (130).

Again and again this machinery repeats its mechanical reminders of passing time in a way that is almost malignant: "One could almost be positive that there was a malicious leer upon the hideous creature's face, and a mischievous delight in its twitchings" (131). Fanny, misled by a spire (a clock-tower?), is the victim of this "malice." She explains to Troy: "I thought that church with the spire was All Saints, and I was at the door at half past eleven to a minute as you said. I waited till a quarter to twelve, and found then that I was in All Souls" (131). Troy's insistence upon punctuality "to the minute" identifies him with the "grotesque clockwork" that imposes its mischievous time upon Fanny. Yet, just as Oak's perception of sidereal time is translated into clock time, so Troy's perception of clock time continually bumps up against sidereal time. This has already been observed in his encounter with Bathsheba, where his sword creates an impression of meteors and aurorae, and it is evident again at the point of Fanny's demise.

On her final journey to the Casterbridge workhouse, rejected and destitute, Fanny's subjection to abstract time is complete, but that subjection can only be expressed with reference to the temporality eclipsed in her experience. So, the night is said to be "moonless and starless," and unbroken cloud shuts out "every speck of heaven" (302). Sidereal and seasonal time are obscured and in place of these natural indicators a manor-house clock marks the hour "in a small attenuated tone." Again, when she arrives at the workhouse another clock marks the moment: "it was getting on towards six o'clock" (308). We have already seen that this night is associated with fallen Pleiads, and now it can be observed that this is not just a matter of a mythological resonance which casts Troy in the role of a hunter. It also indicates the fact that cosmological time is destined to defeat by the march of the new time of clocks, factory hours, and railway timetables. The stars are fallen, to be replaced with what Hardy calls the "Casterbridge aurora" (303)—an urban parody of Oak's guiding light that supplants its cosmic original.

There seems to be in *Far From the Madding Crowd*, then, a pattern of allusion to two contrasting modes of construing time. While the valorization of cosmological time and the concomitant devaluing of abstract time are suggested by the moral goodness and victory of Oak and by the moral badness and death of Troy respectively, the interdependence of the two modes suggests a less than straightforward progression. To change time takes time. Memory, nostalgia, atavism, dispersion intertwine with progress and the new so that time wrinkles, folds, and twists. *Far From the Madding Crowd* seems to register those complicating factors during a period of transition. It shares this characteristic with the Apocalypse—a text in which temporalities clash as resistance to the changes wrought by an age of technological and political upheaval runs out in moral and cosmological conflict. For Hardy the new time imposed by the engines of industrial and civic progress was then eclipsing the former time; it was emerging as a time after time and as an expression of such a rupture in the temporal fabric it could not but reinscribe the vanished horizon of apocalypse, repeating its sense of temporal crisis. When in the last decade of the nineteenth century H. G. Wells attempted to create another fiction that explored the human relationship with time, he too would find that for narratives about time, however changed by scientific discourses and material advances, apocalypse remained inescapable.

EUCHARIST AND APOCALYPSE

Inspired by the time machines of its age, whether trains or refrigerators, H. G. Wells's novella *The Time Machine* (1895) bears witness to the way in which Darwinian origins and thermodynamic endings reshaped interpretations of apocalypse. Rejection of the biblical version of the end left Wells, by his own admission, terrified at the prospect of time without limits. His creation of a scientist who travels through time to the end of the world, then returns to his own time and recounts his experiences to his late nineteenth-century audience, represents an attempt to re-impose narrative shape upon human history in the light of its revised origins.

The manifold biblical resonance in the text suggests that Wells's post-Christian vision of the end of the world is a revision or reinterpretation of apocalypse. For example, the name "Eloi" recalls Jesus's words on the cross ("Eloi, Eloi, lama sabachtani"—"My God, My God. Why have you forsaken me?"). That the post-human creatures who bear this name exist only to be eaten and recall the broken body of Christ should alert the reader to the eucharistic tone in certain passages of Wells's novella. Working this eucharistic element into an eschatological story, *The Time Machine* recalls the profoundly futuristic character of Christianity's central ritual.

In exploring these biblical themes in *The Time Machine* it becomes clear that, despite Wells's supplanting of the Bible's temporal horizon with a non-apocalyptic vision of the world's end (based on evolutionary theory and thermodynamics), his (ironic) deployment of eucharistic and apocalyptic motifs disrupts this vision, making his imposition of narrative closure upon human history a matter of reinterpreting the Apocalypse.

In the novella Wells describes the world in the year 802,701, as seen by a time traveller. The latter discovers that the human race has evolved into two separate species, one of which (the Morlocks) preys upon the other (the Eloi).[16] Both of these names have biblical resonances. The "Morlocks" seem to have been named after Moloch (or Molech)—the god of the Ammonites—to whom, the Bible tells us, children were sacrificed by fire (see, for example, Leviticus 18:21, 2 Kings 23:10). The name "Eloi," as already observed, recalls Christ's words on the cross. At the most basic level, these biblical connections suggest to the reader the God-forsakenness of the Eloi and the predatory character of the Morlocks, implying that the relationship between the two species is one of blood-sacrifice. But far from constituting a religious or soteriological system, the sacrifice of the Eloi takes place in a time when any redemptive possibilities have long-since become obsolete. The post-religious slaughter of the subhuman innocents in 802,701 dramatizes the message that evolutionary theory, by removing the teleological imperative from human development, has denied the world any apocalyptic consummation. When the time traveller voyages to the end of the world, after leaving 802,701, this important anti-apocalyptic aspect of the novella appears even more clearly. There he encounters a world too cold to support life, dying in a "remote and awful twilight" (76). The then-new science of thermodynamics gave grounds for just this kind of scientific eschatology: its formulation of the law of entropy predicted that the universe would eventually reach an inhospitable mean temperature, and that, consequently, all life would be extinguished.

The novella's allusive nomenclature demythologizes the world's end and, simultaneously, replaces the substitutionary death of Christ with an evolutionary version of sacrifice. Peter Kemp points out that Wells often draws attention in his work to "the fact that life consists in battening, that in order for one organism to survive another must be sacrificed."[17] As sacrificial victims of the struggle for survival, the strategically-named Eloi embody the contrast between sacrifice as an evolutionary principle and as a religious value, and their plight subordinates one of Christianity's central themes to the Darwinian principle of the survival of the fittest. While Jesus taught that "the meek shall inherit the earth," natural selection—the cumulative effect of infinitesimal beneficial adaptations in organisms—can be seen as determining a very different outcome. T. H. Huxley argued that "the followers of the 'golden rule' ['Do as you would be done by'] may indulge in hopes of heaven, but they must reckon with the certainty that other people will be masters of the earth."[18] The sacrifice of the Eloi to the nutritional needs of the Morlocks clearly reflects this Huxleyan challenge to Christ's teaching. Wells, who studied under Huxley for a short time, envisaged an epoch in the distant future during which the subterranean, darkness-loving Morlocks would inherit the earth by brute force, subjugating the physically weaker Eloi. In this formulation the Christian, biblical account of human history, the axial point of which is the crucifixion of Jesus, is sacrificed to the anti-apocalyptic evolutionary narrative.

It is this coalescence of eucharistic and eschatological intimations in *The Time Machine* that recalls the profoundly futuristic orientation of Christianity's most important rite—the eucharist, or communion service. Jesus's words at the Last Supper (the model for later eucharistic celebrations), establish this tone: "I will not drink henceforth of this fruit of the vine, *until that day* when I drink it new with you in my Father's kingdom" (Matt. 26:29, my emphasis). Christian tradition has, since the earliest times, viewed the crucifixion as an eschatological event, one that guaranteed the eventual establishment of God's kingdom on earth. The writer to the Hebrews asserts: "once *in the end of the world* hath he appeared to put away sin by the sacrifice of himself" (Heb. 9:26b, my emphasis). That the act of remembering the crucifixion in the eucharist is also an anticipatory gesture is evident from Paul's first letter to the Corinthian Church: "For as often as ye eat this bread, and drink this cup, ye do show the Lord's death *till he come*" (1 Cor. 11:26, my emphasis).

Such biblical resonances in *The Time Machine* can be seen to undermine certain aspects of its non-apocalyptic, anti-eschatological vision. That is to say that Wells's use of eucharistic and apocalyptic language and imagery can be read as disrupting this vision at a number of points, turning his imaginative depiction of cosmic decline back towards a biblical end. But this is not to argue that Wells's text should be invested with either an atavistic desire for a return to theological categories of explanation or a covert commitment to Christian interpretations of time. Rather, it is to demonstrate that the Apocalypse cannot be circumvented in Victorian renegotiations of time and narrative; its imposition of an end, however thoroughly defunct that end may have become, constantly recalls to itself all modes of narrative closure in Western, Christian, and post-Christian literature. In other words the articulation of the end joins narrative to apocalypse at every turn because it is time's acquisition of an end in the apocalyptic tradition that marks the epoch of Western narrative.

THE TIME TRAVELLER'S LAST SUPPER

That Wells was obsessed with eating and drinking (as well as with the shape of future kingdoms) has been shown by Peter Kemp with great zest and with more than a little scholarly stamina. In *H. G. Wells and the Culminating Ape* he offers nearly seventy pages of examples from an impressive array of Wellsian sources, depicting a vast textual larder of "memorable meals and toothsome moments garnished with odd eatables."[19] At one point in this extended literary menu he notes Wells's dislike of what the latter referred to as Christianity's ceremonial "God-eating," and "symbolical cannibalism."[20] But he also provides abundant evidence of Wells's abiding fascination with human edibility to a variety of predators. Wells' qualms about Christianity's prandial rite may well be reflected in the approximation of cannibalism in *The Time Machine* (one post-human species preys upon another), as well as in the fact that those consumed bear the name "Eloi."

Kemp, for all his dogged persistence in exposing Wells's food fetishism (including his squeamish response to Holy Communion and his contrasting relish of predatory instincts), does not point out the eucharistic undertones of *The Time Machine*. The novella begins in an "after-dinner atmosphere" (3), with a group of men sitting around a fire in the house of the Time Traveller. The following Thursday, over another dinner at the same house, tales of the year 802,701 and of the final setting of the sun are recounted. On this latter occasion the guests have to begin their meal in the absence of the host: " 'It's half-past seven now,' said the Medical Man. 'I suppose we'd better have dinner?' 'Where's—?' said I, naming our host" (11–12). By virtue of its paradoxical character—not naming the host while referring to the act of naming him—the phrase draws attention to itself as a strategy of evasion, applying the name-avoiding word "host" to its subject for the first and only time. The rhetorical gesture which both names and fails to name the host raises the linked questions of his identity and of the significance of his absence. Since the appellation "host" marks both an absence with which the guests are preoccupied and an expectation of imminent return, it allows the reader to hear a eucharistic tone in the description of this all-male supper, so that "naming our host" may be a matter of identifying the Time Traveller with Christ.

The eucharistic meaning of the word "host" (i.e., the bread or wafer which represents the broken body of Christ) may be no more than a faint echo here, but its resonance is strengthened by elements of the description of the Time Traveller when he eventually arrives: "His face was ghastly pale; his chin had a brown cut on it—a cut half healed; his expression was haggard and drawn, as by intense suffering. . . . I saw his feet as he went out. He had nothing on them but a pair of tattered, bloodstained socks" (12–13). The registering of intense suffering in the host's face, and the reference to his bloodied feet, contribute to the paschal tone of the meal. As he sits at the dinner table, his consumption of wine and meat is stressed, recalling the bread (symbolically, the *body* of Christ) and wine consumed in the eucharist. That there is some kind of sacramental aspect to the all-male dinner party is suggested by the gradual change in the Time Traveller's appearance as the meal progresses. His initial battered, bruised, and bloodstained form recovers in phases. The change begins with his first glass of wine: "He drained it, and it seemed to do him good: for he looked around the table, and the ghost of his old smile flickered across his face" (12). His second glass enhances this effect: "His eyes grew brighter, and a faint colour came into his cheeks" (13). The final moment of restoration comes after he has been "to wash and dress": "He was dressed in ordinary evening clothes, and nothing save his haggard look remained of the change that had startled me" (14). Washing and reclothing, of course, are extremely important metaphors in Christian soteriology; the book of Revelation associates both with Christ's death: "These . . . have washed their robes, and made them white in the blood of the Lamb" (Rev. 7:14).

The "ghost of his old smile" (along with two other "ghost" references in the brief opening section of the framing narrative), and his generally altered visage combine to give the Time Traveller something of the look of a revenant. With these passional and eucharistic parallels in mind, it is not difficult to understand the symbolism of his temporal exit from 802,701, made from the interior of a suggestively *cruciform* structure. The Morlocks have hidden his time machine inside the pedestal of a great white sphinx which he has earlier described thus: "the wings, instead of being carried vertically at the sides, were spread so that it seemed to hover" (19). Alongside these eucharistic memorials of the crucifixion and resurrection of Christ, several incidents in the Johannine account of Jesus's post-resurrection appearances are also evoked by the description of the Time Traveller's return. His demand for meat parallels Jesus's question to Peter and Thomas on the shore of the Sea of Tiberias: "Children, have ye any meat?" (John 21:5). The distant air of the Time Traveller as he refuses to answer any questions until he has eaten might be compared with Jesus's strange insistence, on the morning of the resurrection, that he should not be touched (John 20:17). Again, the altered appearance of the returned Time Traveller, which shocks the narrator and which gives rise to vaguely comic suggestions that he may be playing the "Amateur Cadger" or moonlighting as a crossing sweeper (13), bears comparison with the post-resurrection change in Jesus marked by Mary Magdalen's failure to recognize him and by her mistaking him for a gardener (John 20:15). The Time Traveller's promise to make a revelatory return contributes an extra detail to the effect: ". . . I'll come down and explain things" (13).

The eucharistic affinities of Time Traveller's last supper (we know from the end of the novella that it was the last of his Thursday-night gatherings) are not a matter of straightforward allusion. Some features of the story suggest that the Christic parallels are parodic. Clearly his longing for meat aligns the Time Traveller (and, by association, the risen Christ?) with the flesh-eating Morlocks, *against* whom he has fought on the side of the vegetarian Eloi. This seemingly unconscious affinity with his elective enemies is emphasized by his being "dazzled by the light" as he enters the dining room (12): the Morlocks, who emerge from their underground lair only at night, are similarly dazzled both by daylight and by the Time Traveller's matches. Furthermore, the latter responds in kind to the violence of the Morlocks, even admitting at one point that he "longed very much to kill a Morlock or so" (60). A little later he confesses that he would not have been averse to attacking a few more of them with his rod of iron: "I threw my iron bar away, almost sorry not to use it" (70). John Huntington writes: "Even when he meets the Eloi, the Time Traveller's first thoughts are violent: 'They looked so frail that I could fancy flinging the whole dozen of them about like nine-pins.'"[21] On the other hand, the Eloi, while they conform to a Christian image of the "gentle Jesus," are completely unable to save themselves. It is only by replicating the Morlocks' aggression, and by exceeding their predatory violence, that the Time Traveller can hope to escape being identified with the Eloi in their death.

The Time Traveller's Christic qualities and his defense of the helpless Eloi combine with his Morlock-like belligerence and hunger for meat to produce a range of characteristics which confront Christian values (such as meekness, charity, and a belief in divine providence) with "Nature red in tooth and claw."[22] But while this might be understood as a critique of Christianity inspired by Huxleyan evolutionism, it also reflects the gospels' own depiction of Christ: on the one hand he appears as a compassionate healer and as a teacher of forgiveness; on the other hand he is described as the outraged scourge of temple-defiling money-changers.[23] The division of his actions between aid and aggression is matched by the double rhetoric in which he proclaims the coming kingdom of God—a rhetoric which combines pacific with violent figures sometimes in the same discourse:

> Think not that I am come to send peace on earth: I came not to send peace, but a sword. For I am come to set a man at variance against his father, and the daughter against her mother . . . whosoever shall give to drink unto one of these little ones a cup of cold water only in the name of a disciple [. . .] he shall in no wise lose his reward. (Matt. 10:34–42)

This duality is encoded in Revelation's vision of the lion and the lamb—images of Christ as both predator and prey: "And one of the elders saith unto me, Weep not: behold the Lion of the tribe of Juda. . . . And I beheld . . . a Lamb as it had been slain." (Rev. 5:5–6).

The Time Traveller's Apocalypse

Although *The Time Machine* employs little overt biblical allusion, Bernard Bergonzi sees in it various mythical elements, some of which are drawn from Christian lore. The Time Traveller's descent into the unlit, underground domain of the Morlocks, he says, "suggests a parody of the Harrowing of Hell, where it is not the souls of the just that are released but the demonic Morlocks, for it is they who dominate the subsequent narrative."[24] But it may be that there is another, more specifically apocalyptic layer of allusion here. The opening up of the underworld and the release of the creatures of darkness has a parallel in Revelation 9:1–3:

> I saw a star fall from heaven unto the earth: and to him was given the key of the bottomless pit. And he opened the bottomless pit; and

there arose a smoke out of the pit, as the smoke of a great furnace;
and the sun and the air were darkened by reason of the smoke of the
pit. And there came out of the smoke locusts upon the earth: and
unto them was given power, as the scorpions of the earth have
power.

A number of details in this passage have echoes in events that
the Time Traveller describes as taking place subsequent to his
venturing below the surface. As a direct result of the emergence
of the Morlocks, a forest is engulfed by fire and by "masses of
black smoke" (68). Eventually, having moved further into the future, the Time Traveller also witnesses the darkening of the sun
and the air at the end of time: "the pale stars alone were visible.
All else was rayless obscurity. The sky was absolutely black"
(75).

If such resonances are faint and need to be teased out, *The
Time Machine*'s one explicit reference to the Bible has a clearly
apocalyptic tone. It occurs early on when one of the Time Traveller's guests, pondering his host's dishevelled appearance, wonders if he has "his Nebuchadnezzar phases" (13). The reference
is to the book of Daniel—the one example of a fully apocalyptic
text included in the Old Testament. As Patrick Parrinder has
pointed out, the figure of Nebuchadnezzar's sojourn amongst the
beasts of the field can be read as "a prophetic parable of human
destiny," foreshadowing the evolutionary decline of humanity
and implying the possibility that another species will eventually
usurp our dominant place.[25] This association of the Time Traveller with Nebuchadnezzar neatly summarizes Wells's project of
rewriting the End. In his essay "Zoological Regression" (1891)
he refers to the "Coming Beast" as a creature who may "rise in
the fulness of time and sweep *homo* away into the darkness from
which his universe arose."[26] The phrase "the fulness of time"
(borrowed from the New Testament's repertoire of messianic
language) suggests that Wells viewed the overthrow of humanity
as an almost teleological principle—one which could replace the
Bible's apocalyptic end with an alternative form of narrative closure.

In his visions of the Eloi, the Morlocks, and the non-human
creatures that inhabit the earth in its twilight age, Wells was rewriting Darwin's vision of the end as well as that predicted in
the Bible. In *The Origin of Species* Darwin suggested that the

evolutionary process could produce infinite refinement: ". . . as natural selection works solely by and for the good of each being, all corporeal and mental endowments will tend to progress towards perfection."[27] T. H. Huxley, in his 1893 lecture on evolution and ethics, took a rather different view: the process, he claimed, would eventually begin to work backwards: "The theory of evolution encourages no millennial anticipations. If, for millions of years, our globe has taken the upward road, yet, some time, the summit will be reached and the downward route will be commenced."[28] Wells envisaged just such a decline, using the division between the "Capitalists" who lived at ease and the "Labourers" who worked in the dark Victorian factories, mills, mines, and service tunnels as the model for a foreseeable, retrograde, evolutionary split in humankind (43). The Morlocks, begotten of laboring-class ancestors, are compared with sloths, apes, spiders, lemurs, and rats, in a vocabulary which stresses not only the Darwinian continuum of all forms of animate life, but also the evolutionary demise of humanity.

Yet, despite this post-Darwinian vision of humanity's animal origins and destiny, the Morlocks are also called "damned souls" (68)—creatures of an older cosmogony. This phrase is an indication of the way in which Wells's text encodes an ambivalence about its own replacement of apocalypse with evolutionary and entropic decline. The designation of the Morlocks as "damned souls" occurs during a curiously Dantean episode. Pursued through a forest by Morlocks, the Time Traveller has set a fire that spreads rapidly. At the center of the blazing forest the fugitive arsonist comes across "a hillock or tumulus" (67):

Upon the hill-side were some thirty or forty Morlocks, dazzled by the light and heat, and blundering hither and thither against each other in their bewilderment . . .

At last I sat down on the summit of the hillock, and watched this strange incredible company of blind things groping to and fro, and making uncanny noises to each other, as the glare of the fire beat on them . . .

For the most part of that night I was persuaded it was a nightmare. I bit myself and screamed in a passionate desire to awake. I beat the ground with my hands, and got up and sat down again, and wandered here and there, and again sat down. Then I would fall to rubbing my eyes and calling upon God to let me awake. Thrice I saw Morlocks put their heads down in a kind of agony and rush into the flames (67–68).

The Time Traveller refers to the hillock as "a kind of island in the forest" (68). Dante, we may recall, described Purgatory as an island mountain, and it is in ascending the Purgatory-like mount that the Time Traveller looks down upon the Morlocks caught in the blaze as upon a nightmare vision of Hell: "these damned souls going hither and thither and moaning . . ." (68). Evolution, it seems, enacts some kind of eschatological judgement: some "souls" are "damned" by natural selection. Furthermore, the fiery torment with which the Morlocks are punished is meted out by the fire-starting Time Traveller himself. Consonant with this act of judgement, his violent confrontation with the Morlocks casts him in the apocalyptic role of a messianic figure who rules with "a rod of iron" (Rev. 2:27; 19:15). Having broken a lever from a machine discovered in a derelict museum, he carries it with him as a weapon: "I rolled over, and as I did so my hand came against my iron lever . . . holding the bar short, I thrust where I judged their faces might be. I could feel the succulent giving of flesh and bone under my blows . . ." (66). Revelation 2:27 conjures a similarly gruesome image: "And he shall rule them with a rod of iron; as the vessels of a potter shall they be broken to shivers."

At the beginning of the chapter that follows on from the Time Traveller's purgatorial night, his narratorial tone, if not exactly penitent, is certainly somewhat chastened by his experience. He returns to the point of his first, naively optimistic view of the far-future landscape and casts over it a colder eye: "I thought of my hasty conclusions upon that evening and could not refrain from laughing bitterly at my confidence. . . . I understood now what all the beauty of the Upperworld people covered" (69). Climbing above the flames and escaping the infernal fate of the Morlocks, the Time Traveller has gained a new perspective—a perspective that might be called "apocalyptic" in that he now sees *beneath the cover* of Upperworld beauty. But his revelation is an inverse apocalypse. While apocalyptic literature sought to explain the dark affairs of the "lower," earthly world in terms of events in the "world above," the Time Traveller discovers the truth about the Upperworld by uncovering a sinister lower region. Echoes, maybe, of James Thomson's *The City of Dreadful Night*.

In John's Apocalypse it is Christ who uncovers Upperworld mysteries to the visionary. He is characterized as the master of time, as "the Alpha and Omega, the beginning and the ending" (1:8, 11), holding sway over past, present, and future, and able to reveal "the things which are, and the things which shall be hereafter" (1:19). Such texts have produced, within Christianity, a vision of Christ as a kind of magnificent time-lord, as one well-known nineteenth-century hymn makes clear: "Crown him the Lord of years, / The Potentate of time."[29] Given this time-over-coming potency, there is a degree of irony in the acknowledgment that his return is deferred; nevertheless, the postponement of Parousia (return) was written into the New Testament itself, as Christ's lateness in coming back began to be noted by the early Christians. The writers of the canonical epistles were occasionally forced to excuse his delay to impatient believers: "The Lord is not slack concerning his promise, as some men count slackness . . . the day of the Lord will come . . ." (2 Pet. 3:9–10). The importance to Christian faith of Christ's ever-imminent return is evident in a passage from Paul's first letter to the Corinthians which I have already quoted: "For as often as ye eat this bread, and drink this cup, ye do show the Lord's death *till he come*" (1 Cor. 11:26, my emphasis). The eucharist is thus the focus of both the memorial and the proleptic aspects of Christian faith: it recalls Jesus's "Last Supper" and looks forward to the "marriage supper of the Lamb" (Rev. 19:9). But it also serves to mark the deferral of the promised return: every time it is celebrated, the believer tacitly acknowledges Christ's lateness, the fact that he has not yet come.

In Revelation the "marriage supper of the Lamb" follows the consummation of the world age. Like the apocalyptic Lamb, Wells's Time Traveller also appears at a meal, fresh from the end of the world. He comes to his last supper after having observed the entropic demise of the sun and the earth. Repeating the irony of Christ's delay, he is *late* for this meal as a result of travelling through time, and his lateness is what prompts the Christ-evoking phrase: " 'Where's—?,' said I, naming our host." Not only is this ironic lateness an important Christological, apocalyptic moment, but it also draws attention to a related eucharistic parallel. Since the laboratory which contains the time machine is located in his house, the host is spatially present while being temporally absent. This strange logic of time travel repeats the paradox of the host's presence/absence in the eucharist: the "real presence" of Christ in the elements (the bread and wine) is, as we have seen, also the mark of his continuing absence, of the fact that he has yet to come back.

However parodic they may be, the Christic parallels ultimately compromise the novella's anti-apocalyptic vision. *The Time Machine* ends with the speaker of the framing narrative (into which the Time Traveller's own account is set) worrying over his friend's delayed return, and fearing an infinite postponement: "I am beginning now to fear that I must wait a lifetime. The Time Traveller vanished three years ago. And, as everybody knows now, he has never returned" (81). The universalizing of the sense of deferral ("everybody knows") recalls the delayed Parousia, while the time-laden phrases "a lifetime," "three years," "never," reinforce the irony of that lateness. In the opening sentence of the epilogue, still musing on the whereabouts of the vanished host, the narrator asks: "Will he ever return?" The end, it seems, is still in doubt. His wondering continues:

I, for my own part cannot think that these latter days of weak experiment, fragmentary theory, and mutual discord are indeed man's culminating time! I say, for my own part. He, I know . . . saw in the growing pile of civilisation only a foolish heaping that must inevitably fall back upon and destroy its makers in the end. (83)

Just as it shows us a double image of Christ as lion and lamb, the text of Revelation also encodes both of these possible futures, depicting the collapse of "the growing pile of civilisation" in the fall of Babylon, and envisaging a more glorious "culminating time" in its depiction of the Millennium and of the New Jerusalem.

RECREATING ABOLISHED HORIZONS

Wells's Darwinian—or more accurately Huxleyan—education led him away from the eschatological certainties of his evangelical upbringing. Armageddon, the Last Judgement and the triumphant return of Christ, the consummation of the world as described in Revelation, vanished in the open-ended, unimaginable time-scale of geological formations and of the infinitely

slow processes of natural selection, to be replaced by a "black-
ness and a vagueness about the endless vista of years ahead, that
was tremendous—that terrified."[30] Wells's terror is understandable. As Frank Kermode has said: "tracts of time unpunctuated
by meaning derived from the end are not to be borne."[31] Paul Ricoeur's extended analysis of the reciprocity of time and narrative
uncovers the depth of our need to implicate time in the diegetic
structures of emplotment: ". . . time becomes human time to
the extent that it is organised after the manner of a narrative;
narrative, in turn, is meaningful to the extent that it portrays the
features of temporal experience."[32] Darwin and Huxley each in
his own way imposed a narrative of human temporality upon the
measureless expanse of evolutionary time. Darwin did so by
means of expressions of belief in the ability of science to throw
light upon "the origin of man and his history," and in natural
selection as tending to produce perfection.[33] Huxley's humaniz-
ing emplotment involved asserting the opposite: the human
story would ultimately be one of rise and fall, of gaining an evolutionary "summit" and of descending once more into sub-hu-
manity. It is worth noting here that Northrop Frye has described
the biblical account of history as the archetypal form of this kind
of undulating narrative pattern.[34]

In telling a story about the end of the world, Wells, like Hardy,
was bound by the sheer force of cultural imperatives—the
weight of both the will-to-narrative and the Western, Christian,
biblical tradition—to construe his anti-apocalytpic tale as a rewriting of biblical eschatology and of its central event—the
death of Christ. Just as the book of Revelation projects Christ
into the age of human fulfilment and world-consummation, the
Time Traveller humanizes the vast expanses of non-human,
post-theological time by visiting its future extremity and by re-
porting its non-apocalyptic end to his late-nineteenth-century
(*fin de siècle*) audience of bourgeois males. In doing so he necessarily returns geologico-evolutionary time to a narrative structure, creating an anthropocentric story with a beginning, a
middle, and an end.

In *The Sense of an Ending* Kermode claims that, despite oft-
repeated disconfirmations of apocalyptic prediction and
counter-prediction, our drive to impose plots upon human experience remains undefeated. Even a plot as apparently counter-
diegetic as that of *Ulysses*, he insists, contains a good deal of

end-imposing emplotment.[35] While on the one hand we banish our teleological expectations by disconfirming our prognoses, on the other hand, "we recreate the horizons we have abolished, the structures that have collapsed; and we do so in terms of the old patterns, adapting them to our new worlds."[36] If Wells was intimidated by time's ungodly expansion, his first published work of fiction, *The Time Machine*, might be seen as an ambivalent response to that shock. Ambivalent because it both transgresses apocalyptic expectations and, simultaneously, "recreates the horizons" which it thus abolishes. It does so precisely "in terms of the old patterns" of Christian eucharistic and eschatological thought, "adapting them to . . . new worlds."

Something like this necessity had been identified by George Eliot in a brief preamble to the first chapter of *Daniel Deronda* (1876). The opening words of her final novel make clear that the renegotiation of temporality in the Victorian era did not remove the demand for narrative limits; it merely brought to consciousness their fictive status:

> Men can do nothing without the make-believe of a beginning. Even science, the strict measurer, is obliged to start with a make-believe unit, and must fix on a point in the stars' unceasing journey when his sidereal clock shall pretend that time is at Nought. His less accurate grandmother Poetry has always been understood to start in the middle; but on reflection it appears that her proceeding is not very different from his; since Science, too, reckons backwards as well as forwards, divides his unit into billions, and with his clock-finger at Nought really sets off *in medias res*. No retrospect will take us to the true beginning; and whether our prologue be in heaven or on earth, it is but a fraction of the all-presupposing fact with which our story sets out.[37]

Eliot's acknowledgement of the fictionality of beginnings surely owes much to the ways in which both the scientific discourses and the literary imaginations of the age grappled with the abolition of temporal horizons.

Sally Shuttleworth and Gillian Beer, among others, have explored the ways in which Eliot's engagement with nineteenth-century science not only emerged in the interests of her characters but also provided her with key metaphors.[38] Diana Postlethwaite notes that "the new physical, experimental natural sciences of the Victorian Age played a major role in George El-

iot's intellectual development."[39] More significantly for this discussion Shuttleworth demonstrates that the science of her age
also shaped Eliot's approach to the construction of plots, issuing
in the experimental endings and beginnings of *Middlemarch* and
Daniel Deronda:

> While the Finale to *Middlemarch* questioned the absolute nature of
> endings, the opening words of *Daniel Deronda* draw attention to the
> arbitrary nature of beginnings. By suggesting that the novelist's
> choice of a beginning is merely a fictional construct, George Eliot
> challenges the dominant assumptions of the realist text. She takes
> direct responsibility in *Daniel Deronda* for her own constructive
> role as novelist.[40]

That "constructive role" Shuttleworth contends, stemmed from
the "new experimental methodology" that enabled Eliot to draw
on the principles of explanation employed in diverse scientific
fields such as geology, physics, astronomy, and philology, as well
as evolutionary biology.[41]

Wells's fiction might be seen as a direct descendant of Eliot's
weaving of science into literature. *The Time Machine* established this relationship (and helped to found the genre of science
fiction) in terms of the very concerns with the provisionality of
time that are foregrounded in the opening of *Daniel Deronda.*
There Eliot confesses that human achievement always depends
upon some kind of narrative shape that enforces the imposition
of a fictional beginning in order to render intelligible the processes of change, development, growth, decline, renewal that
constitute the human relationship with time. Despite the trou-
bling expansion of time beyond the ken of finite minds, or
maybe because of it, Victorian writers reinscribed the limits, not
now as cosmic absolutes but as provisional boundaries that enabled understanding within a restricted purview.

The Time Machine explores the idea implicit in Eliot's later
fiction: that the "make-believe of a beginning" entails the make-
believe of an end. To abolish the horizon in one direction is also
to abolish it in the other, and to replace one is to replace both.
Thus, Eliot might be seen to have raised questions about the relationship between time and narrative that *The Time Machine*
would later dramatize.

Shuttleworth makes clear too that in the brief prologue to

Daniel Deronda Eliot was gesturing towards the limits of realism, hinting at an awareness of its provisional status, its own fictiveness as an account of reality, in a way that suggests the opening of a narrative space between English realism and the intensified self-scrutiny of modernism. Time perception, of course, would be crucial to this transition, and this necessarily had an impact upon the forms, conventions, and functions of narrative. That the measured pace, the drawn out duration, and the careful dating of Victorian realist novels gave way to the stream of internal time consciousness of Virginia Woolf and James Joyce owes a great deal to the processes of temporal discontinuity that this chapter has traced. What happens to time in Victorian writing necessarily also happens to narrative.

The opening of *Daniel Deronda* is of moment in this context for one further reason: along with the provisionality of its temporality goes a concomitant unsettling of spatial definition, so that the location of narrative is ambiguous: is it heaven or earth? Eliot's point seems to be about the impossibility of beginnings: life has always already begun, but the best resource we have for understanding it is narrative, and that, as Frank Kermode has pointed out in *The Sense of Ending*, will always imply the imposition of beginnings, middles, and ends, however cryptically, minimally, or obliquely imagined. This is always, in a sense, a question of cosmogony, of drawing out the lines of demarcation necessary for the calling into being of some kind of world, of asking again in what kind of space could time and nature begin or end? The very inconceivability of such a space, or non-space (which might put us in mind of the *khora* as discussed by Jacques Derrida), is what gives rise to the fictionalizing of origins.[42] Eliot's reference to a prologue which might take place in heaven or on earth is an allusion to the double prologue of Goethe's *Faust*, but it also evokes, consciously or otherwise, both Genesis and Revelation, each of which begins in an ambiguous space— the space of unlocatable beginnings and endings. In the following chapter I consider the ways in which certain Victorian texts replicate the dystopia of the Apocalypse by locating characters, scenes, actions in a space which seems to be opened up by the death of one world view and the delayed emergence its replacement.

5

The Third Space

THE CENTRAL MARGIN

> Modern scholars tell us that land occupation is at the root of
> the genre we know as apocalyptic. Apocalyptic arises out of
> exile from the land. . . . That land is the beloved, desired by
> God; but some fear that we have been displaced into the false
> city. . . . The dream is one of reoccupying the promised
> land. . . . That reoccupation . . . will be the consummation . . .
> at once the founding of the new city, and the restoration of
> the garden.
>
> —David Lawton, *Faith, Text and History*

THE BOOK OF REVELATION IS THE PARADOXICAL CENTRAL MARGIN OF
Christianity. In the sense described by David Lawton (above), it
is a marginal text: an evocation of dreams conjured by exile, ex-
teriority, and a longing for the closure or consummation of return. It is marginal, too, in the sense that it has a controversial
history in relation to the biblical canon that has made it an occasionally uneasy and contentious appendage to the gospel. It was
accepted into the canon of scripture only after a great deal of argument with regard to its authorship. The Eastern church
fathers were particularly opposed to its inclusion. Eusebius
(265–340) thought that if it was authored by the apostle John
then it was acceptable, otherwise it was best forgotten. This suggests that there were strong doubts about the religious legitimacy of its strange and complicated narrative and its other-
worldly descriptions that could be laid to rest only by the establishing of apostolic authorship. If the apostle wrote it then it
must have some kind of orthodox value, however unorthodox its
content might appear. A checkered history of interpretation and
reinterpretation, of religious and political appropriation and re-

appropriation was to follow its eventual inclusion in the Bible of the western church.

In the early centuries of the church's history a kind of apocalyptic calculus was highly popular. This involved the manipulation—by figures such as Hippolytus—of certain biblical numbers to arrive at a date for the end of the world, an approach that was eventually overthrown by Augustine's insistence that apocalyptic predictions had no bearing on contemporaneous events (they were applicable only to the future). The futurist interpretation of the Apocalypse all but silenced millenarian expectations until Joachim of Fiore, a twelfth-century abbot from Calabria, proposed a new pattern of historical progress through three great world ages.[1]

Throughout the Middle Ages readers of Revelation saw the outworking of John's visions of the end in the events of their own times. But the legitimacy of predicting end-time events and the return of Christ was subjected to searching questions in the thirteenth century, leading to heated academic debate over a long period of time. The arguments were not just theological. Millenarian expectations always imply some kind of dissatisfaction with the political status quo, as they look forward to an age of justice and peace which will overthrow the kingdoms of the world. In fact, the book of Revelation has been used throughout Christian history as a text that warrants various forms of political and religious imposition in the name of a divine narrative order that underwrites earthly power. It has also been used as a source of legitimation for subversive and dissenting discourses, whether one thinks of prophetic agitators such as Thomas Muntzer in Reformation Germany, or radical activists groups such as the Diggers and the Levellers in seventeenth-century England. Such ambiguity runs out in the fact that while the gospels and epistles of the Christian Bible characterize Jesus and the primitive church as eschatological figures, heralds of the soon to be revealed kingdom prophesied in the Jewish tradition, the occasional claims that the end is imminent have tended to marginalize the claimants and turn them into heretics. The sociocultural system predicated upon the end cannot countenance its actual arrival, since that would be to acknowledge the provisionality and temporary status of the extant authority. Thus while Christianity would have been altogether inconceivable without apocalypticism, making it a central, fundamental tenet of the belief system, the inherent threat to social stability represented by those who take it literally is not to be borne; it must be perpetually excised, excommunicated, exiled.

Such banishments were not unknown to the Victorian church. In his magisterial two-volume ecclesial history of the period, Owen Chadwick records the periodic upsurges in apocalyptic and millennial religion throughout the era. In the aftermath of the Napoleonic wars the sense of impending doom was rife: "In a panic the Book of Revelation rose easily to the surface of Christian minds. The French Revolution encouraged English evangelicals to study the signs of the times, and Catholic emancipation stirred again the apocalyptic mysteries."[2] Again in the period following the defeat of the first Reform Bill in 1831, the public disturbances seemed ominous. The bishops, who had mostly voted against the bill, were seen as having betrayed the interests of their flock, and the established church was vilified in the popular imagination as a result. Pamphleteering, agitation, and rioting directed scorn and, occasionally, physical violence at the clergy, causing some to see in the developments of their age the unfolding of an apocalyptic pattern. That such a time should produce millennial movements and sects within the church is unsurprising. Edward Irving, a Scottish Presbyterian minister, became the figurehead of just such a group in the early 1830s. He interpreted outbreaks of glossolalia in his church as pentecostal signs of the end and amassed a large following. When he was charged by the Presbyterian authorities with heresy and deprived of his ministry, he led some eight hundred people into a new church known as the Catholic Apostolic Church.[3]

Then there was the charismatic Irish evangelical, J. N. Darby, who led an extreme group in Dublin. His principle of openness and inclusivity meant that there was no priesthood; all were free to conduct meetings and to speak. A proponent of the belief in the rapture of believers at the return of Christ, he taught his followers to expect, and to be ready for, that return at any moment. Unable to square these ideas with the doctrines and practices of the mainstream, he too established a new denomination—the Plymouth Brethren—in 1830.

In 1841–42, the Mormons appeared in Britain. By the middle of the decade there were more of them in the country than there were Quakers. They proclaimed an apocalyptic gospel which centered on the imminent appearance of the earthly kingdom of

God at Nauvoo, Illinois. "Israel" would live in millennial bliss on the banks of the Mississippi. In the mid-century, "earthquakes, murders, eruptions, floods, tornadoes, fires, shipwrecks, thunder, blood-red flag in the sky over Hull, luminous electric ball over Windermere, were observed as signs of the End."[4] The millennial dreams of the sect appealed strongly to Britain's poorer classes, especially in the coal mining communities of the South Wales valleys. But despite successes which saw more than two thousand people sail for the new world from Liverpool in the years 1841–43, numbers began to decline after English churchmen and newspapers denounced Mormonism as immoral because of the practice of polygamy.

The rapid growth of Evangelicalism and non-conformism through the middle decades of the century was often linked with apocalyptic beliefs and expectations which could not be comfortably accomodated within the established church. It came to form a key aspect of the non-conformist credo and to mark out evangelicals within the Anglican fold:

> The focus and arbiter of instructed evangelical opinion, the *Christian Observer*, announced in January 1860 that Garibaldi's imminent destruction of the papacy showed the second coming to be near. Dr William Marsh of St Thomas in Birmingham was known in the city as Millennial Marsh. . . . Radicals and Chartists came from far and near to hear Marsh read from the Book of Revelation and discourse of a city paved with gold and built upon precious stones. In 1845 Marsh declared in a sermon his expectation that antichrist would be revealed within about twenty-five years and the Second Coming would be at hand.[5]

While Marsh remained within the Anglican communion, his ideas were mocked and marginalized within that church. Thomas Arnold characterized such literalistic readers of the Bible as "good Christians" who had "low understanding," "bad education," and "ignorance of the world."[6] It was the politically marginal, those outside of the establishment, the "radicals" and reformers, who flocked to hear Millennial Marsh's discourses on a world beyond the control of earthly powers—powers that they sought to resist. The kind of literal readings that led people to look for signs of the end and to expect the second coming tended increasingly to be associated with Evangelicalism in the Victorian era, as the new, less credulous approaches to biblical criticism came to predominate through the century, prompting the production of sceptical and demythologizing readings among liberals. Theological and critical developments helped to marginalize Revelation to the extent that, as suggested in the introduction, it almost seemed to many people to be of no use at all.

The strange status of the Apocalypse, its marginality to the canon, its occasional use as a critique of the existing social order among politically marginalized groups, is mirrored by the tropological and narrative space that it occupies. The narrator claims to be in exile on the island of Patmos "for the Word of God, and for the testimony of Jesus Christ" (1:9). Whether the reader is to understand this exile as a self-imposed writing retreat or as a forcible incarceration is not clear, but the geographically marginal location serves to highlight the work's thematic dislocation from the ordinary, everyday, sublunary world. Immediately after noting his physical (dis)location the narrator observes: "I was in the Spirit on the Lord's day," rendering the liminality of his context spiritual as well as physical, temporal as well as spatial: his *mise-en-scène* is the nexus of worlds—an indefinable cosmic embrasure from which he can look out on two worlds, seeing beyond the confines of time and space into the eternal.

Looking two ways, occupying some kind of interstitial opening can be understood as—in certain ways—typical of Victorian literary culture. In *The Lucid Veil* David Shaw makes just this point. His chapter on "The Agnostic Imagination" characterizes the advent of agnosticism as a kind of displacement most apparent in the poetry of Matthew Arnold and Arthur Hugh Clough.[7] Of the major Victorian poets these two are "the most uprooted."[8] In poems such as Arnold's "Stanzas from the Grande Chartreuse," with its account of languishing between liberation from, and longing for, the certainties of faith, Shaw senses the opening of an "agnostic void" that makes of the poet

> the quintessential displaced person, suffering from an utter personal, theological, and historical homelessness . . . displaced in time as well as space. For this restless agnostic . . . an inability to locate the unspeakable object of worship produces the anguish of a man born out of his time, the anguish of a religious man without religion.[9]

In his lack of a definite location Arnold becomes "the most representative Victorian critic," looking "two ways at once."[10]

Such displacement finds equivalents in Tennyson's image of St. Simeon Stylites atop his pillar, caught "betwixt the meadow and the cloud," and living "a life of death," his private guilt, doubt, and anguish interpreted as sainthood by onlookers; and the "dangerous edge of things . . . the giddy line midway" where Browning's Bishop Blougram dwells.[11] It can also be mapped onto the studied religious ambiguity of poems like Clough's "That there are powers," the last line of which contains the disquieting double negative that suspends both belief and disbelief: "I will not say they will not give us aid."[12]

Even a poet as devout as Christina Rossetti seems at times to have found herself unable to place unambiguously either God or the believing subject. "A Christmas Carol," as Shaw points out, shifts uneasily between the stable of the nativity and the celestial activity of "angels and archangels." The God of the poem is one whose place is neither in heaven nor on earth:

> Our God, Heaven cannot hold Him
> Nor earth sustain;
> Heaven and earth shall flee away
> When he comes to reign.[13]

So while the poet insists that "a stable-place sufficed," she is unable to provide her own version of a stable place for the divinity. In the final stanza, pleading her poverty, the narrative voice is thus unable to place her own devotion alongside either the angelic adoration or the embodied love of Mary. Neither can she offer the material gifts of shepherds or wise men; instead she is thrown back on the offering of that ambivalent symbol, her "heart," with its connotations of both the physical and the spiritual.

WOMEN ON THE EDGE

To the reader of Victorian fiction too, especially that written by women, the non-space of John's visions may seem oddly familiar. This is because the social marginalization of women is so often figured in the literature as an interest in boundaries, interstices, edges, embrasures: locked doors, curtained retreats, broken windows, climbed walls, attics. These are especially fa-

miliar to readers of the Brontë novels, of course, written by
women who dwelt at the edges of British life, not simply inasmuch as they were women, but also because of the isolated rural
location of the Haworth parsonage where they grew up. The
manifold edginess of the Apocalypse, its isolated geographical
matrix, its relationship to the canon, its plying of the boundary
between human and inhuman worlds, thus finds frequent echoes in the works of the Brontës. The opening of *Wuthering
Heights*, for example, shows the inhuman Heathcliff, leaning
over a gate in an image which proleptically expresses both his
transgressive character and the abiding interest of the novel in
the breaching of limits. From then on such images abound: in
the third chapter a window is broken by Lockwood, and his
reach through the shattered pane bridges the gap between life
and death as his hand grasps the cold fingers of Catherine's
ghostly form; another window is broken and climbed through by
Heathcliff in a violent incident which almost results in Hareton
Earnshaw's death; yet another forms the frame for Catherine's
posture in her last days as she hovers between life and death. So
these boundaries mark not only architectural and social defini-
tions, but also that ultimate human margin—the line between
life and death, between this world and another.

In *The Tenant of Wildfell Hall* female marginality is signalled
by Helen Graham's status as tenant rather than owner of the
hall. Nor is she tenant of the whole building; rather she is confined to one wing by the dilapidation of the whole. It is on notic-
ing this restriction that the narrator of this part of the novel,
Gilbert Markham, encounters Helen's young son engaged in the
scaling of a garden wall, as though to signal both the transgressive and escaped condition of himself and his mother, and their
uneasy position beyond the pale (in the literal sense of that old
saying—beyond the fence or boundary). Again, in an exchange
between the heroine and her husband-to-be, a male perception
of the significance of female texts is given telling expression.
Finding the indented traces of an erased portrait of himself on
the reverse of one of Helen's drawings, Huntingdon observes: "I
perceive, the backs of young ladies' drawings, like the post-
scripts of their letters, are the most important and interesting
part of the concern."[14] This echoes a similar sentiment expressed in *Agnes Grey*. We may well be reminded of Catherine
Earnshaw's diary, handwritten in the margins of printed works

and characterized by Lockwood as a use of books "not altogether for a legitimate purpose."[15] Physically, socially, and textually sidelined, both Catherine Earnshaw and Helen Graham are yet central characters in the novels they inhabit. So too with the heroine of *Jane Eyre*. In the present context Charlotte's novel is especially interesting in the way that it interweaves obvious allusions to, and subtle reminders of, the book of Revelation in its pages, associating them with moments at which the heroine's socially anomalous position is foregrounded.

Such a reading has itself been sidelined by Gilbert and Gubar's celebrated treatment of the novel. Their hermeneutic procedure in *The Madwoman in the Attic* brings to light the way in which the text explores Jane's psychological states through the depiction of various figures who serve as her doubles but studiously avoids its apocalyptic resonances, despite drawing attention to features which are strongly suggestive of Revelation. When, for example, they note the biblical models for St. John Rivers, they compare him with John the Baptist in his "contempt for the female," and with the writer of the gospel whose "masculine abstraction" of the Word funds Rivers's male-oriented, loveless gospel, but no mention is made of the St. John who was the visionary of Patmos.[16] Again, when they address the novel's ending they focus on its allusion to *The Pilgrim's Progress* but fail to engage with its specific quotation of Revelation's final words. Thus they note that Ferndean, Jane's final location, suggests not that Celestial City which will be the eternal home of Bunyan's pilgrim, but "a natural paradise, the country of Beulah 'upon the borders of heaven,'" while neglecting to observe that such a liminal position is precisely what gives rise to apocalyptic visions like that of the imprisoned Bunyan. Despite the essay's tracing of Jane's Bunyan-esque journey through despondency and desperation towards self-realization, the exilic origins of the ancient genre that underlies Bunyan's vision of Christian destiny and is replicated at certain moments in Brontë's text, is not acknowledged. I will return to this theme shortly.

Valentine Cunningham's reading of the novel *does* engage with its apocalyptic ending, and in doing so helps to explain, albeit tacitly, why Gilbert and Gubar might have been reluctant to pursue the point. Cunningham focuses on the ways in which *Jane Eyre* can be seen to be a novel about reading, and shows that the processes of interpretation are inseparable from issues of slavery, mastery, colonization, and authority. What is at stake in the apocalyptic ending of the novel, then, is the putative authority of the male as reader and interpreter of the biblical text, as colonial/missionary adventurer, as spiritual leader, and as paterfamilias: to posit goals, destinies, closure, is to assert an all-encompassing mastery over texts and the world they purport to represent. Jane seems to reject this authority on all counts and to discover for herself what Cunningham calls "another kind of Christianity than Rivers', another kind of prayer, another kind of relationship with Christ than Rivers proposed."[17] She rejects Rivers and with him the hermeneutic mastery he seems to represent. All the stranger, then, that the novel should end with an almost encomiastic tribute to the missionary endeavor of this propagator of patriarchal religion. Gilbert and Gubar make no attempt to account for what seems like a rehabilitation of St. John in the denouement:

> A more resolute, indefatigable pioneer never wrought amidst rocks and dangers. Firm, faithful, and devoted, full of energy and zeal, and truth, he labours for his race; he clears their painful way to improvement; he hews down like a giant the prejudices of creed and caste that encumber it. He may be stern; he may be exacting; he may be ambitious yet; but his is the sternness of the warrior Greatheart, who guards his pilgrim convoy from the onslaught of Apollyon . . . his is the ambition of the high master-spirit, which aims to fill a place in the first rank of those who are redeemed from the earth—who stand without fault before the throne of God, who share the last mighty victories of the Lamb, who are called, and chosen, and faithful.[18]

The resoundingly apocalyptic tone of this paean, envisioning the victory of the Lamb and the triumph of the saints (Rev. 7:14), segues into Rivers's own letter and its expression of longing for parousia drawn from the closing of Revelation. There is, in other words, an eschatological coalescence which seems to rule irony out of Jane's tone. As Cunningham notes, a palpable difficulty is presented to the reader by this rehabilitation of Rivers, given the fact that he appears as something of a threat to Jane's freedom and self-realization earlier in the novel. The explanation he proffers is suggestive:

> Satisfyingly apocalyptic and ultimate in tonality though the melding of the last words of this book into the last words of the Big Book

might be (to some), there is, it appears, a word, a letter . . . yet to come: "I know that a stranger's hand will write to me next." Admittedly, it's anticipated that this text of the stranger from India will also carry on in the same vein as Rivers' own last letter and say, using the words of the Master in Christ's parable (Matthew 25:21) "that the good and faithful servant has been called at length into the joy of his Lord." But still, St John Rivers is to be denied, after all, the last word.[19]

Cunningham's glee in the office of the stranger is understandable; for readers with feminist or libertarian sympathies (among whom I would include myself), the recuperation of Rivers is an uncomfortable and not very welcome reinstatement of male religious authority. Yet Cunningham's admission that the stranger is unlikely to deviate from this patriarchal and imperialist norm weakens somewhat the impact of the posthumous letter. Furthermore, when he insists that Rivers will be denied the last word he is actually straying beyond the timeframe of the novel: the letter from the hand of a stranger is imagined, projected by Jane as a likely occurrence, rather than recounted as something that has happened. However definite she is that this letter will arrive soon, its occurrence remains futural when the novel closes. Not only so, but Jane's certainty about its imminent arrival is echoed by Rivers's assurance of the imminence of the parousia: are they both tokens of an infinite deferral? Rivers, in his identification with the end, becomes almost an emblem of indefeasible deferral. Whether or not they are to be read this way, Rivers's death, like the second coming, is projected beyond the end of the novel; as far as the text itself is concerned, Rivers *does* have the final word. Even had this not been so, the portrait of him as a valiant missionary laboring to establish the kingdom of God would remain problematical, unassimilable in readings such as Gilbert and Gubar's. Once again, it is the influence and recrudescence of the Apocalypse which interrupts familiar readings of Victorian texts.

If neither Gilbert and Gubar's nor Cunningham's reading of *Jane Eyre* provides altogether convincing explanations of the final lionization of Rivers, it is because they take insufficient account of the apocalyptic dimensions of the novel and consequently fail to interpret him as a figure whose significance registers most strongly in an apocalyptic economy. This must be due in part to the fact that apocalyptic is usually understood in terms of time and the imposition endings, while *Jane Eyre*'s deployment tends to be spatial, to be a matter of seeing the world from those liminal spaces assigned to, or assumed by, the socially marginalized. For *Jane Eyre* is, par excellence, a novel of edges, exile, exclusion.

A Room at the End of the World

Mary Poovey has argued that the socially anomalous status of the governess, a figure at the heart of so many early and mid-Victorian novels, can be understood simultaneously to both epitomize and destabilize the hierarchical system of domesticity: "Because the governess was like the middle-class mother in the work she performed, but like both a working-class woman and man in the wages she received, the very figure who theoretically should have defended the naturalness of separate spheres threatened to collapse the difference between them."[20]

Policing the development and desires of her charges, channelling them into the normative patterns of behavior, the governess was also expected to control herself according to the same constraints. Her position was supposed to immure her sexuality: she was thought to be inaccessible to the servants beneath her and untouchable to the gentlemen above her in the domestic structure. This, Poovey argues, meant that she both embodied and superintended morality, but also served as a boundary figure between the gentlewoman and her working-class counterpart. Thus any threat to the stability of the role was a threat to the order in which it functioned as a definitive and conservative presence.

That Charlotte Brontë's heroine is to become a governess and so a figure who plies both the social margins and various kinds of symbolic physical extremity is prefigured in her early life. The reader of *Jane Eyre* is well aware of Jane's anomalous position from the opening chapter. She is an orphan and a dependent, unwelcome in the Reed household, persecuted by those who are the closest she has to a family. She is first encountered already under an exclusion order placed upon her by Mrs. Reed, which keeps her at a distance from the other children until she can show herself to be more like them, more "sociable," more "childlike," more "contented." Exiled from her family, she takes up a suitably edgy position in a window seat, behind a drawn curtain, looking at the introduction to a borrowed book. Cunningham neatly catalogues the "arresting array of dangerous edges or thresholds" on display in this opening chapter:

> Jane bleeds at the edge where the reader is, the opening of our book, because the complexly edged retreat she contrived for herself in the window seat, between the curtain and the window panes, and in the introductory pages of her book, proves too edgy for comfort, and is no safe haven at all. She bleeds on the threshold where Reed carefully disposes her—"Go and stand by the door, out of the way of the mirror and the windows"—trying in vain to dodge the hurled book and striking her head "against the door and cutting it. The cut bled, the pain was sharp." A woman of these many margins, she bleeds at the edge of her own body, from her vulnerable female skin. She's then physically banished to the red room, out of the way, upstairs.[21]

The book of Revelation, too, is a bleeding edge at the extremity of the book—a canonical margin filled with blood—and it is in the description of the red room that the first echoes of its imagery are heard in Brontë's text. The room is a sequestered space, a place of exile in more ways than one: "This room was chill, because it seldom had a fire; it was silent, because remote from the nursery and kitchens; solemn, because it was known to be so seldom entered" (45). Furthermore, like the trangressed boundaries of *Wuthering Heights*, it is associated with the margin between life and death: Mr. Reed "breathed his last" and "lay in state" there (46). In such a space, chill, silent, remote, and solemn, beyond the bounds of normal domesticity, outside of the family circle, the judgement of God may be revealed: "God," according to Miss Abbot, whose name conjures images of both seclusion and religious authority, "may punish her: He may strike her dead in the midst of her tantrums" (45). Alone in this inhospitable cell, Jane's impression of her environs is peppered with clear and specific images of Apocalypse. The room is said to center upon a huge bed, with architectural mahogany pillars, hung with "deep red damask"; it stands out "like a tabernacle in the centre" (45; cf, Rev. 15:5). That this apocalyptic resonance is no accident is confirmed when the second most prominent feature of the room is also described in terms of St. John's visionary furniture: "an ample-cushioned easy-chair near the head of the bed, also white, with a footstool before it, and looking, as I thought, like a pale throne" (45). When the white throne appears in Revelation, it is as the seat of final judgement: "And I saw a great white throne, and him that sat upon it, from whose face the earth and the heaven fled away; and there was found no place for them" (Rev. 20:11). Just like those judged at the end of the world, Jane finds herself before the pale throne and is cast out, having no place found for her.

Subsequent allusions to the Apocalypse in this passage are more muted, but the weighty, unequivocal presence of the tabernacle and the white throne can sensitize the reader to their significance. We find, for example, that just as St. John witnesses the opening of the long-sealed scrolls of human destiny (Rev. 5:1–9) and is told to eat another sealed document in order to be able to prophesy (Rev. 10), Jane is aware of Mrs. Reed's occasional recourse to this room and to "a certain secret drawer in the wardrobe, where were stored divers parchments, her jewel casket, and a miniature of her deceased husband; and in those last words lies the secret of the red-room—the spell which kept it so lonely in spite of its grandeur" (46). The jewel case, presumably, contains what George Eliot would later call "fragments of heaven," and associate with the description of the New Jerusalem in Revelation 21. But there is also the suggestion of a mystery at work in the contents of the secret drawer—a mystery of last words kept hidden away, yet to be revealed, controlling Jane's destiny. Significantly, it will be the novel's own St. John who opens the scroll of Jane's fortune and reveals to her her ultimate status as wealthy heiress (chapter 33).

Rivers's destiny-delivering arrival at the door of Jane's suitably cut-off cottage (made all but inaccessible by a snow storm), appears momentarily supernatural, heralded as it is by meteorological portents: "I heard a noise: the wind, I thought, shook the door. No; it was St John Rivers, who, lifting the latch, came in out of the frozen hurricane, the howling darkness, and stood before me: the cloak that covered his tall figure all white as a glacier. I was almost in consternation, so little had I expected any guest from the blocked up vale that night" (403). Not only do his size and whiteness evoke the image of the angel "clothed with a cloud" who delivers the Apocalyptic document to St. John (Rev. 10), but the snow-bound garments are reminiscent, too, of those whose garments are said to be washed in the blood of the Lamb in Revelation 7. This is precisely the image that will recur in the problematical hymn in praise of this man at the novel's close. This suggests that St. John Rivers is a rather more complex figure than is generally realized. His recuperation is not the shock that Cunningham suggests it is; Brontë has carefully prepared us for the image of him as a representative of apocalyptic religion. It is no surprise, then, that he should appear in two very different lights, since the Apocalypse itself is represented in the novel as having two distinct and irreconcilable poles: judgement and condemnation, as against consummation and fulfilment.

Rivers to be Crossed

At one level, St. John Rivers represents the problem of Revelation as a text that offers both promise and threat. It imposes an authoritative and oppressive closure while offering the promise of restoration, renewal, radical change. In *Jane Eyre* Charlotte Brontë manages to convey, within the constraints of a (broadly) realist novel, both of these possibilities as modes of narrative outcome. During the period Jane spends at Marsh End, when Rivers appears in his most displeasing aspect, his attempt to turn Jane into the subservient wife of a missionary is couched in terms of judgement based upon the pronouncements of Rivers's ancient namesake:

> For the evening reading before prayers, he selected the twenty-first chapter of Revelation . . . he sat there, bending over the great old Bible, and described from its page the vision of the new heaven and the new earth—told how God would come to dwell with men, how He would wipe away all the tears from their eyes, and promised that there should be no more death, neither sorrow nor crying, nor any more pain, because the former things were passed away.
> The succeeding words thrilled me strangely as he spoke them: especially as I felt, by the slight, indescribable alteration in sound, that in uttering them his eye had turned on me.
> "He that overcometh shall inherit all things; and I will be his God, and he shall be My son. But," was slowly, distinctly read, "the fearful, the unbelieving . . . shall have their part in the lake which burneth with fire and brimstone, which is the second death."
> Henceforward, I knew what fate St John feared for me. (442)

Here, both versions of Apocalypse are in view, and both seem to
be embodied in the reader of the biblical text. We may recall that
Rivers has already appeared in the role of God's messenger deliv-
ering the "inheritance of all things" to Jane—the revelation of
her bequest from the rich Madeira uncle. Now he bears the
mixed message of promise and threat, seeming to Jane to bend
the doom-laden words of fiery judgement towards her as she
thrills to the vision of eternal bliss. We may also recall that this
very threat has been hurled at Jane before, when, as a child, the
malevolent Mr. Brocklehurst branded her a liar who would have
her portion in the "lake burning with brimstone and fire" (66).

On the very same evening that Rivers reads the words of Revelation 21, another voice sounds in Jane's head, offering her what
Cunningham calls "another kind of Christianity than Rivers',
another kind of prayer, another kind of relationship with Christ
than Rivers proposed." It is the voice of Rochester, heard as
though in a visionary trance. The voice cries her own name:
"'Jane! Jane! Jane!'—nothing more" (444). An alternative vision
has emerged from the reading of Revelation—the vision of self
realization, of receiving one's own name, just as promised to the
faithful of the Church of Pergamos (Rev. 2:17). Rivers, then,
stands between the undifferentiated condemnation of Brocklehurst's cold, loveless, and cruel religion, and the religion of renewal and fulfilment which Jane finally espouses. His name
suggests not only that he embodies this apocalyptic choice but
also his status as boundary figure: he is not only "St. John," but
also "Rivers." Rivers form natural, geographical limits, markers
of borders, signifiers of transition from one state to another. Rivers also mark the limits or margins of the text, running through
the opening and closing scenes of the biblical canon: the garden
of Eden was located at the head of four rivers according to Genesis 2:10, and, of course, a river runs through the center of the
New Jerusalem, suggesting that it represents a return to paradise—the renewal of the earth and humanity's reinstatement in
the garden. Similarly, the Promised Land can only be reached by
crossing the Jordan.

That it is Rochester's voice Jane hears calling her across the
river into the alternative state of blessing is not without its apocalyptic significance. During the courtship at Thornfield, he has
appeared temporarily as an antichrist: "My future husband was
becoming to me my whole world; and more than the world; al-

most my hope of heaven. He stood between me and every thought of religion, as an eclipse intervenes between man and the broad sun. I could not, in those days, see God for his creature: of whom I had made an idol" (302). Among the portents that herald the approach of the end in Revelation, as in Jesus's catalogue of eschatological events (Matt. 24:29), is a solar eclipse: "the sun became black as sackcloth of hair, and the moon became as blood" (Rev. 6:12). Some two pages further on from Jane's admission of religious defection, the moon is described as a "blood-red" disc (304). Again, the idol who leads people astray from God in Revelation 13 is a figure of the beast or antichrist—the epitome of rebellion against the Lamb. Thus, in response to Rochester at this time, Jane says, she was disinclined to be "lamb-like," and notes her own identification with a variety of almost demonic creatures in his teasing pet names for her—malicious elf, sprite, changeling (302). That Rochester does not remain for Jane a figure of rebellion against God is manifest in her response to the seemingly telepathic contact with him that follows the reading of Revelation 21:

> "Down superstition!" I commented, as that spectre rose up black by the black yew at the gate. "This is not thy deception, nor thy witchcraft: it is the work of nature. . . ." I mounted to my chamber; locked myself in; fell on my knees; and prayed in my way—a different way to St John's, but effective in its own fashion. I seemed to penetrate very near a Mighty Spirit; and my soul rushed out in gratitude at His feet. I rose from the thanksgiving—took a resolve—and lay down, unscared, enlightened—eager but for the daylight. (445)

Rochester is no longer a figure of darkness or eclipse, but of daylight; he no longer draws Jane away from God, but into a renewed sense of the divine which takes her out of judgement and the fear of condemnation into an enlightened and fearless freedom. It is from this latter point of view that Jane will ultimately be able to look kindly upon Rivers, seeing in his embodying of the Apocalypse a figure of transition moving her towards forgiveness, a reminder of the shucking off of guilt, the ability "to stand without fault before the throne of God" (477).

This issue of viewpoint is crucial to *Jane Eyre* and is another feature of its apocalyptic imagery. Jane's viewpoint is, characteristically, from the margins of rooms, where she becomes an un-

observed observer of a world that is never quite her own. This
has already been shown in the novel's opening, with Jane's confinement to the red room. Again, as already noted, when
Brocklehurst first appears as a precursor to her exile at Lowood
school he quotes Revelation at her. The bifurcation of its interpretation that I have been tracing begins at this point. For, despite its use as a proof text in Jane's exclusion from family, and
from the destiny of the righteous, she tells her oppressor that,
along with the one other biblical exemplar of the apocalyptic
genre, Daniel, Revelation is one of the few bits of the Bible that
she actually likes (65). Her childish enjoyment of the text suggests that there is something about it which does not correspond
to the condemnatory uses to which it is put by her accuser.

In chapter 17 Jane is once again found behind a curtain,
"seeing without being seen." The curtain acts as a token of both
revelation and concealment, offering Jane insights into Thornfield life unavailable to others. As if to remind us that this vision
is a matter of glimpsing a place and a way of life doomed to destruction, Jane hears "four equestrians" galloping up the drive
(195). While their arrival does not unleash war, famine, pestilence, and death, it does mean hunger for those excluded from
the dinner party, and a suggestion of the threat of fire and chaos
is made as Jane visits the kitchen. Thornfield will, of course, ultimately go the way of the damned—consigned to the fire from
which Rochester emerges as a brand plucked from the burning.
If the pageant of the rich guests observed by the hidden Jane is
suggestive of the inhabitants of Babylon who "glorified themselves" and "lived deliciously," the ruined house in its desolation will evoke that city in its fallen state (Rev. 18). By then, Jane
has heeded the warning to leave the place behind, having heard
a voice within, reminding her of Jesus's incitement to suffer self-
immolation or mutilation rather than be cast into the fires of
hell (Matt. 5:29–30; JE, 325). Just such a warning is given to the
people of Babylon before its destruction: "Come out of her, my
people, that ye be not partakers of her sins, and that ye receive
not of her plagues" (Rev. 18:4). Rochester is saved, if not by
plucking out his own eyes as Jesus advocates, then at least by
losing the use of them, albeit temporarily.

The end of Thornfield by fire is one version of Apocalypse—
the vision of judgement and destruction. The post-Thornfield
reinscription of Apocalypse in the closing passage offers an alter-

native mode of construing narrative closure in terms of liberation and renewal. What has allowed this alternative to emerge is
precisely Jane's confinement to the social edges and margins, the
comfortless spaces, the wilderness in which she wanders as an
outcast after leaving Thornfield, and the anomalous position she
occupies as a governess. Had she been a full member of Thornfield society, a true citizen of Babylon, then she would never
have heard the command to flee from the wrath to come and
would have perished with the rest. This pattern is reiterated in
the Ferndean episode that closes the narrative. Its name contrived to contrast specifically with Thornfield, Ferndean offers a
vision of peace after paschal suffering—a New Jerusalem to supplant destroyed Babylon. Yet its initial delineation is noticeably
lacking in echoes of Revelation's description of the celestial city.
In fact it is another marginal space, hidden away in the depth of
a woodland. As Jane approaches it for the first time the scene is
a dreary and forbidding one. The sky is overcast, and the house
appears to be mouldy and decaying. The garden is devoid of
flowers; grass and gravel are all around (455). So forlorn does it
look that Jane can hardly believe it to be occupied at all. But, of
course, prior to Jane's arrival, it has been inhabited by a man who
thinks of himself as a ruin akin to his own destroyed mansion.
Its dark, colorless appearance mimics Rochester's own sightless-
ness and echoes the fate of Thornfield as the subject of judgement. It is only Jane's arrival in this out of the way setting that
opens again the hope of renewal, that gives rise to an alternative
vision of the end. She introduces color to the scene, describing
to Rochester the "brilliant" green of the fields, the "sparkling"
blue of the sky, and the colorful emergence of the flowers (464).
As Rochester's slow recovery of his spirits and his sight progresses, hints of the heavenly city begin to emerge in blue and
gold:

> One morning at the end of the two years, as I was writing a letter to
> his dictation, he came and bent over me, and said—
> "Jane, have you a glittering ornament round your neck?"
> I had a gold watch-chain: I answered "Yes."
> "And have you a pale blue dress on?"
> I had. . . .
> He cannot now see very distinctly . . . but he can find his way with-
> out being led by the hand: the sky is no longer a blank to him—the

earth no longer a void. When his first-born son was put into his arms, he could see that the boy had inherited his own eyes as they once were—large, brilliant, and black. On that occasion, he again, with a full heart, acknowledged that God had tempered judgement with mercy. (476–7)

It is this sense of renewal and rebirth, giving both earth and sky back their form and color—"a new heaven and a new earth," as Revelation 21:1 puts it—that restores the balance of judgement and mercy and that opens the way for that last eulogizing account of the figure who bridges the two apocalyptic possibilities—St. John Rivers. He appears in his most positive light now because destructive retribution has not had the last word.

If, on the one hand, the end of *Jane Eyre* allows the emergence of a positive, life-enhancing version of the end as a matter of renewal and rebirth, rather than of world conflagration, it also encodes a choice between spiritual fulfilment (perceived as the product of self-denial in the interests of an other-worldly reward), and a thankful grasping of the opportunities offered by this world. It delineates both of these choices as matters of the interpretation of the Apocalypse by locating its heroine on the margins, looking always at two worlds, belonging fully to neither, and thus able to access a perspective unavailable to the denizens of either. This technique remains within a realist framework of representation precisely because it focuses on the issue of interpretation and steadfastly refuses to collapse that human process into one of supernatural revelation. At the same time its use of space opens a margin that effectively broadens the real, both in the sense that it focuses attention on the social embrasure occupied by the governess, and, in doing so, evokes the Apocalypse as a vision of potential transformation.

THIRD SPACE

Conscientiously transgressing the realist framework of representation and openly advocating unequivocal belief in the supernatural, Marie Corelli's *fin-de-siècle* novel *The Sorrows of Satan* (1895) could hardly be more unlike *Jane Eyre*.[22] It belongs to the opposite end of the Victorian era, when realism was losing its grip on English fiction, giving way to a renewed interest in the

supernatural (*inter alia*), whether we think of Rider Haggard's
She (1887), Oscar Wilde's *The Picture of Dorian Gray* (1890), or
Bram Stoker's *Dracula* (1897). Yet Corelli too had to inhabit and
to focus attention upon certain margins, edges, or equivocal
spaces, and in doing so she appealed to the Apocalypse both as a
literal scene of divine judgement and as a metaphor for certain
social transpositions that might compensate for the exclusions
she suffered as a popular female writer.

Indeed Corelli's very popularity formed one kind of margin as
it excluded her from the emergent canons of literary art during
the formation of the modernist ideology that sought to distin-
guish between "popular" literature and "high" literature.[23]
While Brontë occupied a geographical and gender margin, Corelli found herself writing in a cultural margin in the sense that
her work was almost uniformly despised by critics who considered her something of a joke. Thus, in Corelli's opinion, writers
as a breed are looked down upon: "a man gifted with original
thoughts and the power of expressing them, appears to be regarded by everyone in authority as much worse than the worst
criminal, and all the 'jacks-in-office' unite to kick him to death
if they can."[24] On the other hand, *The Sorrows of Satan* stands
as one of the founding novels of the "bestseller" category, such
were the volume and scope of its readership. According to Brian
Masters, "It had an initial sale greater than any previous novel in
the language, making it the first best-seller in English history."[25]

Despite being part of a massively popular social phenomenon,
Corelli saw herself as resisting regrettable trends such as the
emergence of "new literature" with its eroticism and amorality
and the rise of the New Woman. The "new literature" had rejected "ideas of domestic virtue" (297) and awakened "a disgust
of life, and a hatred of one's fellow creatures" (330). The New
Women of the late Victorian age were the "strutting embryos of
a new sex which will be neither male nor female" (66); they were
"unnatural hybrids of no-sex" (178). At times she seems to
loathe the very culture that offered her unprecedented popularity; she describes her own age as "decadent" and "ephemeral"
and as having a "rotten core" (62–63), high society of her day as
characterized by "concealed vice and accusing shame" (236), and
the clergy as downright demonic: "wherever a clergyman is, the
devil may surely follow!" (238). But if Corelli despised gender

hybrids, she was herself a hybrid creature in many ways—a tissue of paradoxes.

Paradoxes such as those already mentioned make Corelli appear to occupy an anomalous position in the literary world of the *fin de siècle*, and they seem to multiply almost virally in her life and work. Annette R. Federico offers a list of some of them:

> From the start of her career Corelli was scorned by reviewers yet adored by readers . . . she was a highly successful woman who insisted publicly on women's intellectual equality . . . yet she cultivated an image of hyperfemininity and abhorred the New Woman; she was unmarried and lived intimately with another woman her entire life, yet her books dwell on displays of heterosexual passion . . . she was anti-intellectual yet wished to appear well educated in history and modern languages. Corelli's novels attack or expose Victorian vice, hypocrisy, and injustice with all the fire and brimstone the public could crave, yet they also indulge the pleasures of social, moral, and sexual transgression.[26]

To this list must be added R. B. Kershner's identification of yet another Corellian cleft stick: he characterizes her as a "hybrid" of modernism who had a great deal in common with James Joyce, and who turns up in his work in various ways, and yet who has been commonly dismissed as being on the wrong side of modernism's cultural divide.[27] Paradoxes, or "contrary energies" as Federico calls them, suggest edges, margins, borders, since they indicate that some kind of boundary line runs through the person or text displaying them; such a person or text is internally divided. Federico's catalogue suggests that Corelli occupied positions somewhere between each of the following and their contraries—feminism, lesbianism, anti-intellectualism, and moralism. But it would be misleading to suggest that Corelli was in any sense equivocal about her attitudes and beliefs; on the contrary, her biographers depict a woman of unshakeable religious, moral, and social convictions. She was not a weak-minded waverer; she merely seems to have had an extraordinary talent for occupying a variety of anomalous positions—an affinity for a kind of third space—a neither/nor, or a both/and.

When we first meet the hero of *The Sorrows of Satan*, Geoffrey Tempest, he occupies a social margin worthy of his creator, as a struggling writer who appears to exemplify the moral superiority of the poor but sincere artist, writing a work of genuine

worth, but meeting with the disapprobation of shortsighted publishers. He lives in squalid digs, and is reduced to writing beg-
ging letters to wealthy friends in order to survive. But eventually
he is corrupted by the wealth provided for him by the ministra-
tions of the devil himself (in the guise of Prince Lucio Rimanez)
by whom he is befriended, unaware of his new friend's true diabolical identity. It is this corruption that moves him from the
edge of respectable society into its heart, allowing Corelli to depict the rich and influential people of her time as completely un-
principled in valuing only wealth and status. They despise
Tempest when he is a worthy, struggling, would-be writer and
venerate him only when he becomes a shallow and vain socialite. But Tempest's new-found kudos does not bring him the kind
of public acclaim enjoyed by the popular novelist Mavis
Clare—a character who has been seen by many critics as a vain-
glorious self-portrait of Corelli.

As a result of Rimanez's interventions in his financial status,
Tempest is able to afford to publish his own novel, but he has to
pay reviewers to praise it in print. These, of course, are the very
reviewers who have poured scorn upon the popular works of
Clare/Corelli. Such hacks are in the employ of the devil as far as
Corelli is concerned. When Tempest is finally made aware that
he has been befriended by none other than Satan himself, and
he rejects the demonic help that has propelled him to fame and
fortune, he returns to his former penurious condition, sadder,
but wiser, and devotes himself to writing worthy works. In a
sense then, *The Sorrows of Satan* is a parable of late Victorian
publishing and of the margins it creates. But it is also a study of
liminal states, especially those produced by late capitalist culture: states of commodification, objectification, and alienation—social, sexual, and artistic.

For example, Lady Sibyl Elton, whom Tempest marries, is a
beautiful socialite corrupted by reading New Woman novels and
by the "social education" that fashioned her for the marriage
market; she learned at the age of seventeen (according to her
own extended suicide note), that she was "for sale" (323). As her
husband, Tempest's treatment of her serves to deepen rather
than to alleviate her sense of being commodified: "he has treated
me precisely as he might treat a paid mistress—that is, he has
fed me, clothed me, and provided me with money and jewels in
return for making me the toy of his passions—but he has not

given me one touch of sympathy" (319–20). Of course, Tempest himself is a victim of the same commodifying culture, not only in his relation to the publishing world, but also in that his wealth attracts approbation and association denied to him during his existence as a poor man.

Even before Tempest is drawn into a fateful relationship with the captivating Rimanez, his condition seems liminal in a variety of ways:

> Spiritually I was adrift in chaos—mentally I was hindered both in thought and achievement—bodily, I was reduced to want. . . . I was driven into a corner by my fellow-men who grudged me space to live in. (8)

> I was somewhat in a listless state bordering on stupor. (9)

> I was in a vague light-headed condition . . . in which nothing seems tangible or real . . . my brain was in a whirl—my thoughts were all dim and disconnected—and I appeared to myself to be in some whimsical dream from which I should wake up directly. (24)

The product of poverty, semi-starvation, and social dislocation, Tempest's initial self-estrangement and alienation are temporarily ameliorated by the fortune of five million pounds that Rimanez procures for him, propelling him into high society, fame, and sybaritic excess. But it returns full force as the illusion breaks down and Tempest begins to suspect, and then to understand, the true nature of his sponsor. Chapter 26 begins with a strong sense of Tempest's renewed disorientation:

> I cannot now trace the slow or swift flitting by of phantasmal events . . . wild ghosts of days or weeks that drifted past, and brought me gradually and finally to a time when I found myself wandering, numb and stricken and sick at heart, by the shores of a lake in Switzerland. . . . (241)

This loss of both time consciousness and self consciousness and the displacement implied by suddenly "finding" oneself in foreign climes foreshadows the apocalyptic climax which is reached precisely by means of the kind of spatial dislocation suggested in the above quotation; it is the product of travel, of (both literally and metaphorically) being at sea. Rimanez is finally revealed as the devil on a seagoing yacht, travelling to a spatialized version of the world's end. I will return to this apocalypse shortly, after considering the figure of Rimanez as himself a displaced wanderer, one who plies the world's margins.

LOCATING THE END

Corelli's early biographers/commentators Coates and Bell observe that "No other writer has given such a conception to the devil's character and position."[29] They may have slightly overstated the case, since the depiction of a man befriended in ignorance by the devil owes more than a little to James Hogg's *Confessions of a Justified Sinner* (1824). Nevertheless Corelli does appear to have invented her own version of the Lucifer myth in order to enable a humanized devil to wander the earth, seeking not "whom he may devour," but people who will resist his temptations and thus bring him closer to redemption. Rimanez outlines this myth to Tempest in chapter 6, recounting God's sentence upon himself: "Each human soul that yields unto thy tempting shall be a new barrier set between thee and heaven; each one that of its own choice doth repel and overcome thee, shall lift thee nearer to thy lost home! When the world rejects thee, I will pardon and again receive thee—but *not till then*" (53). Of course, Satan's sorrows abound in decadent and ephemeral *fin-de-siècle* London because no one seems remotely interested in resisting temptation. Apart, that is, from the saintly Mavis Clare. The fate of the age, then, is sealed: it is an apocalyptic age that is doomed by its own vices:

> Any era that is dominated by the love of money, has a rotten core within it and must perish. All history tells us so, but no one accepts the lesson of history. Observe the signs of the time—Art is made subservient to the love of money—literature, politics, and religion the same—you cannot escape from the general disease. The only thing to do is to make the best of it—no one can reform it. . . . (63)

In its working out of this myth of social and religious decline the novel is necessarily one in which exile plays a key role—chiefly the exile of Satan from heaven, but also the concomitant exile from society of writers and Christians who do not belong in the decadent and ephemeral world through which the devil moves with unchecked ease. Rimanez characterizes himself as a homeless wanderer: "I live nowhere for long. I am of a roving disposition, and am never tied down to one corner of the earth" (98). Like Charlotte Brontë's Jane, he has faced divine judgement and been condemned to seek out a place for himself as best he may. While he pretends that this is a matter of free choice, his nostalgic longing for his heavenly home emerges from time to time, if only as an undertone in his rejection of the church's vision of heaven (based on descriptions found in the book of Revelation): "Personally I should decline to go to any heaven which was only a city with golden streets; and I should object to a sea of glass, resenting it as a want of invention on the part of the creative Intelligence" (122).

Because of Rimanez/Satan's position as an exiled angel, able to view the human world *sub specie aeternitatis,* a perspective is opened up which makes humanity itself appear marginal and insignificant in the universe: "man is a pygmy, and his aims are pygmy like himself. For noble forms of life seek other worlds!—there *are* others" (30). The earth appears on more than one occasion to be a far-flung outpost of divine interests. Rimanez sneers at its paltriness: "I hate the planet; were there not, and are there not, other and far grander worlds that a God should have chosen to dwell on than this one!" (203). Once again, Corelli seems to be guilty of what she despises in the literature of her own age: "a disgust of life, and a hatred of one's fellow creatures" (330). Or, at least, Rimanez is guilty of it. But since his voice is the most distinctive and preponderant in the novel, and since he is attributed with far greater knowledge and intellect than the mere mortals around him, it is difficult to avoid being bombarded by his sneering misanthropy. On the other hand, the persistence and multiplication of the condition of exile that is associated with his tirades against humans and their world might also be seen as a function of what we have observed Florence Nightingale to have explored in *Cassandra*—the exile of female consciousness. Rimanez/Satan's perspective universalizes the condition of exile in a way that perhaps feminizes the world, or at least relativizes male power. This may also help to explain the negative tendency of the novel's apocalyptic tone, its depiction of a society ripe for some kind of judgement:

"The world is a veritable husk of a planet; humanity has nearly completed all its allotted phases, and the end is near."

"The end?" echoed Lady Sibyl, "Do you believe the world will ever come to an end?"

"I do, most certainly. Or, to be more correct, it will not actually perish, but will simply change. And the change will not agree with the constitution of its present inhabitants. They will call the transformation the Day of Judgement. I should imagine it would be a fine sight." (121)

This inclination towards remedial destruction is, in part, a matter of reading the signs of the times. As already observed, Corelli suggests that those signs are very evident in late Victorian Britain, especially in London, which Tempest (in a familiar gesture), refers to as "the restless modern Babylon" (172).

Yet time is not really the main issue when it comes to Corelli's apocalyptic sensibilities. For although the novel directs the reader's attention to distinctively damnable qualities that characterize her own era, time is internal rather than cosmic: "time is what the Soul makes it, and no more" (383). Given this internalization of time and the variety of ways in which the novel creates, depicts, and actually embodies liminal states, the locating of apocalyptic possibilities in terms of *spatial* transgression is rather more typical of its rhetorical strategy.

Once again, towards the novel's end, on board Rimanez's yacht—"The Flame"—Tempest finds himself confined, "driven into a corner": "I stood in the black obscurity of my cabin, trying to rally my scattered forces. . . . I tried to open my door. It was locked outside!—I was a prisoner!" (365–66). Thus begins the extraordinary climactic phase of the book. Corelli now opens before the reader a vision of the world's end for which she has been preparing. As with the myth of Lucifer, she is not content merely to stage the Apocalypse in familiar terms; she presents it with her customary imaginative twist, reinventing the myth as she goes.

Tempest believes that he is on board the diabolical vessel for a sailing holiday to aid recuperation following the suicide of his wife. He has embarked in complete ignorance of his true destination. He finds himself locked in the cabin after Rimanez has openly told him that he is his enemy and has displayed something of his monstrous form. "The Flame" now sails into a violent storm during which Tempest hears a voice crying: "Breakers ahead! Throughout the world, storm and danger and doom! Doom and Death!—but afterwards—Life!" (366). The storm is at once literal and metaphorical, encouraging the reader to associate the physical location of the yacht and its precarious situation with the dire warnings about the character of the times that pepper the narrative; the hero's surname now takes on its greatest significance as a reminder of that metaphorical value. The wind and the waves seem to Tempest to roar out "Ave Sathanas!" (366–67)—evoking an age that effectively worships the devil because its values are utterly corrupt; it has rejected God in both its philosophical theory and its social practice, in favor of the worship of money.

There follows an extended sermon from Rimanez explaining why it is evident that the end of the world is near:

> For vulgar cash, the fairest and noblest scenes of nature are wantonly destroyed without public protest—the earth, created in beauty, is made hideous—parents and children, wives and husbands are ready to slay each other for a little gold—Heaven is barred out—God is denied—and Destruction darkens over this planet. . . . When the world is totally corrupt—when Self is dominant . . . when gold is man's chief ambition—when purity is condemned—when poets teach lewdness, and scientists blasphemy—when love is mocked, and God forgotten—the End is near. (372)

Evidently, there is an important temporal dimension to this that cannot be disguised—the repetition of "when" makes that abundantly clear. But there is also a distinctive spatial dimension to Corelli's apocalypse to which I wish to draw attention here.[29] The scene, after all, takes place in transit, on board a seagoing yacht that Rimanez commands to be steered "Onward, to the boundaries of the world! . . . Onward where never man hath trod—steer on to the world's end!" (375–76). In this command the spatial and the temporal seem to be conflated, and this is confirmed by what follows. The yacht sails on into waters that become increasingly icy until eventually it passes beyond "the barriers of ice . . . into a warm inland sea" (377). This place on the other side of the frozen wastes, it transpires, is the earth's lost Paradise. Once again it is the role of Rimanez to explain:

> Here, where the distorted shape of man hath never cast a shadow!— here—where the arrogant mind of Man hath never conceived a sin!—

here where the godless greed of man hath never defaced a beauty, or slain a woodland thing!—here, the last spot on earth left untainted by Man's presence! Here is the world's end!—when this land is found, and these shores profaned—when Mammon plants its foot upon this soil—then dawns the Judgement Day! . . . This place is neither hell nor heaven nor any space in between—it is a corner of thine own world on which thou livest. (378)

This spatializing of apocalypse has its roots in the depiction of hubris that plays so important a role in Corelli's diagnosis of her age. Rimanez's unique perspective is often used to point it out: "Oh, never mind the elements. Man has nearly mastered them or soon will do so, now that he is getting gradually convinced there is no Deity to interfere in his business" (34). Nor is human arrogance limited to asserting control over its own planet: "Why in heaven's name do you not let other planets alone? Why do you strive to fathom their mysteries and movements? If men, as you say, have no business with any planet save this one why are they ever on the alert to discover the secret of mightier worlds—a secret it may some day terrify them to know!" (75).

Corelli thus fuses different senses of *transgression*—the willful and overweening desire to cross both spiritual *and* material boundaries—in order to fuse the spatial and the temporal in a vision of destruction that humanity brings upon itself. Yet Paradise is also a figure of transgression in itself. It occupies a place that is "neither hell nor heaven nor any space in between—it is a corner of thine own world." That is to say: it both is and is not the human world: our own, and yet not our own, since to touch it is to call down divine retribution, to bring an *end* to our own world. It is like the Tree of Knowledge of good and evil in Eden— both accessible and inaccessible to humankind—there as a temptation, a portent, a threat, and a possibility, an embodied limit or threshold of human experience.

The human/non-human, open/closed garden is liminal to human experience in an even more striking sense. As he marvels at the beauty of the pristine place Tempest is visited by the dead: "And now many familiar faces shone upon me like white stars in a mist of rain—all faces of the dead—all marked with unquenchable remorse and sorrow" (377). The garden here seems to function in much the same way as a physical barrier in a Brontë novel—it suggests not only physical and social margins, but also metaphysical ones. All the more curious then, that in this context it is also an echo of a more familiar domestic space—Mavis Clare's garden which Tempest has previously visited on two occasions. The popular novelist is evoked during the Paradise episode, just before the appearance of the dead, by the song of an unknown bird that sounds to Tempest "like that of a *mavis* in spring" (377, my emphasis), and the reader cannot but recall Tempest's visit to the novelist's garden and to his hearing there "the piping of a thrush up somewhere among the roses," more than a hundred pages earlier (252). We might sense again in this collocation that Derridean *hauntology* evoked by Nightingale—the presence/absence that places the *unheimlich* at the heart of the domestic. But it also displaces the domestic—transports it to the world's end, melding it with the apocalyptic *mise en scene*.

So, there is a sense here in which the Apocalypse is once again domesticated, is drawn into the realm of the familiar, the homely, and the reassuring. There is, of course, a price to pay for such a gesture—a price which can be appreciated in the texts by Rossetti and Nightingale I have already considered in these pages, and which reimposes itself here: to domesticate the Apocalypse is also to defamiliarize home, to allow in the *unheimlich* with its potential to disrupt, threaten, or even overthrow familiar categories of experience. But it is also to insist upon the placing of limits around human aspirations and to exact the promise that human failure, turpitude, finitude, and overreaching ultimately shall not determine the world's destiny. This, it seems to me, helps to explain why a spatialized Apocalypse is particularly attractive to some Victorian women writers—it limits the human sphere, imposing on the projections and ramifications of male power a boundary that echoes that placed around their own "sphere" of operation and influence in the Victorian age.[30] But there is another, perhaps more significant aspect to this phenomenon. As long as the Apocalypse is thought in terms of temporal endings it has the ring of finality, of closure, of the shutting down of possibilities. That Corelli did not wish to construe it in this way has already been made evident in the quoting of Rimanez's words about the world's "end": "it will not actually perish, but will simply change."

Despite the rhetoric of fire and brimstone in the novel there is always this underlying sense of massive upheaval putting things right, at great cost—necessarily—but not at the cost of ultimate consummation. Spatializing the Apocalypse, using it to envisage a place that is neither hell nor heaven but real possibility inherent in the human world—even if the human world will require supernatural intervention in order to realize its potential—allows us to think of it in terms of passage, progression, or even transcendence. The fact that both Charlotte Brontë's and Marie Corelli's texts translate temporal ends into spatial difference can be seen as a function of the various ways in which the marginalization of women in the Victorian era forced a renegotiation of limits. It might be said that in *Jane Eyre* and *The Sorrows of Satan* women, so often viewed as irreducibly physical, as occupiers of space, recast narrative ends to include their own destinies and to limit male ambitions for control. The gardens at Ferndean and at the house of Mavis Clare figure as images of both the apocalyptic reversal of male power and ambition and as idealized spaces of female control.

Such an interpretation may require the gendering of the way this rhetoric works in Victorian texts. For, whether we think of Mathilde Blind's use of it as a metaphor for renewal and re-emergence, Florence Nightingale's sense of the return of Christ in female form, Charlotte Brontë's intimations of re-creation, or even Christina Rossetti's disguised self-reflection, it seems that the specific uses made of the Apocalypse by Victorian women tend away from destruction and from finality, towards the overthrow of the dominant (male) order of things in favor of imaginative reconstruction—a new heaven and a new earth, maybe.

Conclusion

FROM TIME TO TIME

ACCORDING TO ALEXANDER WELSH, "THE REVELATION OF ST JOHN was frequently present to the nineteenth-century imagination . . . and the Victorians found it useful on many occasions."[1] The foregoing chapters offer substantial evidence that Welsh's assertion is well grounded. He refers to the sense of "obscure imminence" inherent in Victorians' frequent references to time: "The literature of the period abounds with references to time, which threatens and retreats, creates and resolves anxiety, sanctions and obliterates moral acts."[2] Welsh sees Dickens as arguing that time will ultimately bring a day of judgement because truth will be revealed by its passage. While nineteenth-century historicism ran counter to such notions in the sense that it posited both the endlessness and irreversibility of time, as Welsh says, it simply "renewed the need to envision an ending."[3] He calls upon Tennyson, Comte, Marx, Dickens, Eliot, Scott, and Thackeray as witnesses. Janet L. Larson's treatment of the theme, which like Welsh's focuses firmly on Dickens, also tends to see Victorian deployments of apocalyptic as a matter of the inculcation of ends—not necessarily as imposed by divine fiat, but as inherent in social trends, human proclivities, or the dynamics of culture.[4] Again, David Carroll's discussion of George Eliot's *Felix Holt* characterizes its apocalypticism in terms of a "cosmic crisis after which things could never be the same again."[5] The cosmic crisis in view is not the product of divine intervention; it relates to the historical and political events associated with the Reform Act of 1832: a "secularised apocalypse which reveals the relationship of past, present and future."[6]

Welsh's, Larson's, and Carroll's approaches are exemplary of the way the relationship between English literature and the Apocalypse has been understood by critics. By contrast, my concern in these pages has been to treat apocalyptic in a rather

190

broader sense than do these readings of Dickens and Eliot—to think of it as interwoven with a range of rhetorical figures, images, themes, and ideas which do not necessarily have to do directly with narrative closure or with what Frank Kermode calls "the sense of an ending." As Kermode demonstrates, the imposition of some kind of end is inherent in narrative; it is part of the very definition of what narrative is and what it entails.[7] But I take the apocalyptic affinities of Victorian literature to be something more than the inevitable effect of narrativity. It is for this reason that I have not dealt in any detail with the well-known epochal statements associated with the *fin de siècle*, with what Max Nordau famously called "the Dusk of Nations." Ideas of degeneration, deepening gloom, social and moral dissolution that trouble the pages of *Dorian Gray*, of *Dracula*, of *She*, etc., seem to me to "protest too much," to noisily outbid the long drawn out undertone of religious and philosophical uncertainty that—consciously or otherwise—resonates with Johannine anxiety. One might almost argue that the most obvious signs of apocalyptic consciousness, the openly expressed fear of, or desire for, some kind of temporal crisis or rift, represent the disarming of hitherto potent threats by exposure—an apocalyptic gesture in itself, of course. They might remind us of Kant's disparaged "mystagogues" who confuse the rational and the oracular in their philosophical descriptions—those who leap to judgement on the basis of revelation, proclaiming in their delirium the end or death of philosophy. For the texts of the *fin de siècle* often reincorporate the supernatural and frequently make unargued announcements about the end of the world, or at least of the epoch.

In "Of an Apocalyptic Tone recently Adopted in Philosophy" Jacques Derrida's discussion of Kant's essay on this "overlordly" tone attempts to unpick or to deconstruct the distinction that Kant is making between the voices of reason and of prophecy, finding that the very idea of a "tone" in written language is elusive and ineluctable, and that the apocalyptic always exceeds attempts to contain it, since it outmaneuvers generic classifications, reasserting itself in every attempt to enclose a category or to bring something to an end, whether a regrettable trend in philosophy, the epoch of metaphysics, history, literature, progress, or humanity, etc.[8] Since the confusion (or interweaving, depending upon one's attitude to Enlightenment reasoning) of the rational and the oracular announces something like the end of philosophy, Derrida's argument offers another way of understanding the relationship between Victorian literature and the Apocalypse. There are two moments of comparison to be recognized here. Firstly, it is clear that many *fin-de-siècle* texts demonstrate the interweaving and co-implication of rational and declamatory discourses, bringing together Darwinian themes with Bible-inspired ideas of temporal closure (*The Time Machine*), philosophical aesthetics with sin and judgement (*Dorian Gray*), the sexual and social liberation of women with unfounded assertions of creeping degeneracy (*Gallia*), and so on. Secondly, it has to be acknowledged that this coalescence is a continuation of the literary tradition that brought High Realism together with biblio-mythological narrative patterns, whether one thinks of the pervasive influence of Bunyan's allegory of the Christian life in *The Pilgrim's Progress* or the direct allusion-making of the Brontës, Eliot, and Hardy. In this sense apocalyptic is clearly perceptible as a chracteristic mode of Victorian writing.

In one sense this is a matter of epistemological diffraction, of what David Shaw has shown to be the emergence of a number of competing approaches to knowledge and the knowable, as science competed with poetry, idealism with empiricism, and holistic theories with atomic theories.[9] The conflict served to expose and to valorize the limits of the human, of reason, observation, analysis, and language, and focused attention on what Shaw, borrowing from Tennyson, calls the "lucid veil": the encountering of perceptual limits as indices both of what they may conceal and of human finitude as such. As the preceding chapters have shown, metaphors, rhetoric, and images associated with such limits are endemic in Victorian writing—whether those limits are spatial, temporal, physical, psychological, or textual.

But this epistemological conflict has another aspect which Shaw does not address: it is an issue with implications for the philosophy and politics of gender. This is not simply by virtue of the interpretation of apocalypse as discussed in chapter 5—the possibility of transcending the limitations of a woman's sphere—but also because the temporal dimension of apocalypse, its function as the bearer of eschatological meaning, is subject to the questions posed to the concept of time by thinkers such as

Luce Irigaray and Julia Kristeva. For Irigaray western philosophy has tended to characterize time as interior to the subject and space as exterior, so that "the subject, the master of time, becomes the axis, managing the affairs of the world. Beyond him lies the eternal instant of God, who brings about the passage between time and space."[10] This has meant that woman has typically been associated with space and man with time. As Margaret Whitford puts it: "Woman has always been for man his space, or rather his *place*, but has no place of her own. This deprives her of identity for herself."[11] Apocalypse could be read in this light as a male discourse designed to totalize human experience in the interests of man, to assert his mastery in the name of God the Father; or it could even be reducible to what Alice Jardine calls a "paranoid reaction" to "women's massive awakening."[12] The Victorian era was one in which such an awakening was already taking place, and as has been made evident in the foregoing discussions of *Cassandra* and *Jane Eyre*, it led Nightingale and Brontë (among others) to engage directly with the problematics of space and time in order to question into visibility the way in which these categories were constituted.

An additional question is raised: why should women writers engage with the Apocalypse or deploy its figures if they are excluded or reduced by its temporality? In "Women's Time" Kristeva raises a closely related issue: the definition of historical time and its significance to feminism.[13] She argues that female subjectivity has been problematized by a certain conception of time: "time as project, teleology, linear and prospective unfolding; time as departure, progression, and arrival—in other words, the time of history."[14] Early feminism—that of suffragists and the existential struggle—sought out a place within historical time that would allow women to identify with the dominant rationality. The second generation of feminists rejected the goal of identification with the dominant mode and its linear history, seeking out instead the specificities of female psychology that were irreducible to male categories. The characteristic temporality of the second generation, Kristeva asserts, is cyclical or mythical. She claims that the late 1970s saw the emergence of a third, mixed mode that combined questing for the insertion of women into history with a refusal to accept the limits of historical subjection. While she admits that this analysis is "too Hegelian"—as I must admit my own to be—Kristeva advocates the third way. This is not a chronology, she insists, so much as *"signifying space,* a both corporeal and desiring mental space," that does not exclude "the parallel existence of all three in the same historical time, or even that they be interwoven one with the other."[15]

It appears then that as an expression of "the time of history"—at least in its teleological, progressional, linear aspects—the Apocalypse is vulnerable to the moment of rejection within feminist interpretations of time. But, since it also provided Victorian women such as Blind, Rossetti, Nightingale, Brontë, and Corelli with a site for renegotiating women's time, place, subjectivity, it can also be seen to function as a Kristevan "signifying space" of parallel existences and interweavings. Such a possibility arises because the end of history is never containable within history; the Apocalypse is necessarily lodged within history as the possibility of its overthrow. If male readings tend to interpret this as totalization or closure, female readings tend to read it otherwise—as possibility, renewal, regeneration. To put it another way, the removal of the veil might reveal the secrets of a male god, or the faces of (Victorian) women. This is a matter of interpretation in more than one sense.

Unveiling: the End

At least since Paul's reading of the "Old" Testament, interpretation has been associated with the process of unveiling. Allegorizing the veil with which Moses covered his face when he descended from Mount Sinai with the tablets of the law, Paul equated the Christian revelation with the unveiling of the scripture's meaning: "for until this day remaineth the same veil untaken away in the reading of the old testament; which veil is done away in Christ" (2 Cor. 3:14). The dichotomy of the veiled and the unveiled gave rise to the split between the letter and spirit which in turn produced the hermeneutic traditions of Christian reading practice.[16] Traceable through medieval proliferations of levels of meaning—historical, analogical, moral, spiritual, etc.—through Reformation insistence on the primacy of the literal sense of scripture, understood as subdivided between historical and figural, through Romantic notions of the text as a conductor of the sublime, it emerged in the nineteenth century in a variety of guises. Friedrich Schleiermacher, for example, wrote of interpretative "divination"—the act of imaginative response by means of which the reader inhabits the author's world—a model which treats the text as a kind of veil that can be penetrated by the hermeneutical process. Demythologizing readings of scripture like those favored by Matthew Arnold and George Eliot posit an analogous process: here the defunct myth-opoeic worldview underpinning the Bible's narratives, descriptions, and teachings is the veil that must be removed if the useful moral meaning is to be uncovered.

The theoretical models that emerged in the second half of the twentieth century set their face against the idea that the text was a veil through which truth, reality, or authorial intention might pass. Deflected by the perception that words connect not with a world beyond themselves, but only with each other in a closed system of differences, the reader moved across the textual surface in an endless interpretative glide of shifting significations rather than through it into a world of fixed meanings. Such an approach often seems to take for granted that earlier interpreters presumed language to be perspicuous, and texts—whether written, spoken, or appearing as pages from the "Book of Nature"—to be penetrable. Darwin's troubles with the human eye, with affinity, analogy, and metaphorical language, James Thomson's concern with a "seeming order" that makes observed reality a doubtful prospect, George Eliot's interest in webs and in the equivocal character of language as a mode of representation, Christina Rossetti's worries about textual obscurity, Charlotte Brontë's double interpretation of Revelation, all serve to indicate that Victorian writers were frequently troubled by a sense that interpretation was a matter of reading the veil rather than presuming that it could be removed, of confronting the nature of their own perceptual, epistemological, and ontological limits. That they did not, on the whole, collapse this into either textual idealism or naive assumptions of theological presence is evident in the patterns of allusion to, borrowing from, and deployment of the apocalyptic affinities I have been tracing.

This is counterintuitive in the sense that the Apocalypse might seem to some to be the ultimate site of an insistence upon a transcendent reality that is, if not accessible, then at least lucidly inferrable. But John's text must also be seen, for reasons already adduced, as itself a veil: it couples cryptic, allusive, and riddling language with esoteric, genre-specific, and nonce symbols. It purports to be an unveiling, but what it reveals is never clear. The unclarities are layered: impossible visual images coalesce with an unfollowable narrative; obscure numerological references entwine with an unstatable temporality. Even its account of its own textual history is layered to such an extent that the reader cannot calculate their precise relation to an original text. Just look at the opening verse: "The Revelation of Jesus Christ, which God gave unto him, to show unto his servants . . . and he sent and signified it by his angel unto his servant John." If there appears to be a clearly defined line of provenance from God to Jesus, from Jesus to an angel, from an angel to John, and from John to the churches in Asia Minor, this is complicated by the inclusion of letters which seem to be dictated by an unknown voice and addressed to the "angels" of seven churches, and by various books and scrolls whose content may or may not contribute to what we read. "And there is," as Derrida puts it, "no certainty that man is the exchange of these telephone lines or the terminal of this endless computer."[17] The Victorian resonance is clear: the lines of development that criss-crossed the Victorian era, the various cultural "sendings" of science, technology, sociology, politics, religion, made it inordinately difficult to know how to locate humanity as a product of nature, or a commodity of exchange, or a denizen of a denatured, urban world, or a child of God, or a political animal. These lines of force might indeed not have had humanity at their center since they seem to invoke the inhuman whether in its divine, natural, economic, or temporal guise, and to exceed, threaten, transcend, or condition human existence in ways that were only dimly understood.

Such uncertainties came to be expressed in ways that evoked the Apocalypse because the latter is a text that simultaneously unveils and veils human destiny and because its very obscurity grounds the reflection of the reader and their time, inviting the gaze of the wanderer "between two [or more] worlds." In a culture richly patterned by traditions of biblical knowledge but increasingly uncertain what those patterns meant or how they related to newer forms of knowledge, the Apocalypse was present as one thread among many. One could perhaps explore relations between Victorian writing and Job, the Psalms, Ecclesiastes, the gospels, etc. What makes Revelation particularly telling, it seems to me, is that its presence is persistent but muted, almost as though it were covered over by the utilitarian, realist, pragmatic concerns of the day.

If the foregoing chapters have been interested primarily in the half-concealed heritage of Bible-informed culture rather than in its conscious interpretation and reinterpretation of biblical texts, this is because such affinities reveal not only the source of much cultural anxiety—the problematizing of the Bible as sacred scripture by the discoveries of science, textual criticism, archaeology, and psychology—but also that these very discourses are themselves embedded in an ideological formation colored by the Bible, by its interpretation and deployment. This has emerged in various ways and in a number of different guises: in the way in which Darwin's vision of Nature evokes John's visions of supernature; in the reflections of both the New Jerusalem and Babylon that many writers saw in the new urban sprawls; in the persistence of the image of the veil and the evident ambivalence about the possibility of seeing beyond it; in the way imaginative writing reinscribes temporal horizons erased by science; in the renegotiations of social and cultural space demanded by the changing dynamics of class, gender, and economics. The book of Revelation is one stratum of the Victorian cultural formation. It is not necessarily the easiest to unearth since it is often deep-laid. It is present but veiled, you might say, by an age that thought it to be (almost) of no use, yet that used it in ways that reveal something of the motivation for its veiling. Like many Victorian writers, we may find that in engaging with their texts we too are required to read the veil and to wonder at its strange lucidity.

Notes

NOTES TO INTRODUCTION

1. Klaas Runia, "Eschatology and Hermeneutics," *European Journal of Theology* 3, no. 1 (1994): 17–33, 20.
2. Christopher Rowland argues that eschatological concerns should not be seen as a defining characteristic of apocalyptic literature, since some apocalyptic texts have little to say about the end times, while some non-apocalyptic texts contain eschatological material. C. Rowland, *The Open Heaven: A Study of Apocalyptic in Judaism and Early Christianity* (London: SPCK, 1982), 26.
3. David E. Aune, *The New Testament in Its Literary Environment* (Cambridge: James Clarke and Co., 1988), 241.
4. Richard Bauckham, *The Climax of Prophecy: Studies on the Book of Revelation* (Edinburgh: T and T Clark, 1993), 177.
5. John J. Collins, *The Apocalyptic Imagination: An Introduction to the Jewish Matrix of Christianity* (New York: Crossroad, 1989), 26–28.
6. Norman Cohn, *Cosmos, Chaos and the World to Come: The Ancient Roots of Apocalyptic Faith* (New Haven, CT: Yale University Press, 1993), 219. Cohn deals with the relationship between apocalyptic literature and combat myths in considerable detail.
7. Thomas Carlyle, *Sartor Resartus*, ed. Kerry McSweeney and Peter Sabor (Oxford: Oxford University Press, 1987), 111.
8. Matthew Arnold, "Stanzas from the Grande Chartreuse," in *The Poems of Matthew Arnold*, ed. Kenneth Allott (London: Longmans, 1965), 285–94, ll.85–86.
9. George Eliot, *Middlemarch*, ed. W. J. Harvey (Harmondsworth: Penguin, 1965), 35.
10. Elizabeth Barrett Browning, *Aurora Leigh*, ed. Kerry McSweeney (Oxford: Oxford University Press, 1993), 9, ll. 941–64; Arthur Hugh Clough, *Amours de Voyage*, in *The Victorians: An Anthology of Poetry and Poetics*, ed. ValentineCunningham (Oxford: Blackwell, 2000), 444–70, Canto 2, 1, ll.17–20; Thomas Hardy, *Jude the Obscure*, ed. Timothy Hands (London: Everyman, 1995), 21; Robert Browning, *Poetical Works: 1833–1864*, ed. Ian Jack (Oxford: Oxford University Press, 1970), "Christmas Eve," 489–524, ll. 530–34; "Andrea del Sarto," 673–79, ll. 260–62.
11. Elizabeth Gaskell, *North and South*, ed. Angus Easson (Oxford: Oxford University Press, 1982), 151; *Mary Barton*, ed. Stephen Gill (Harmondsworth: Penguin, 1970), 141.
12. Charlotte Brontë, *Shirley*, ed. Andrew and Judith Hook (Harmondsworth: Penguin, 1974), 57.

13. Sebastian Evans, "The Fifteen Days of Judgement," in *The New Oxford Book of Victorian Verse*, ed. Christopher Ricks (Oxford: Oxford University Press, 1987), 437–42.

14. Matthew Arnold, *Culture and Anarchy*, ed. J. Dover Wilson (Cambridge: Cambridge University Press, 1932), 83.

15. Samuel Butler, *The Way of All Flesh*, ed. R. A. Streatfield (London: Jonathan Cape, 1932), 16. Although not published until 1903, Butler's novel was written between 1872 and 1884.

16. Anthony Trollope, *The Way We Live Now*, ed. Frank Kermode (London: Penguin, 1994), 570.

17. George Eliot, *Daniel Deronda*, ed. Barbara Hardy (Harmondsworth: Penguin, 1967), 431.

18. "In 1855 the 'newspaper tax,' which had in 1836 been reduced from 4d to 1d, was abolished; six years later the excise duty on paper, which had kept the price of all publications from sinking to its open market minimum, was abolished too. But these acts are more sensibly viewed as responses to, or products of, deep shifts in public opinion and consumer demand, than as themselves initiators of change. The fact is, that by the fifties a large and still enlarging middle-cum-working-class public was ready to read all the cheap literature it could get. . . . Whatever the causes, the results were clear enough: the decisive creation, during our period, of a mass-market for cheap literature, and an unprecedented explosion of the newspaper press." Geoffrey Best, *Mid-Victorian Britain, 1851–75* (London: Fontana, 1979), 245–46.

19. George Gissing, *The Nether World*, ed. Stephen Gill (Oxford: Oxford University Press, 1992), 345.

20. Charlotte Brontë, *Jane Eyre*, ed. Q. D. Leavis (London: Penguin, 1966), 477.

21. Ibid., 475.

22. Charlotte Brontë, *Villette*, ed. Mark Lilly (London: Penguin, 1979), 595.

23. Ibid., 596.

24. Harold Bloom, *Shelley's Mythmaking* (New York: Cornell University Press, 1969), 122.

25. William Wordsworth, *The Prelude: A Parallel Text*, ed. J. C. Maxwell (Harmondsworth: Penguin, 1971), 6, ll.570–1 of the 1805–6 version, 6, ll. 638–39 of the 1850 version.

26. Spurgeon, 80.

27. Alfred Tennyson, *In Memoriam*, in *In Memoriam, Maud and Other Poems*, ed. John D. Jump (London: Everyman, 1974), 75–153, 131, ll. 133–44.

28. W. David Shaw, *The Lucid Veil* (London: Athlone, 1987), xvi.

Notes to Chapter 1

1. *The Life and Letters of Charles Darwin*, ed. Francis Darwin, rev. ed. (London: John Murray, 1888), 2:312.

2. Gavin Carlyle, *The Battle of Unbelief* (London: Hodder and Stoughton, 1878), 224–25, 229–30.

3. Andrew George, trans., *The Epic of Gilgamesh* (London: Penguin, 1999), ll. 48–65.

4. John A. Wilson, "Egypt: The Function of the State," in *Before Philosophy: The Intellectual Adventure of Ancient Man*, ed. H. Frankfort, H. A. Frankfort, J. A. Wilson, and T. Jacobsen, 71 (Harmondsworth: Penguin, 1963).

5. Jeffrey Gantz, trans., *Early Irish Myths and Sagas* (Harmondsworth: Penguin, 1981), 131.

6. Emily Brontë, *Wuthering Heights* (London: Penguin, 1995), 37.

7. Ibid., 102.

8. Christian Rossetti, "Goblin Market," in *Christina Rossetti: Selected Poems*, ed. C. H. Sisson (Manchester: Carcanet, 1984), 82.

9. Friedrich Nietzsche, "On Truth and Falsity in Their Ultramoral Sense," *Early Greek Philosophy and Other Essays*, trans. M. A. Mugge (London: T.N. Foulis, 1911), 173.

10. Friedrich Nietzsche, *Thus Spake Zarathustra*, in *The Portable Nietzsche*, ed. and trans. Walter Kaufmann (New York: Viking Penguin, 1959), 1.4.126.

11. Agnes Mary Robinson, "Darwinism," in *Victorian Women Poets 1830–1900: An Anthology*, ed. Jennifer Breen (London: Everyman,1994), 128.

12. Mathilde Blind, *The Ascent of Man* (London: Chatto and Windus,1889).

13. Isobel Armstrong, *Victorian Poetry: Poetry, Poetics and Politics* (London: Routledge, 1993), 376.

14. Blind, 7, 9. Page numbers for the following references are given in the text.

15. Jacques Derrida, *Of Grammatology*, trans. G. C. Spivak (Baltimore: Johns Hopkins University Press, 1976), 233.

16. Charles Darwin, *The Origin of Species*, ed. G. Beer (Oxford: Oxford University Press, 1996), 185–91. Page references to this work are given, henceforth, in the text.

17. T. H. Huxley, "The Physical Basis of Life," *The Fortnightly Review*, Feb. 1869, 143.

18. Quoted in James R. Moore, *The Post-Darwinian Controversies: A Study of the Protestant Struggle to Come to Terms with Darwin in Great Britain and America, 1870–1900* (Cambridge: Cambridge University Press, 1979), 261.

19. See *Marx and Engels on Malthus*, ed. Ronald L. Meek, trans. Dorothea L. Meek and Ronald L. Meek (London: Lawrence and Wishart, 1953), 171–88.

20. Friedrich Engels, letter to Lavrov (November 12, 1875) in Meek (ed.),176.

21. Walter E. Houghton, *The Victorian Frame of Mind, 1830–1870* (New Haven, CT: Yale University Press, 1957), 196–217.

22. Elizabeth Gaskell, *North and South* (Oxford: Oxford University Press, 1982), 81.

23. Blind, 12, 13, 17.

24. Charles Darwin, *The Descent of Man, and Selection in Relation to Sex* (London: John Murray, 1871), 386–87.

25. Gavin de Beer, introduction to *Charles Darwin, Thomas Henry Huxley: Autobiographies*, ed. G. de Beer (London: Oxford University Press, 1974), xi.

26. Valentino Gerratana, "Marx and Darwin," *New Left Review* 82 (1973).

27. M. McGiffert, "Christian Darwinism: The Partnership of Asa Gray and George Frederick Wright, 1874–1881" (Ph.D. diss., Yale University, 1958). Quoted (approvingly) in James Moore, 13.

28. Gillian Beer, *Darwin's Plots: Evolutionary Narrative in Darwin, George Eliot and Nineteenth-Century Fiction* (London: Routledge and Kegan Paul, 1983), 94; Paul Ricoeur, *The Rule of Metaphor: Multi-disciplinary Studies in the Creation of Meaning in Language,* trans. R. Czerny, K. McLaughlin, and J. Costello, SJ (London: Routledge and Kegan Paul, 1978), 22–24.

29. Beer, *Darwin's Plots,* 38.

30. Ernst Benz, *Evolution and Christian Hope: Man's Concept of the Future from the Early Fathers to Teilhard de Chardin,* trans. Heinz G. Frank (London: Victor Gollancz, 1967), 229.

31. Dov Ospovat, *The Development of Darwin's Theory: Natural History, Natural Theology, and Natural Selection, 1838–1859* (Cambridge: Cambridge University Press, 1981), 116–28.

32. Charles Darwin, quoted in Ospovat, 181.

33. On the rise of philology in the nineteenth century, see J. W. Burrow, "The Uses of Philology in Victorian England," in *Ideas and Institutions of Victorian Britain,* ed. Robert Robson (London: G. Bell and Sons, 1967).

34. Gillian Beer, *Open Fields: Science in Cultural Encounter* (Oxford: Clarendon, 1996), 95–114.

35. Ibid., 110.

36. Ibid., 112–3.

37. Hans Aarsleff, *The Study of Language in England, 1780–1860* (Minneapolis: University of Minnesota Press, 1983), 208.

38. Lawrence Frank, "Reading the Gravel Page: Lyell, Darwin, and Conan Doyle," *Nineteenth-Century Literature* 44, no. 3 (1989): 364–87, 367.

39. Beer, *Open Fields,* 108.

40. Jacques Derrida's treatment of the subject of metaphor's relationship to philosophical texts is in view here, specifically his argument that since the term *metaphor* is itself metaphorical, every definition will repeat the term to be defined. So, philosophy can never fully define nor control metaphor: "Classical rhetoric . . . cannot dominate, being enmeshed within it, the mass out of which the philosophical text takes shape. Metaphor is less in the philosophical text (and in the rhetorical text coordinated with it) than the philosophical text is within metaphor. And the latter can no longer receive its name from metaphysics, except by a catachresis." Jacques Derrida, *Margins of Philosophy,* trans. Alan Bass (Brighton: Harvester Press, 1982), 258.

41. J. Hillis Miller, *The Form of Victorian Fiction* (Notre Dame: University of Notre Dame Press, 1968), 118–19. Hillis Miller focuses on the well-known image of the pier-glass in *Middlemarch.* He suggests that the candle-flame which produces the effect of making random surface-scratches on the pier-glass appear to form a "concentric arrangement" might be thought to elucidate the role of the author in organizing characters and events into a social fabric. Similarly, Darwin's perception that nature can be truly represented by a tree might be an effect of his observational techniques.

42. James Krasner, *The Entangled Eye: Visual Perception and the Representation of Nature in Post-Darwinian Narrative* (New York: Oxford University Press, 1992), 5.

43. Ibid., 35.

44. Michel Foucault, *The Foucault Reader,* ed. Paul Rabinow (Harmondsworth: Penguin, 1986), 81.

45. Ibid., 83.

46. Darwin, *The Descent of Man*, 389.

47. Darwin, *Autobiography*, 54.

48. In his *Autobiography* Darwin intimates that at the time when the *Origin* was written he was a "theist," and that sometime later he became an "agnostic" (54).

49. Richard Bauckham, *The Climax of Prophecy: Studies on the Book of Revelation* (Edinburgh: T and T Clark, 1993), 233. Bauckham's argument, here, is that John sought to characterize faithfulness to Christ to the point of martyrdom as an active engagement with the forces of evil rather than as passive resistance, and that the military metaphor of apocalyptic tradition well served this purpose.

50. Beer, *Darwin's Plots*, 65.

51. Ibid., 90. Beer, at this point, is actually pointing out the features common to scientific theorizing and the making of fiction. While she does note the prophetic function of major scientific theories (also claimed by the novel—"which seeks to register emergent forms for consciousness before they are capable of manifesting themselves within a society"—91), she makes no mention of the apocalyptic affinities evident in her own description.

52. Henry Drummond, "The City Without a Church," in *The Greatest Thing in the World and Other Essays* (London: Collins, no date). Although I can find no publication date for this collection, the introduction suggests that a date between 1885 and 1890 is quite likely for the writing of "The City Without a Church." Page references to this work are given, henceforth, in the text.

53. St. George Mivart, *On the Genesis of Species* (London: Macmillan, 1871), 17.

54. Ibid., 5.

55. Adrian Desmond and James Moore, *Darwin* (Harmondsworth: Penguin, 1991), 585.

56. Ibid., 590.

57. Ibid., 591.

58. Ibid., 671.

59. Ibid., 675.

60. Ibid., 677.

61. Mathilde Blind, "The Red Sunsets, 1883," in *The Ascent of Man*, 155.

62. Owen Howell, *The Dream of the Opium Eater* (London: George King Matthews, c. 1850), 16.

NOTES TO CHAPTER 2

1. On the relation between order and chaos in apocalyptic literature, see Norman Cohn, *Cosmos, Chaos and the World to Come: The Ancient Roots of Apocalyptic Faith* (New Haven, CT: Yale University Press, 1993).

2. Robert Browning, "Christmas Eve," in *Browning: Poetical Works 1833–1864* (Oxford: Oxford University Press, 1970), 489–524, ll. 530–34.

3. John Mason Neale, "Jerusalem the Golden," in *The Victorians: An An-*

thology of Poetry and Poetics, ed. Valentine Cunningham (Oxford: Blackwell, 2000), 427–28, ll. 73–74.

4. Thomas Hardy, *Jude the Obscure* (London: Everyman, 1995), 21.

5. Elizabeth Barrett Browning, *Aurora Leigh* (Oxford: Oxford University Press, 1993), 9, ll. 954–64.

6. Prince Albert, speech at a banquet at the Mansion House, London, 1850, in *Culture and Society in Britain 1850–1890: A Source Book of Contemporary Writings,* ed. J. M. Golby (Oxford: Oxford University Press, 1987), 1–2.

7. Janet L. Larson, *Dickens and the Broken Scripture,* 188.

8. Charlotte Brontë, *Villette* (London: Penguin, 1979), 106.

9. Robert Buchanan, "The Cities," in Cunningham (ed.), 823–24.

10. Matthew Arnold, "Alaric at Rome," in *The Poems of Matthew Arnold,* ed. Kenneth Allott (London: Longmans, 1965), 3–12, 31, l. 182.

11. William Morris, *News from Nowhere,* in *Three Works by William Morris: News from Nowhere, The Pilgrims of Hope, A Dream of John Ball* (London: Lawrence and Wishart, 1973), 250.

12. David Carroll has read *Felix Holt* as an apocalyptic text, depicting a "world in crisis on the verge of revolution" in the years leading up to and following the 1832 Reform Act: "In all cases, whether of hope or despair, the moment of vision which makes choice possible arises from the collision of two world-views, one conformed to, one challenged or rebelled against. In political terms it represents the imminent collapse of a world, in personal terms the collapse of a world-view." David Carroll, *George Eliot and the Conflict of Interpretations: A Reading of the Novels* (Cambridge: Cambridge University Press, 1992), 232. See also Mary Wilson Carpenter, *George Eliot and the Landscape of Time: Narrative Form and Protestant Apocalyptic History* (Chapel Hill: University of North Carolina Press, 1986).

13. George Eliot, "In a London Drawingroom," in Cunningham (ed.), 499.

14. Charles Dickens, *Bleak House* (Harmondsworth: Penguin, 1971), 49.

15. Ibid., 81.

16. Ibid., 50.

17. Lyn Pykett, *Charles Dickens,* 130–31.

18. Charles Dickens, *The Uncommercial Traveller* (London: Mandarin, 1991), 146.

19. Ibid., 246–54, 247.

20. Timothy Clark, "Dickens through Blanchot: the nightmare fascination of a world without interiority," in *Dickens Refigured: Bodies, Desires and Other Histories,* ed. J. Schad (Manchester: Manchester University Press, 1996) 23–38, 35.

21. Ibid., 136.

22. Ibid., 136–37.

23. Ibid.

24. Ibid., 143.

25. Robert Crawford, "James Thomson and T. S. Eliot," *Victorian Poetry* 23, no. 1 (1985): 23–41; Edwin Morgan, introduction to *The City of Dreadful Night* by James Thomson (Edinburgh: Canongate, 1993), 7–24; William Sharpe, "Learning to Read *The City,*" *Victorian Poetry* no. 22, 1 (1984): 65–84.

26. James Thomson, "The Sleeper," in *The Poetical Works of James Thomson,* ed. Bertram Dobell (London: Reeves & Turner, 1895), 84.

27. Ibid., lxiii.

28. Sharpe, 68.

29. Ibid., 83.

30. James Thomson, "Insomnia," in *Poetical Works*, 225–32, ll. 1–4.

31. Ibid., 227, ll. 48–52.

32. Peter C. Noel-Bentley, " 'Fronting the Dreadful Mysteries of Time': Durer's *Melencolia* in Thomson's *City of Dreadful Night*," *Victorian Poetry* 12, no. 3 (1974): 193–203.

33. Noel-Bentley, 194.

34. Thomson, *Poetical Works*, 215, ll. 29–35.

35. James Thomson, "Sunday Up the River," in *The City of Dreadful Night and Other Poems* (London: Watts and Co, 1932), 47–64, 3.

36. For a discussion of the derivation of this image, see Michael R. Steele, "James Thomson's Angel and Sphinx: A Possible Source," *Victorian Poetry* 12, no. 4 (1974): 373–75.

37. Noel-Bentley, 197.

38. Ibid., 196.

39. On time, narrative, and the succession of generations, see Paul Ricoeur, *Time and Narrative*, trans. Kathleen Blamey and David Pellauer (Chicago: University of Chicago Press, 1988), 3:109ff.

40. Geoffrey Galt Harpham, *The Ascetic Imperative in Culture and Criticism* (Chicago: University of Chicago Press, 1987).

41. Crawford, 33.

42. Florence Nightingale, *Cassandra/Suggestions for Thought*, ed. Mary Poovey (London: Pickering and Chatto, 1991), 227. Page numbers for this book are given in the text from here on.

43. An extended version of this discussion of Nightingale's text can be found in my article "Passion of the Female Christ: The Gospel according to Cassandra," *Prose Studies* 21, no. 3 (1998): 69–88.

44. George P. Landow, "Aggressive (Re)interpretations of the Female Sage: Florence Nightingale's Cassandra," in *Victorian Sages and Cultural Discourse: Renegotiating Gender and Power*, ed. Thais E. Morgan (New Brunswick: Rutgers University Press, 1990) 32–45.

45. Jacques Derrida, *Specters of Marx: The State of the Debt, the Work of Mourning and the New International*, trans. Peggy Kamuf (New York: Routledge, 1994), 10, 50–51.

46. This is another misquotation of the biblical text. Acts 2:17 reads: "your sons and your daughters shall prophesy, and your young men shall see visions, and your old men shall dream dreams." This is a slight variation of Joel 2:28.

47. Nightingale, 214.

48. Donald Thomas, *The Victorian Underworld* (London: John Murray, 1998).

NOTES TO CHAPTER 3

1. Thomas Carlyle, *Sartor Resartus*, ed. Kerry McSweeney and Peter Sabor (Oxford: Oxford University Press, 1987), 195.

2. Ibid., 42.

3. Ibid., 193.

4. Ibid., 195.

5. Ibid., 196.

6. Ibid., 196–7.

7. Ibid., 197.

8. James Thomson, *The City of Dreadful Night* (Edinburgh: Canongate, 1993), 21, ll. 68–69.

9. Nathaniel Hawthorne, "The Minister's Black Veil," in *Nathaniel Hawthorne's Tales*, ed. James McIntosh (New York: Norton, 1987), 104.

10. Ibid., 106–7.

11. Edgar Allan Poe, from an unsigned review of *Twice Told Tales*, in Hawthorne, 331.

12. Charles Dickens, "The Black Veil," in *Sketches by Boz*, ed. Dennis Walder (London: Penguin, 1995), 428.

13. Ibid., 432.

14. Ibid., 433.

15. Alfred Tennyson, "The Two Voices," in *In Memoriam, Maud and Other Poems*, ed. John D. Jump (London : Everyman, 1974), 26–38, ll. 10–11.

16. Ibid., "The Two Voices," ll.445–47.

17. Tennyson, "In Memoriam," 56, ll. 27–28.

18. Christina Rosssetti, "Winter: My Secret," in *Christina Posseth: Selected Poems*, ed. C. H. Sisson (Manchester: Carcanet, 1984), 73.

19. Coventry Patmore, "The Paragon," in Cunningham (ed.), 557–58, ll. 25–28.

20. E. S. Dallas, *The Gay Science*, quoted in *The Nineteenth-Century Novel: A Critical Reader*, ed. Stephen Regan (London: Routledge, 2001), 57.

21. Ibid., 55.

22. James Henry, "Very Old Man," in *The New Oxford Book of Victorian Verse*, ed. Christopher Ricks (Oxford: Oxford University Press, 1987), 331.

23. Edward Fitzgerald's translation of "The Rubaiyat of Omar Khayyam," in Ricks (ed.), 345–55, 32, ll. 126–27.

24. Olive Schreiner, *The Story of an African Farm* (Harmondsworth: Penguin, 1939), 263.

25. Charlotte Brontë, *Jane Eyre*, ed. Q. D. Leavis (London: Penguin, 1966), 311.

26. Sandra M. Gilbert and Susan Gubar, *The Madwoman in the Attic* (New Haven, CT: Yale University Press, 1984), 359–60.

27. Emily Brontë, *Wuthering Heights*, ed. Pauline Nestor (London: Penguin, 1995), 122.

28. Mary Elizabeth Braddon, *Lady Audley's Secret*, ed. David Skilton (Oxford: Oxford University Press, 1988), 253.

29. Mrs Henry Wood, *East Lynne*, ed. Norman Page and Kamal Al-Solaylee (London: Everyman, 1994), 397.

30. Carlyle, 57; George Eliot, *Middlemarch*, ed. W. J. Harvey (Harmondsworth: Penguin, 1965), 111.

31. Eliot, *Middlemarch*, 74, 448, 574, 581.

32. Ibid., 177.

33. Ibid., 297.

34. Ibid., 170.

35. Carlyle, 67.

36. Christina G. Rossetti, *The Face of the Deep: A Devotional Commentary on the Apocalypse* [1892], 3rd ed. (London: SPCK, 1895). These are the opening words of the book, contained in a prefatory note. Page references for this volume are given in the text.

37. The issue of gendered interpretation is never dealt with explicitly in *The Face of the Deep*, but there are points at which it appears to be implied: "The curiosity of Eve brought sin into the world . . . Curiosity may have seduced Lot's wife into looking back. . . . These two instances suggest Curiosity as a feminine weak point inviting temptation, and doubly likely to facilitate a fall when to indulge it a woman affects independence. Thus we see Eve assume the initiative with Adam, and Lot's wife take her own way behind her husband's back" (520). This investment in the mythical origins of female dependence has clear ramifications for Rossetti as a female interpreter; "ever to write modestly under correction" (177, 415) is her avowed aim, and one suspects that such correction is likely to be of male provenance. An appeal to the words of a preacher who once impressed her gives the same impression: "That preacher's authority sanctions (I hope) what I endeavoured to think out on a former text (ch. i, ver. 4)," 154.

38. Dolores Rosenblum, "Christina Rossetti: The Inward Pose," in *Shakespeare's Sisters: Feminist Essays on Women Poets*, ed. Sandra M. Gilbert and Susan Gubar (Bloomington: Indiana University Press, 1979), 83.

39. Of course, Rossetti's use of veils and her fascination with the relationship between surfaces and depths has a certain Freudian dimension. This is clear in lines from Rossetti's poem "The Heart Knoweth its Own Bitterness" (1857), which are reminiscent of the erotic mysticism of Teresa of Avila and St. John of the Cross:

> I long for one to stir my deep—
> I have had enough of help and gift—
> I long for one to search and sift
> Myself, to take myself and keep.
>
> You scratch my surface with your pin,
> You stroke me smooth with hushing breath:—
> Nay pierce, nay probe, nay dig within,
> Probe my quick core and sound my depth.

The poem ends with the recognition that the fulfilment sought will not be available to the seeker in this world where "harvests fail" and where "breaks the heart"; only complete union with Christ will suffice: "I full of Christ and Christ of me." Its complaint of superficiality in the addressee's response, contrasted with satiety in communion with Christ, sets up an opposition between movement across a surface and penetration into an interior depth, in a gesture which equates truth with depth, and surfaces with dissimulation.

40. Christina G. Rossetti, "L. E. L.," in *Poetical Works*, ed. William Michael Rossetti (London: Macmillan, 1904), 344–45.

41. Christina G. Rossetti, "In Progress," in *Poetical Works*, 352.

42. On this reading of Revelation see Richard Bauckham, *The Climax of Prophecy: Studies on the Book of Revelation* (Edinburgh: T and T Clark, 1993), especially chapter 10: "The Economic Critique of Rome in Revelation 18."

43. Both Lona Packer and Jan Marsh, in their respective biographies, note the biographical significance of Rossetti's condemnation of spiritualism in *The Face of the Deep*. Packer writes: "The interest in 'spirit-rapping' had started in England in the 1850s and had reached a fashionable climax in the mid-sixties. . . . Both William and Gabriel [Christina's brothers] attended the fashionable seances of the American Davenport brothers, who in 1864 were 'electrifying London' by their amazing psychic feats. Of them all, Christina alone was not taken in. Upon hearing her brothers' reports of the seances, she suspected what later turned out to be the case, that 'simple imposture' was the "missing key" to the inexplicable." Lona Mosk Packer, *Christina Rossetti* (Berkeley: University of California Press, 1963), 212.

Commenting on the same events Jan Marsh notes Rossetti's fondness of Robert Browning's "Mr Sludge the Medium," a poem attacking Daniel Home—an infamous hoaxer of communication with the dead, *Christina Rossetti: A Literary Biography* (London: Jonathan Cape, 1994), 340.

44. P. G. Stanwood, "Christina Rossetti's Devotional Prose," in *The Achievement of Christina Rossetti*, ed. David A. Kent (Ithaca: Cornell University Press, 1987), 226.

45. See, for example, the anecdotes on 174–75 and 470.

46. Marsh, 550.

47. The tendency to interpret passages of politico-economic significance in terms of individual morality is exemplified by Rossetti's treatment of allusions to Rome (as already discussed), and by her comments on the Apocalyptic famine (Rev. 6): "When the pinch of famine comes they will be prepared to bear it who already for charity's sake have learned and practiced to suffer hunger. They who have kept the Fast of God's choosing by dealing their bread to the hungry will even in extremity know Whom they have trusted" (202). Again, when pondering the destruction of a third of the world's ships (Rev. 8:9), Rossetti judges commercial interests as though they were indices of individual moral failings: ". . . ships by association suggest commerce; and commerce, alas! too often covetousness. Or if we turn to war-ships, stubbornness seems only too probable in connection with them" (251).

48. Rosenblum, 82.

49. Marsh, 260.

50. Christina G. Rossetti, *Commonplace and Other Short Stories* (London: F. S. Ellis, 1870).

51. William Thackeray, *Vanity Fair*, ed. J. I. M. Stewart (London: Penguin, 1968), 100.

52. Hugh Stutfield, "Tommyrotics," *Blackwood's Magazine* 157 (1895), 836.

53. John Ruskin, *Unto This Last and Other Writings*, ed. Clive Wilmer (London: Penguin, 1985), 228.

54. W. David Shaw, *The Lucid Veil: Poetic Truth in the Victorian Age* (London: Athlone, 1987), 141.

55. Matthew Arnold, "Empedocles on Etna," in *The Poems of Matthew Arnold*, ed. Kenneth Allott (London: Longmans, 1965), 147–94, ll. 276–354.

56. James Longenbach, "Matthew Arnold and the Modern Apocalypse," *PMLA* 104 (1989), 849.

NOTES TO CHAPTER 4

1. Carlyle, 197.

2. F. M. L. Thompson, "The Revolution in World Agriculture," in *The Nineteenth Century: The Contradictions of Progress*, ed. Asa Briggs (London: Thames and Hudson, 1970), 159.

3. Charles Dickens, *Dombey and Son*, ed. Peter Fairclough (London: Penguin, 1970), 120–21.

4. Ibid., 982–83 n. 2

5. Ibid., 483.

6. Ibid., 869.

7. Ibid., 871.

8. Alfred Tennyson, *In Memoriam, Maud and Other Poems*, ed. John D. Jump (London: Everyman, 1974), 105.

9. John Clare, "Sonnet: I am," in *The New Oxford Book of Victorian Verse*, ed. Christopher Ricks (Oxford: Oxford University Press, 1987), 173.

10. Howard Babb, "Setting and Theme in *Far From the Madding Crowd*," quoted in Ian Gregor, *The Great Web: The Form of Hardy's Major Fiction* (London: Faber and Faber, 1974), 50.

11. Gregor, 49.

12. Thomas Hardy, *Far From the Madding Crowd* (London: Macmillan, 1965), 2. Page numbers for this edition are given in the text from here on.

13. On the question of gender politics in relation to *Far From the Madding Crowd*, see, for example, Rosemarie Morgan, *Women and Sexuality in the Novels of Thomas Hardy* (London: Routledge, 1988), especially chapter 2, 30–57; Linda M. Shires, "Narrative, Gender, and Power in *Far From the Madding Crowd*," in *The Sense of Sex: Feminist Perspectives on Hardy*, ed. Margaret R. Higgonet (Urbana: University of Illinois Press, 1993), 49–65.

14. Peter J. Casagrande, "A New View of Bathsheba Everdene," in *Critical Approaches to the Fiction of Thomas Hardy*, ed. Dale Kramer (London: Macmillan, 1974), 50–73.

15. Geoffrey Harvey, *The Complete Critical Guide to Thomas Hardy* (London: Routledge, 2003), 62.

16. H. G. Wells, *The Time Machine* (London: Everyman, 1995). Page numbers for this edition are given in the text.

17. Peter Kemp, *H. G. Wells and the Culminating Ape: Biological Themes and Imaginative Obsessions* (London: Macmillan, 1982), 34.

18. T. H. Huxley, "Prolegomena to 'Evolution and Ethics,'" in *Evolution and Ethics, 1893–1943*, ed. T. H. Huxley and Julian Huxley (London: The Pilot Press, 1894), 52.

19. Kemp, 7.

20. Ibid., 39.

21. John Huntington, *The Logic of Fantasy: H. G. Wells and Science Fiction* (New York: Columbia University Press, 1982), 177, n. 6.

22. Alfred Tennyson, *In Memoriam*, 105.

23. The story of Jesus's purging of the temple can be found in all four gospels: Matthew 21:12–13; Mark 11:15–17; Luke 19:45–46; John 2:13–16.

24. Bernard Bergonzi, "*The Time Machine:* An Ironic Myth," in *H. G. Wells: A Collection of Critical Essays,* ed. Bernard Bergonzi (Englewood Cliffs, NJ: Prentice-Hall, 1976), 48.

25. Patrick Parrinder, *Shadows of the Future: H. G. Wells, Science Fiction and Prophecy* (Liverpool: Liverpool University Press, 1995), 49. The story of Nebuchadnezzar's metamorphosis into a "beast of the field" can be found in the book of Daniel, chapter 4.

26. H. G. Wells, "Zoological Regression," *The Gentleman's Magazine* 271, (1891): 253.

27. Charles Darwin, *The Origin of Species*, ed. Gillian Beer (Oxford: Oxford University Press, 1996), 395.

28. T. H. Huxley, "Evolution and Ethics" (1893), in Huxley and Huxley (ed.), 83. On the subject of evolutionary degeneration in *The Time Machine*, see Parrinder, 49–64; see also Robert M. Philmus, "The Logic of 'Prophecy' in *The Time Machine*," in Bergonzi (ed.), 56–68.

29. The hymn is "Crown him with many crowns," by Matthew Bridges (1800–94), revised by Godfrey Thring (1823–1903).

30. H. G. Wells, *The Future in America: A Search after Realities* (London: Chapman and Hall, 1906), 10.

31. Frank Kermode, *The Sense of an Ending: Studies in the Theory of Fiction* (London: Oxford University Press, 1967), 162.

32. Paul Ricoeur, *Time and Narrative*, trans. Kathleen McLaughlin and David Pellauer (Chicago and London: University of Chicago Press, 1984), 1:3.

33. Darwin, *Origin of Species*, 394.

34. Northrop Frye, *The Great Code* (London: Routledge and Kegan Paul, 1982), 171.

35. Kermode, 45.

36. Ibid., 58.

37. George Eliot, *Daniel Deronda*, ed. Barbara Hardy (Harmondsworth: Penguin, 1967), 35.

38. Sally Shuttleworth, *George Eliot and Nineteenth-Century Science: The Make-Believe of a Beginning* (Cambridge: Cambridge University Press, 1984); Gillian Beer, *Open Fields: Science in Cultural Encounter* (Oxford: Clarendon, 1996).

39. Diana Postlethwaite, "George Eliot and Science," in *The Cambridge Companion to George Eliot*, ed. George Levine (Cambridge: Cambridge University Press, 2001), 110.

40. Shuttleworth, 175.

41. Ibid., 14–15.

42. See Jacques Derrida, "Khora," trans. Ian MacLeod, in *On the Name*, ed. Thomas Dutoit (Stanford: Stanford University Press, 1995), 87–127. Focusing on Plato's *Timaeus*, Derrida considers his notion of *khora*. Plato uses this term

to denominate the space, place, or void in which the sensible world replicates the eternal, intelligible forms. Like the ideal Forms, this non-location is always already there, and yet it is not eternal as they are. But neither is it temporal in the way that sensible objects are. It belongs, then, to neither realm: it cannot be perceived by the senses and is not fully apprehensible by reason.

Notes to Chapter 5

1. On Joachim of Fiore see M. Reeves, "The Bible and Literary Authorship in the Middle Ages," in *Reading the Text: Biblical Criticism and Literary Theory*, ed. S. Prickett (London: Blackwell, 1991), 12–63; "Pattern and Purpose in History in the Later Medieval and Renaissance Periods," in *Apocalypse Theory and the Ends of the World*, ed. M. Bull (Oxford: Blackwell, 1995), 90–111.

2. Owen Chadwick, *The Victorian Church* (London: A and C Black, 1966, 1970), 35–36.

3. Ibid., 36.

4. Ibid., 437.

5. Ibid., 451.

6. Ibid.

7. W. David Shaw, *The Lucid Veil: Poetic Truth in the Victorian Age* (London: Athlone, 1987).

8. Shaw, 122.

9. Ibid., 122.

10. Ibid., 223.

11. Alfred Tennyson, "St Simeon Stylites," in *In Memoriam, Maud and Other Poems*, ed. John D. Jump (London: Everyman, 1974), 39–43; Robert Browning, "Bishop Blougram's Apology," in *The Poems, Volume One*, ed. J. Pettigrew and T. J. Collins (London: Penguin, 1981), 617–42.

12. Arthur Hugh Clough, "That there are powers," in *A Choice of Clough's Verse*, selected by Michael Thorpe (London: Faber and Faber, 1969), 373.

13. Christina Rossetti, "A Christmas Carol," in *Christina Rossetti: Selected Poems*, ed. C. H. Sisson (Manchester: Carcanet, 1984), 125–27.

14. Anne Brontë, *The Tenant of Wildfell Hall*, ed. G. D. Hargreaves (London: Penguin, 1979), 172.

15. Emily Brontë, *Wuthering Heights*, ed. Pauline Nestor (London: Penguin, 1995), 20.

16. Sandra Gilbert and Susan Gubar, *The Madwoman in the Attic* (New Haven, CT: Yale University Press, 1984), 365.

17. Valentine Cunningham, *In The Reading Gaol* (Cambridge, MA: Blackwell Publishers, 1994), 356.

18. Brontë, Charlotte. *Jane Eyre*, ed. Q. D. Leavis (London: Penguin, 1966), 477. Page references for this edition are given in the text from this point on.

19. Cunningham, 358.

20. Mary Poovey, "The Anathematized Race: The Governess and *Jane Eyre*," in *The Nineteenth-Century Novel: A Critical Reader*, ed. S. Regan (London: Routledge, 2001), 195.

21. Cunningham, 345.

22. Corelli openly stated her commitment to the supernatural in an article in the *Idler:* "I feel the existence of the supernatural, and feeling it, I must speak of it. I understand that the religion we profess to follow emanates from the supernatural. And I presume that churches exist for the solemn worship of the supernatural. Wherefore, if the supernatural be thus universally acknowledged as a guide for thought and morals, I fail to see why I, and as many others as choose to do so, should not write on the subject." Quoted in Thomas F. G. Coates and R. S. Warren Bell, *Marie Corelli: The Writer and the Woman* (London: Hutchinson and Co., 1903), 46–47.

23. On Corelli's relationship to modernism, see R. B. Kershner, "Modernism's Mirror: The Sorrows of Marie Corelli," in *Transforming Genres,* ed. Nikki Lee Manos and Meri-Jane Rochelson (New York: St. Martin's Press, 1994), 67–86.

24. Marie Corelli, *The Sorrows of Satan,* ed. Peter Keating (Oxford: Oxford University Press, 1895), 5. Page references for this edition are given in the text from this point on.

25. Brian Masters, *Now Barabbas was a Rotter: The Extraordinary Life of Marie Corelli* (London: Hamish Hamilton, 1978), 143.

26. Annette R. Federico, *Idol of Suburbia: Marie Corelli and Late Victorian Literary Culture* (Charlottesville: University Press of Virginia, 2000), 2–3.

27. Kershner, 80–81.

28. Coates and Bell, 168.

29. Corelli had already envisaged a spatialized apocalypse in *Ardath* (1889). In that novel the city of Al-Kyris is destroyed for its atheism and republicanism and its practice of an empty formal religion. The city is projected as existing in a parallel world, which enables the protagonist (Theos) to witness it and yet to survive it and to escape back to his own world.

30. On the Victorian woman's "sphere," see Lyn Pykett, *The "Improper" Feminine: The Woman's Sensation Novel and the New Woman Writing* (London: Routledge, 1992).

Notes to Conclusion

1. Alexander Welsh, *The City of Dickens* (Oxford: Oxford University Press, 1971), 213–14.

2. Ibid., 214.

3. Ibid., 217.

4. Janet L. Larson, *Dickens and the Broken Scripture* (Athens, GA: The University of Georgia Press, 1985).

5. David Carroll, *George Eliot and the Conflict of Interpretations: A Reading of the Novels* (Cambridge: Cambridge University Press, 1992), 201.

6. Ibid., 233.

7. Frank Kermode, *The Sense of an Ending: Studies in the Theory of Fiction.* (London: Oxford University Press, 1967).

8. Jacques Derrida, "Of an Apocalyptic Tone Recently Adopted in Philosophy," trans. John P. Leavy, Jr., *Oxford Literary Review* 6, no. 2 (1984): 3–37.

9. W. David Shaw, *The Lucid Veil: Poetic Truth in the Victorian Age* (London: Athlone, 1987).

10. Luce Irigaray, "Sexual Difference," trans. Sean Hand, in *The Irigaray Reader*, ed. Margaret Whitford (Oxford: Blackwell, 1991), 167.

11. Margaret Whitford, *Irigaray*, 157.

12. Alice Jardine, "Introduction to Julia Kristeva's 'Women's Time,'" *Signs: Journal of Women in Culture and Society* 7, no. 1 (1981): 9.

13. Julia Kristeva, "Women's Time," trans. Alice Jardine and Harry Blake. *Signs: Journal of Women in Culture and Society* 7, no. 1 (1981): 13–35.

14. Ibid., 17.

15. Ibid., 33.

16. I have dealt at length with the hermeneutics of the letter and the spirit in Christian interpretation in Kevin Mills, *Justifying Language: Paul and Contemporary Literary Theory* (London: Macmillan, 1995).

17. Derrida, 27.

Bibliography

Aarsleff, Hans. *The Study of Language in England, 1780–1860.* Minneapolis: University of Minnesota Press, 1983.

Abel, Elizabeth, ed.. *Writing and Sexual Difference.* Brighton: Harvester Press, 1982.

Armstrong, Isobel. *Victorian Poetry: Poetry, Poetics and Politics.* London: Routledge, 1993.

Arnold, Matthew. *The Poems of Matthew Arnold.* Edited by Kenneth Allott. London: Longmans, 1965.

———. *Culture and Anarchy.* Edited by J. Dover Wilson. Cambridge: Cambridge University Press, 1932.

———. *Selected Prose.* Edited by P. J. Keating. London: Viking Penguin, 1970.

Aune, David E. *The New Testament in Its Literary Environment.* Cambridge: James Clarke and Co., 1988.

Austin, Linda M. "James Thomson's Elegy and 'Human Unsuccess.'" *Victorian Poetry* 32, no. 1 (1994): 21–34.

Bailin, Miriam. *The Sick Room in Victorian Fiction: The Art of Being Ill.* Cambridge: Cambridge University Press, 1994.

Baltazar, Lisa. "The Critique of Anglican Biblical Scholarship in George Eliot's *Middlemarch.*" *Literature and Theology* 15, no. 1 (2001): 40–60.

Barr, James. *Biblical Words for Time.* 2nd ed. London: SCM, 1969.

Bauckham, Richard. *The Climax of Prophecy: Studies on the Book of Revelation.* Edinburgh: T and T Clark, 1993.

———. *The Theology of the Book of Revelation.* Cambridge: Cambridge University Press, 1993.

Baudrillard, Jean. *The Illusion of the End.* Translated Chris Turner. Cambridge: Polity Press, 1994.

Beer, Gavin de, ed. *Charles Darwin, Thomas Henry Huxley: Autobiographies.* London: Oxford University Press, 1974.

Beer, Gillian. *Darwin's Plots: Evolutionary Narrative in Darwin, George Eliot and Nineteenth-Century Fiction.* London: Routledge and Kegan Paul, 1983.

———. *Open Fields: Science in Cultural Encounter.* Oxford: Clarendon, 1996.

Bell, Mackenzie. *Christina Rossetti: A Biographical and Critical Study.* London: Thomas Burleigh, 1898.'

213

Benz, Ernst. *Evolution and Christian Hope: Man's Concept of the Future from the Early Fathers to Teilhard de Chardin.* Translated by Heinz G. Frank. London: Victor Gollancz, 1967.

Bergonzi, Bernard, ed. *H. G. Wells: A Collection of Critical Essays.* Englewood Cliffs, NJ: Prentice-Hall, 1976.

Best, Geoffrey. *Mid-Victorian Britain, 1851–75.* London: Fontana, 1979.

Blind, Mathilde. *The Ascent of Man.* London: Chatto and Windus,1889.

Bloom, Harold. *Shelley's Mythmaking.* New York: Cornell University Press, 1969.

Braddon, Mary Elizabeth. *Lady Audley's Secret.* Edited David Skilton. Oxford: Oxford University Press, 1988.

Brake, Laurel, ed. *Essays and Studies 1995: The Endings of Epochs.* Cambridge: D. S. Brewer, 1995.

Brantlinger, Patrick, and William B. Thesing, eds. *A Companion to the Victorian Novel.* Malden, MA; Oxford: Blackwell Publishing, 2002.

Breen, Jennifer, ed. *Victorian Women Poets 1830–1900: An Anthology.* London: Everyman,1994.

Briggs, Asa (ed.). *The Nineteenth Century: The Contradictions of Progress.* London: Thames and Hudson, 1970.

Bristow, Joseph, ed. *Victorian Women Poets.* London: Macmillan, 1995.

Brome, Vincent. *H. G. Wells: A Biography.* Westport, CT: Greenwood Press, 1951.

Brontë, Charlotte. *Jane Eyre.* Edited by Q. D. Leavis. London: Penguin, 1966.

———. *Shirley.* Edited by Andrew and Judith Hook. Harmondsworth: Penguin, 1974.

———. *Villette.* Edited by Mark Lilly. London: Penguin, 1979.

Brontë, Emily. *Wuthering Heights.* Edited by Pauline Nestor. London: Penguin, 1995.

Brontë, Anne. *Agnes Grey.* Edited by Anne Smith. London: Everyman, 1991.

———. *The Tenant of Wildfell Hall.* Edited by G. D. Hargreaves. London: Penguin, 1979.

Brown, P. *The Rise of Western Christendom: Triumph and Diversity AD 200— 1000.* Oxford: Blackwell, 1996.

Brown, Richard. *Change and Continuity in British Society, 1800–1850.* Cambridge: Cambridge University Press, 1987.

Browning, Elizabeth Barrett. *Aurora Leigh.* Edited by Kerry McSweeney. Oxford: Oxford University Press, 1993.

Browning, Robert. *Browning: Poetical Works: 1833–1864.* Edited by Ian Jack. Oxford: Oxford University Press, 1970.

———. *The Poems, Volume One.* Edited by J. Pettigrew and T.J. Collins. London: Penguin, 1981.

Bull, Malcolm, ed. *Apocalypse Theory and the Ends of the World.* Oxford: Blackwell, 1995.

Butler, Samuel. *The Way of All Flesh.* Edited by R.A. Streatfield. London: Jonathan Cape, 1932.

Caird, G. B. *A Commentary on the Revelation of St. John the Divine.* London: A and C Black, 1966.

Campbell, Ian. " 'And I Burn Too': Thomson's *City of Dreadful Night.*" *Victorian Poetry* 16, no. 1–2 (1978): 123–33.

Carlyle, Gavin. *The Battle of Unbelief.* London: Hodder and Stoughton, 1878.

Carlyle, Thomas. *Sartor Resartus.* Edited by Kerry McSweeney and Peter Sabor. Oxford: Oxford University Press, 1987.

Carpenter, Mary Wilson. *George Eliot and the Landscape of Time: Narrative Form and Protestant Apocalyptic History.* Chapel Hill: University of North Carolina Press, 1986.

Carroll, David. *George Eliot and the Conflict of Interpretations: A Reading of the Novels.* Cambridge: Cambridge University Press, 1992.

Chadwick, Henry. *The Early Church.* Harmondsworth: Penguin, 1967.

Chadwick, Owen. *The Victorian Church.* 2 vols. London: A and C Black, 1966, 1970.

Charles, Edna Kotin. *Christina Rossetti: Critical Perspectives, 1862–1982.* Selinsgrove, PA: Susquehanna University Press, a1985.

Charles, R. H. *A Critical and Exegetical Commentary on the Revelation of St. John.* 2 vols. Edinburgh: T and T Clark, 1920.

Charlesworth, James H., ed. *The Old Testament Pseudepigrapha.* Vol. 1, *Apocalyptic Literature and Testaments.* New York: Doubleday, 1983.

Clough, Arthur Hugh. *A Choice of Clough's Verse.* Selected by Michael Thorpe. London: Faber and Faber, 1969.

Coates, Thomas F. G. and R. S. Warren Bell. *Marie Corelli: The Writer and the Woman.* London: Hutchinson and Co., 1903.

Cohn, Norman. *Cosmos, Chaos and the World to Come: The Ancient Roots of Apocalyptic Faith.* New Haven, CT: Yale University Press, 1993.

———. *The Pursuit of the Millennium: Revolutionary Millenarians and Mystical Anarchists of the Middle Ages.* New York: Oxford University Press, 1970.

Collins, John J. *The Apocalyptic Imagination: An Introduction to the Jewish Matrix of Christianity.* New York: Crossroad, 1989.

———. *Apocalypticism in the Dead Sea Scrolls.* London: Routledge, 1997.

Corelli, Marie. *The Sorrows of Satan.* Edited by Peter Keating. Oxford: Oxford University Press, 1895.

Corcoran, Paul. *Awaiting Apocalypse.* Houndmills: Macmillan, 2000.

Cox, Michael, ed. *Victorian Detective Stories.* Oxford: Oxford University Press, 1993.

Crawford, Robert. "James Thomson and T.S. Eliot." *Victorian Poetry* 23, no. 1 (1985): 23–41.

Crosby, Christina. *The Ends of History: Victorians and "The Woman Question."* New York: Routledge, 1991.

Cunningham, Valentine. *In The Reading Gaol: Postmodernity, Texts, and History.* Cambridge, MA: Blackwell Publishers, 1994.

———, ed. *The Victorians: An Anthology of Poetry and Poetics.* Oxford and Malden: Blackwell, 2000.

Darwin, Charles. *The Origin of Species.* Edited by Gillian Beer. Oxford: Oxford University Press, 1996.

———. *The Descent of Man, and Selection in Relation to Sex.* London: John Murray, 1871.

Darwin, Charles. *The Autobiography of Charles Darwin.* Edited by Nora Barlow. London: Colllins, 1958.

Darwin, Francis, ed. *The Life and Letters of Charles Darwin.* London: John Murray, 1888.

David, Deirdre. *Fictions of Resolution in Three Victorian Novels: North and South, Our Mutual Friend, Daniel Deronda.* London: Macmillan, 1981.

Dellamora, Richard. *Apocalyptic Overtures: Sexual Politics and the Sense of an Ending.* New Brunswick: Rutgers University Press, 1994.

Derrida, Jacques. *Of Grammatology.* Translated by G. C. Spivak. Baltimore: Johns Hopkins University Press, 1976.

———. *Margins of Philosophy.* Trans. Alan Bass. Brighton: Harvester Press, 1982.

———. "Of an Apocalyptic Tone Recently Adopted in Philosophy." Translated by John P. Leavy, Jr. *Oxford Literary Review* 6, 2 (1984): 3–37.

———. *Specters of Marx: The State of the Debt, the Work of Mourning and the New International.* Translated by Peggy Kamuf. New York: Routledge, 1994.

———. *On the Name.* Edited by Thomas Dutoit. Stanford: Stanford University Press, 1995.

Desmond, Adrian, and James Moore. *Darwin.* Harmondsworth: Penguin, 1991.

Dickens, Charles. *Sketches by Boz.* Edited by Dennis Walder. London: Penguin, 1995.

———. *Dombey and Son.* Edited by Peter Fairclough. London: Penguin, 1970.

———. *Bleak House.* Edited by Norman Page. Harmondsworth: Penguin, 1971.

———. *The Uncommercial Traveller.* London: Mandarin, 1991.

Dowie, Menie Muriel. *Gallia.* Edited by Helen Small. London: Everyman, 1995.

Drummond, Henry. *The Greatest Thing in the World and Other Essays.* London: Collins, no date.

Egerton, George. *Keynotes and Discords.* London: Virago, 1983.

Eliot, George. *Middlemarch.* Edited by W. J. Harvey. Harmondsworth: Penguin: Viking Penguin, 1965.

———. *Daniel Deronda.* Edited by Barbara Hardy. Harmondsworth: Penguin, 1967.

———. *Selected Essays, Poems and Other Writings.* Edited by A. S. Byatt and Nicholas Warren. London: Penguin, 1990.

Federico, Annette R. *Idol of Suburbia: Marie Corelli and Late Victorian Literary Culture*. Charlottesville: University Press of Virginia, 2000.

Ford, J. Massyngberde. *The Anchor Bible Commentary on Revelation*. New York: Doubleday, 1975.

Frank, Lawrence. "Reading the Gravel Page: Lyell, Darwin, and Conan Doyle." *Nineteenth-Century Literature* 44, no. 3 (1989): 364–87.

Frankfort, H., et al., eds. *Before Philosophy: The Intellectual Adventure of Ancient Man*. Harmondsworth: Penguin, 1963.

Frye, Northrop. *The Great Code*. London: Routledge and Kegan Paul, 1982.

Gantz, Jeffrey, trans. *Early Irish Myths and Sagas*. Harmondsworth: Penguin, 1981.

Gaskell, Elizabeth. *Cranford and Cousin Phyllis*. Edited by Peter Keating. Harmondsworth: Penguin, 1976.

———. *North and South*. Edited by Angus Easson. Oxford: Oxford University Press, 1982.

———. *Mary Barton*. Edited Stephen Gill. Harmondsworth: Penguin, 1970.

George, Andrew, trans. *The Epic of Gilgamesh*. London: Penguin, 1999.

George, Wilma. *Darwin*. Glasgow: Fontana, 1982.

Gerratana, Valentino. "Marx and Darwin." *New Left Review*, 82 (1973): 60–82.

Gilbert, Sandra M., and Susan Gubar. *The Madwoman in the Attic: The Woman Writer and the Nineteenth-Century Literary Imagination*. New Haven, CT: Yale University Press, 1984.

———, eds. *Shakespeare's Sisters: Feminist Essays on Women Poets*. Bloomington: Indiana University Press, 1979.

Gilmour, Robin. *The Novel in the Victorian Age: A Modern Introduction*. London: Arnold, 1986.

———. *The Victorian Period: The Intellectual and Cultural Context of English Literature, 1830–1890*. London: Longman, 1993.

Gissing, George. *The Nether World*. Edited by Stephen Gill. Oxford: Oxford University Press, 1992.

Glasson, T. F. *The Revelation of John*. Cambridge: Cambridge University Press, 1965.

Golby, J. M., ed. *Culture and Society in Britain 1850–1890: A Source Book of Contemporary Writings*. Oxford: Oxford University Press, 1987.

Gregor, Ian. *The Great Web: The Form of Hardy's Major Fiction*. London: Faber and Faber, 1974.

Hand, Sean, ed. *The Levinas Reader*. Oxford: Blackwell, 1989.

Hardy, Barbara. *Forms of Feeling in Victorian Fiction*. London: Methuen, 1986.

Hardy, Thomas. *Far From the Madding Crowd*. London: Macmillan, 1965.

———. *Jude the Obscure*. Edited byTimothy Hands. London: Everyman, 1995.

Harpham, Geoffrey Galt. *The Ascetic Imperative in Culture and Criticism*. Chicago: University of Chicago Press, 1987.

Harvey, Geoffrey. *The Complete Critical Guide to Thomas Hardy*. London: Routledge, 2003.

Hawthorne, Nathaniel. *Nathaniel Hawthorne's Tales.* Edited by James McIntosh. New York: Norton, 1987.

Herrin, J. *The Formation of Christendom.* Oxford: Blackwell, 1987.

Higgonet, Margaret R., ed. *The Sense of Sex: Feminist Perspectives on Hardy.* Urbana: University of Illinois Press, 1993.

Hippolytus, *The Writings of Hippolytus I.* Edited by Rev. A. Roberts and J. Donaldson. Translated by Rev. J. H. Macmahon and Rev. S. D. F. Salmond. Edinburgh: T and T Clark, 1868.

Houghton, Walter E. *The Victorian Frame of Mind, 1830–1870.* New Haven, CT: Yale University Press, 1957.

Howell, Owen. *The Dream of the Opium Eater.* London: George King Matthews, c. 1850.

Hughes, Philip Edgecumbe. *The Book of the Revelation: A Commentary.* Leicester: IVP, 1990.

Huntington, John. *The Logic of Fantasy: H. G. Wells and Science Fiction.* New York: Columbia University Press, 1982.

Huxley, T. H. "The Physical Basis of Life." *The Fortnightly Review,* Feb. 1869.

Huxley, T. H. and Julian Huxley. *Evolution and Ethics, 1893–1943.* London: The Pilot Press, 1894.

Irigaray, Luce. *The Irigaray Reader.* Edited by Margaret Whitford. Oxford: Blackwell, 1991.

Jardine, Alice. "Introduction to Julia Kristeva's 'Women's Time.'" *Signs: Journal of Women in Culture and Society* 7, no. 1 (1981): 5–12.

Joeres, Ruth-Ellen Boetcher, and Elizabeth Mittman, eds. *The Politics of the Essay.* Bloomington: Indiana University Press, 1993.

Johnson, P. *A History of Christianity.* London: Weidenfeld and Nicholson, 1976.

Jordan, John O., ed. *The Cambridge Companion to Charles Dickens.* Cambridge: Cambridge University Press, 2001.

Judge, Edwin A. "The Mark of the Beast, Revelation 13:16." *Tyndale Bulletin* 42, no. 1 (1991): 158–60.

Kacher, Robert M. "Repositioning the Female Christian Reader: Christina Rossetti as Tractarian Hermeneut in *The Face of the Deep.*" *Victorian Poetry* 35, no. 2 (1997): 193–214.

Kahane, Claire. *Passions of the Voice: Hysteria, Narrative, and the Figure of the Speaking Woman, 1850–1915.* Baltimore: The Johns Hopkins University Press, 1995.

Kemp, Peter. *H. G. Wells and the Culminating Ape: Biological Themes and Imaginative Obsessions.* London: Macmillan, 1982.

Kent, David A., ed. *The Achievement of Christina Rossetti.* Ithaca: Cornell University Press, 1987.

Kermode, Frank. *The Sense of an Ending: Studies in the Theory of Fiction.* London: Oxford University Press, 1967.

Kramer, Dale, ed. *Critical Approaches to the Fiction of Thomas Hardy*. London: Macmillan, 1974.

Krasner, James. *The Entangled Eye: Visual Perception and the Representation of Nature in Post-Darwinian Narrative*. Oxford: Oxford University Press, 1992.

Kristeva, Julia. "Women's Time." Translated by Alice Jardine and Harry Blake. *Signs: Journal of Women in Culture and Society* 7, no. 1 (1981): 13–35.

Larson, Janet L. *Dickens and the Broken Scripture*. Athens, GA: The University of Georgia Press, 1985.

Lawton, David. *Faith, Text and History: The Bible in English*. New York: Harvester Wheatsheaf, 1990.

Ledger, Sally, and Roger Luckhurst, eds. *The Fin de Siècle: A Reader in Cultural History c. 1880–1900*. Oxford: Oxford University Press, 2000.

Leighton, Angela. *Victorian Women Poets: Writing Against the Heart*. New York: Harvester Wheatsheaf, 1992.

Levine, George. *The Cambridge Companion to George Eliot*. Cambridge: Cambridge University Press, 2001.

Longenbach, James. "Matthew Arnold and the Modern Apocalypse." *PMLA* 104 (1989): 844–55.

Luckhurst, Roger, ed. *Late Victorian Gothic Tales*. Oxford: Oxford University Press, 2005.

Manos, Nikki Lee, and Meri-Jane Rochelson, eds. *Transforming Genres: New Approaches to British Fiction of the 1890s*. New York: St. Martin's Press, 1994.

Marsh, Jan. *Christina Rossetti: A Literary Biography*. London: Jonathan Cape, 1994.

Masters, Brian. *Now Barabbas was a Rotter: The Extraordinary Life of Marie Corelli*. London: Hamish Hamilton, 1978.

McCord, Norman. *British History, 1815–1906*. Oxford: Oxford University Press, 1991.

McGann, Jerome J. "Christina Rossetti's Poems: A New Edition and a Revaluation." *Victorian Studies* 23, no. 2 (1980): 237–54.

———. "The Religious Poetry of Christina Rossetti." *Critical Inquiry* 10 (1983): 127–44.

Meek, Ronald L., ed. *Marx and Engels on Malthus*. Translated Dorothea L. Meek and Ronald L. Meek. London: Lawrence and Wishart, 1953.

Miller, J. Hillis. *The Form of Victorian Fiction*. Notre Dame: University of Notre Dame Press, 1968.

Mivart, St. George. *On the Genesis of Species*. London: Macmillan, 1871.

Moore, George. *Esther Waters*. Edited by David Skilton. Oxford: Oxford University Press, 1999.

Moore, James R. *The Post-Darwinian Controversies: A Study of the Protestant Struggle to Come to Terms with Darwin in Great Britain and America, 1870–1900*. Cambridge: Cambridge University Press, 1979.

Morgan, Rosemarie. *Women and Sexuality in the Novels of Thomas Hardy.* London: Routledge, 1988.

Morgan, Thais E., ed. *Victorian Sages and Cultural Discourse: Renegotiating Gender and Power.* New Brunswick: Rutgers University Press, 1990.

Morris, Leon. *Revelation: An Introduction and Commentary.* London: Tyndale, 1969.

Morris, William. *Three Works: News from Nowhere, The Pilgrims of Hope, A Dream of John Ball.* London: Lawrence and Wishart, 1973.

Nietzsche, Friedrich. *Early Greek Philosophy and Other Essays.* Translated by M. A. Mugge. London: T. N. Foulis, 1911.

———. *The Portable Nietzsche.* Edited and translated by Walter Kaufmann. New York: Viking Penguin, 1959.

Nightingale, Florence. *Cassandra/Suggestions for Thought.* Ed. Mary Poovey. London: Pickering and Chatto, 1991.

Noel-Bentley, Peter C. " 'Fronting the Dreadful Mysteries of Time': Durer's *Melencolia* in Thomson's *City of Dreadful Night.*" *Victorian Poetry* 12, no. 3 (1974): 193–203.

O'Gorman, Francis, ed. *The Victorian Novel.* Malden, MA: Blackwell, 2002.

O'Leary, Stephen D. *Arguing the Apocalypse: A Theory of Millennial Rhetoric.* New York: Oxford University Press, 1994.

Ospovat, Dov. *The Development of Darwin's Theory: Natural History, Natural Theology, and Natural Selection, 1838–1859.* Cambridge: Cambridge University Press, 1981.

Packer, Lona Mosk. *Christina Rossetti.* Berkeley: University of California Press, 1963.

Palmer, Alan. *The Banner of Battle: The Story of the Crimean War.* London: Weidenfeld and Nicholson, 1987.

Parrinder, Patrick. *Shadows of the Future: H. G. Wells, Science Fiction and Prophecy.* Liverpool: Liverpool University Press, 1995.

Prévost, Jean-Pierre. *How to Read the Apocalypse.* Translated by John Bowden and Margaret Lydamore. London: SCM, 1993.

Prickett, Stephen, ed. *Reading the Text: Biblical Criticism and Literary Theory.* London: Blackwell, 1991.

"Psychosis." *Our Modern Philosophers: Darwin, Bain and Spencer, or The Descent of Man, Mind and Body.* London: T. Fisher Unwin, 1884.

Pykett, Lyn. *The "Improper" Feminine: The Woman's Sensation Novel and the New Woman Writing.* London: Routledge, 1992.

———. *Charles Dickens.* Houndmills: Palgrave, 2002.

Rabinow, Paul, ed. *The Foucault Reader.* Harmondsworth: Penguin, 1986.

Ramsey, James B. *Revelation: An Exposition of the First 11 Chapters.* Edinburgh: Banner of Truth, 1977.

Rainbow, Paul A. "Millennium as Metaphor in John's Apocalypse." *The Westminster Theological Journal* 58, no. 2 (1996): 209–21.

Regan, Stephen, ed. *The Nineteenth-Century Novel: A Critical Reader.* London: Routledge, 2001.

Ricks, Christopher, ed. *The New Oxford Book of Victorian Verse*. Oxford: Oxford University Press, 1987.

Ricoeur, Paul. *The Rule of Metaphor: Multi-disciplinary Studies in the Creation of Meaning in Language*. Translated by R. Czerny, K. McLaughlin and J. Costello SJ. London: Routledge and Kegan Paul, 1978.

———. *Time and Narrative*. Translated by K. Blamey, K. McLaughlin, D. Pellauer. 3 vols. Chicago: University of Chicago Press, 1984–88.

Robson, Robert, ed. *Ideas and Institutions of Victorian Britain*. London: G. Bell and Sons, 1967.

Romanes, George John. *Darwin and After Darwin: An Exposition of the Darwinian Theory and a Discussion of Post-Darwinian Questions*. London: Longmans, Green and Co., 1892.

Rosenblum, Dolores. "Christina Rossetti's Religious Poetry: Watching, Looking, Keeping Vigil." *Victorian Poetry* 20, no. 1 (1982): 33–49.

Rossetti, Christina. *Commonplace and Other Short Stories*. London: F. S. Ellis, 1870.

———. *The Face of the Deep: A Devotional Commentary on the Apocalypse* [1892], 3rd ed. London: SPCK, 1895.

———. *The Poetical Works of Christina Georgina Rossetti with Memoir and Notes*. Edited by William Michael Rossetti. London: Macmillan, 1904.

———. *Christina Rosetti: Selected Poems*. Edited by C. H. Sisson. Manchester: Carcanet, 1984.

Rowe, Henry K. *History of the Christian People*. New York: Macmillan, 1931.

Rowell, George, ed. *Nineteenth-Century Plays*, 2nd ed. Oxford: Oxford University Press, 1972.

Rowland, Christopher. *The Open Heaven: A Study of Apocalyptic in Judaism and Early Christianity*. London: SPCK, 1982.

Runia, Klaas. "Eschatology and Hermeneutics." *European Journal of Theology* 3, no. 1 (1994): 17–33.

Ruskin, John. *Unto This Last and Other Writings*. Edited by Clive Wilmer. London: Penguin, 1985.

Sanders, Andrew. *Charles Dickens*. Oxford: Oxford University Press, 2003.

Schad, John. *Victorians in Theory: From Derrida to Browning*. Manchester: Manchester University Press, 1999.

Schad, John, ed. *Dickens Refigured: Bodies, Desires and Other Histories*. Manchester: Manchester University Press, 1996.

Schreiner, Olive. *The Story of an African Farm*. Harmondsworth: Penguin, 1939.

Sharpe, William. "Learning to Read *The City*." *Victorian Poetry* 22, no. 1 (1984): 65–84.

Shaw, W. David. *The Lucid Veil: Poetic Truth in the Victorian Age*. London: Athlon, 1987.

Showalter, Elaine. "Florence Nightingale's Feminist Complaint: Women, Religion, and *Suggestions for Thought*." *Signs* 6, no. 3 (1981): 395–412.

———. *A Literature of Their Own: From Charlotte Bronte to Doris Lessing.* 2nd ed. London: Virago, 1982.

Shuttleworth, Sally. *George Eliot and Nineteenth-Century Science: The Make-Believe of a Beginning.* Cambridge: Cambridge University Press, 1984.

Skilton, David, ed. *The Early and Mid-Victorian Novel.* London: Routledge, 1993.

Spurgeon, Charles Haddon. *Revival Year Sermons, 1859.* Edinburgh: Banner of Truth Trust, 1959.

Steele, Michael R. "James Thomson's Angel and Sphinx: A Possible Source." *Victorian Poetry* 12, no. 4 (1974): 373–75.

Stokes, John (ed.). *Fin de Siècle/Fin du Globe: Fears and Fantasies of the Late Nineteenth Century.* New York: St. Martin's Press, 1992.

Stutfield, Hugh. "Tommyrotics." *Blackwood's Magazine* 157 (1895): 836.

Sweet, John. *Revelation.* London: SCM, 1979.

Swift, Catherine. *Florence Nightingale.* London: Marshall Pickering, 1993.

Tennyson, Alfred. *In Memoriam, Maud and Other Poems.* Edited by John D. Jump. London: Everyman, 1974.

Thackeray, William. *Vanity Fair.* Edited by J. I. M. Stewart. London: Penguin, 1968.

Thomas, Donald. *The Victorian Underworld.* London: John Murray, 1998.

Thomson, James. *The City of Dreadful Night.* Edinburgh: Canongate, 1993.

———. *The Poetical Works of James Thomson (BV).* Edited by Bertram Dobell. London: Reeves and Turner, 1895.

Thomson, James. *The City of Dreadful Night and Other Poems* (London: Watts and Col, 1932).

Torrance, T. F. *The Apocalypse Today.* London: James Clarke and Co., 1960.

Torrey, Charles C. *The Apocalypse of John.* New Haven, CT: Yale University Press, 1958.

Trollope, Anthony. *The Way We Live Now.* Edited by Frank Kermode. London: Penguin, 1994.

Vaganay, L. C-B. Amphoux. *An Introduction to New Testament Textual Criticism.* Translated by J. Heimerdinger. Cambridge: Cambridge University Press, 1991.

Vyver, Bertha. *Memoirs of Marie Corelli.* London: Alston Rivers Ltd., 1930.

Walvoord, John F. *The Revelation of Jesus Christ: A Commentary.* London: Marshall, Morgan and Scott, 1966.

Wells, H. G. "Zoological Regression." *The Gentleman's Magazine* 271 (1891): 253.

———. *The Time Machine.* London: Everyman, 1995.

———. *The Future in America: A Search after Realities.* London: Chapman and Hall, 1906.

Welsh, Alexander. *The City of Dickens.* Oxford: Oxford University Press, 1971.

Wengst, K. *Pax Romana and the Peace of Jesus Christ.* Translated by J. Bowden. London: SCM, 1987.

Wood, Mrs Henry. *East Lynne*. Edited by Norman Page and Kamal Al-Solaylee. London: Everyman, 1994.

Woodham-Smith, Cecil. *Florence Nightingale 1820–1910*. London: Constable, 1950.

Wordsworth, William. *The Prelude: A Parallel Text*. Edited by J.C. Maxwell. Harmondsworth: Penguin, 1971.

Index

224

—